FAT TIRE RIDER

FAT TIRE RIDER

EVERYONE'S GUIDE TO MOUNTAIN BIKING

Martha J. Kennedy, Michael Kloser
and P. Yuri Samer

VITESSE PRESS • BRATTLEBORO, VERMONT

DEDICATION

To our spouses and families, whose support and encouragement allows our endeavors

and to Joseph A. MacKenna, without whose continued counsel and assistance this project would not have been realized

ISBN 0-941950-29-8

Library of Congress card number 92-61915

Edited by Marilee Attley. Copy edited by Ricia Gordon. Cover and text design by James Brisson. Cover and text photos by P. Yuri Samer (except top two on page 292 by Tom Moran). Illustrations on pages 3–21 by Martha J. Kennedy, pages 180–187 by Michele Fairchild. Typesetting by Pagesetters. Printed by Patterson Printing.

Vitesse Press, 28 Birge Street, Brattleboro, VT 05301

10 9 8 7 6 5 4 3 2 1

••CONTENTS

Getting Competitive about It

Beyond Racing

Mountain Bike Manners

• • FOREWORD

In the dozen or so years that mountain biking has been around it has seen amazing growth and lots of changes. During this short time the bikes and equipment have improved immensely. So what's it all about? After all, when you were a kid you used to ride your bike through the woods. What's the big deal? Well, I'm here to tell you that when you get on a bike that's made to go anywhere and you've got some basic skills and fitness, you're in for a lot of fun. Big Fun. There's simply no denying the feeling when you're cruising a fire road or following a trail free from the pavement.

But if you've got the bug, you might ask, why read about it? Just do it, right? Well, if you're the hardheaded type that likes to figure everything out on your own you'll miss out on the benefit of some great experience. On these pages is a wealth of information collected from three riders and writers who have, luckily for us, taken the time to pass on what they've learned. Choosing the right equipment and sizing, handling skills, trail do's and don't's—everything you'll need to know to get you rolling. If you're interested in going really fast then read about training and racing; you're hearing it from the pros.

Martha and Mike are professional racers. Their approach to training is serious and methodical. Their list of accomplishments shows what their training programs did for them. And Yuri has the all-round exposure to cycling that helps anyone, from novice to hard-core enthusiast. Having been among the ranks in off-road cycling since its inception, Yuri has firsthand experience in frame building, several years of bike shop experience, and an unquenchable thirst for anything and everything related to bikes. Together, these three have amassed what most anybody will need to know to have fun or get serious. As editor, Yuri has added a good dose of humor and left out the babble.

With the help of these guys, you too can feel exhilaration and a sense of accomplishment from a few hours of riding a week. After all, keeping fit is some of the best revenge there is on life. And the challenges are endless: how far, how high, how fast, how much finesse?

Whether you race, tour, or just ride around, you're liable to experience the world in a better way.

—Chris Chance,
Fat City Cycles
Somerville, Massachusetts

••PREFACE

Reading a book about mountain biking is a lot like reading a book about sex. No matter how good the book is, it just can't beat the real thing. But any good instruction book can make the actual experience more rewarding and fun. That's why we wrote *Fat Tire Rider*.

Mountain biking has one of the biggest fun quotients around, which probably comes as no surprise to anyone reading this book. You get to have good, clean (though sometimes muddy) fun in the outdoors while simultaneously getting fit. But whether you're thinking of using your mountain bike for camping, racing, getting closer to wildlife, or simply tooling through the sage with your friends, the success of your venture does depend upon a certain amount of athletic and technological proficiency. You can use this book as a resource to help you develop that proficiency.

The three of us—an Iowa refugee from automotive mechanic school, a printmaker from the upper Midwest with an affection for pitbulls, and a Pacific Northwest adventure scout—repeatedly bumped into each other on trails in remote places like the Matanuska Valley of Alaska. We found we agreed that there was a need for a good book on mountain biking, both to answer the questions we were continually being asked and to encourage more people to get out there on their bikes.

Wouldn't it be great, we thought, if what really mattered in equipment—things like sizing, frameset design, and component function—were presented with the cyclist in mind, whether that cyclist is a nervous novice or a habitual hammerhead? We also agreed that many people, women in particular, but also many men, need to know there is nothing intimidating about mountain biking. They need to learn that it's reasonably safe, great fun, environmentally ethical, and a wonderful means of personal discovery.

We wrote this book because advice on mountain bike training too often amounted to "ride harder, bonk a bit, and see how well you recover." Technical data was too often oriented to obsessed shopheads or seemed designed to bolster commercial interests.

We soon found that writing a book is a lot like specifying components on a bike. Personal preferences and experience come into play. But, just as a manufacturer doesn't put the drivetrain on the left side of the bike simply to do things his way, we approached as many topics as we could in a way that built on pre-existing cycling, mountain biking, or athletic texts. Although we found it possible to use a lot of the existing mountain bike slang and technical terms, we also found it necessary to invent names so we could talk about certain ideas more concisely. (You'll find these names in the glossary, where we've tried to include as many terms relevant to the sport—both slang and technical—as possible.)

Because mountain bikers are both male and female and can be young, old, or in-between, we decided to discuss all topics as they relate to all mountain bikers, so you won't find a separate chapter for women or Juniors, for example. We address all mountain bikers all the time, with asides and bits of information for each gender and age group whenever relevant.

You may wonder how much of the book is Martha, how much Mike, how much Yuri. Actually we found surprisingly little to dicker over—in part because we agreed on many things right from the beginning. (If we hadn't, the project wouldn't have gotten far.) Most of the time there were one or two ideas on things. In a few instances—such as the discussion of inner-tube valve caps—we incorporated all three of our opinions in the text.

Although reading *Fat Tire Rider* won't guarantee you'll beat the champ in mountain bike bowling, we do hope it helps maximize your adventure, excitement, and fun on a mountain bike; dispel some of the phobias that make people insecure about starting out; and relieve you of a lot of the trial-and-error methods we had to use.

··ACKNOWLEDGMENTS

Plenty of people gave freely of their time and shared their knowledge with us for this book.

Our thanks to framebuilders Michael Augsburger, Steve Baker, Joe Breeze, Chris Chance, Glenn Erickson, Gary Fisher, Gary Klein, Tom Ritchey, Mark Slate, and Ross Shafer; Jim Hasenauer at IMBA; Toby Bedford, Gary Klug, and Janice Lettunich at the University of Oregon; Brad Roy at Sacred Heart Hospital's Heart Center, Eugene, OR; Doctors Sally S. Marie and William J. Mills, Jr.; The Eugene Mountain Bike Resource Group; Michael McCoy at Bikecentennial; Phil Miller at the League of American Wheelmen; Duann Hall at NORBA; Chris Carmichael and Philip Milburn at the USCF; U.S. Forest Service staffers Jerry Covault, Terry Egenhoff, Paul Engstrom, Kathryn Schneider, and Della Webb; Lou Gonzalez at the World Bicycle Polo Federation; all the racers and riders who allowed themselves and their bikes to be measured; Bob and Judy Windauer in Columbia Falls, MT; and Victor H. LoGrazzo.

• • Picking It Up

Finding a Bike to Fit You and Your Budget

The fun-and-frolic bug has bit. Your heart soars with thoughts of a new mountain bike. Suddenly you're hit by sticker shock (even if you account for inflation since you purchased your trusty but now rusty Schwinn Varsity). Or maybe you're confused by the plethora of techno-jargon or simply bowled over by all the choices.

But there's no reason you can't ride off happily into the sunset with your new bike. In fact, finding the right bike at the right price can actually be a pleasant experience, leaving you free of suspicion that you were taken advantage of.

How so? By following these six simple rules:

1. Buy from a shop where they eat, drink, and sleep bicycles, preferably mountain bikes. A good bike shop has employees who ride regularly, even commute by bike to work. A good mountain bike shop has employees who ride mountain bikes. This is especially important when it comes to mechanics—those who ride regularly will be familiar with what holds up in real use, will steer store policy toward featuring the better products, and will give you better service.

Ask about nearby trails, local mountain bike clubs, and any park access concerns in the area. A shop with active mountain bikers should be able to provide answers to all those questions. (But be aware that the best trails may be kept secret to keep traffic down or to forestall closure.) Another good sign is free handout literature about mountain bike organizations such as the National Off-Road Bicycle Association (NORBA), and the International Mountain Bikers Association (IMBA).

If the shop is full of healthy personnel who obviously ride bikes, glance at their legs. If they're shaved, with prominent veins and muscle definition, these folks are probably racers. But since there are a lot more road racers than mountain bike racers, ask which they are. It doesn't necessarily mean "forget this place" if they're roadies, but ask who on their staff rides fat tires, and find out what equipment they use and where they ride regularly.

2. Shop for service and repairs as much as for a bike. Assuming a reasonable purchase price and competent assembly, the most important thing a shop can give you will be quality service. And good service begins with competent assembly. Bicycle retailing is one of the few industries left in which the quality of the product depends on the quality of assembly by the retailer. (Ironically, given this situation, there isn't any certification of shops.)

A free tune-up within six weeks of purchase is standard in the industry. Ask if you need an appointment and if they'll give you same-day turnaround on the tune-up.

When you buy a new bike, some shops will offer you a discount on an overhaul if the overhaul appointment is scheduled for the winter off-season. Ask about it. Your interest in maintaining your bike and providing the shop with year-round business should spark a response.

3. Buy only from a shop that allows a complete test ride, unsupervised. Shops are used to letting bikes go out the door for test rides in exchange for security such as your wallet, car keys, or credit cards.

A mountain bike test ride should have two phases—on pavement and on dirt. First, on smooth pavement and in quiet surroundings, test the brakes for stopping power, control modulation (braking force is applied in a smooth curve), and silence. Squealing brakes let you know there's been a basic assembly blunder.

Next, stop the bike and straddle the top tube with both feet on the ground. Firmly apply the front brake and try to roll the bike forward. (Your front wheel shouldn't actually move.) What you should feel in the handlebars is the single force of the bike as a unit held by the front brake. A two-part rocking sensation indicates the

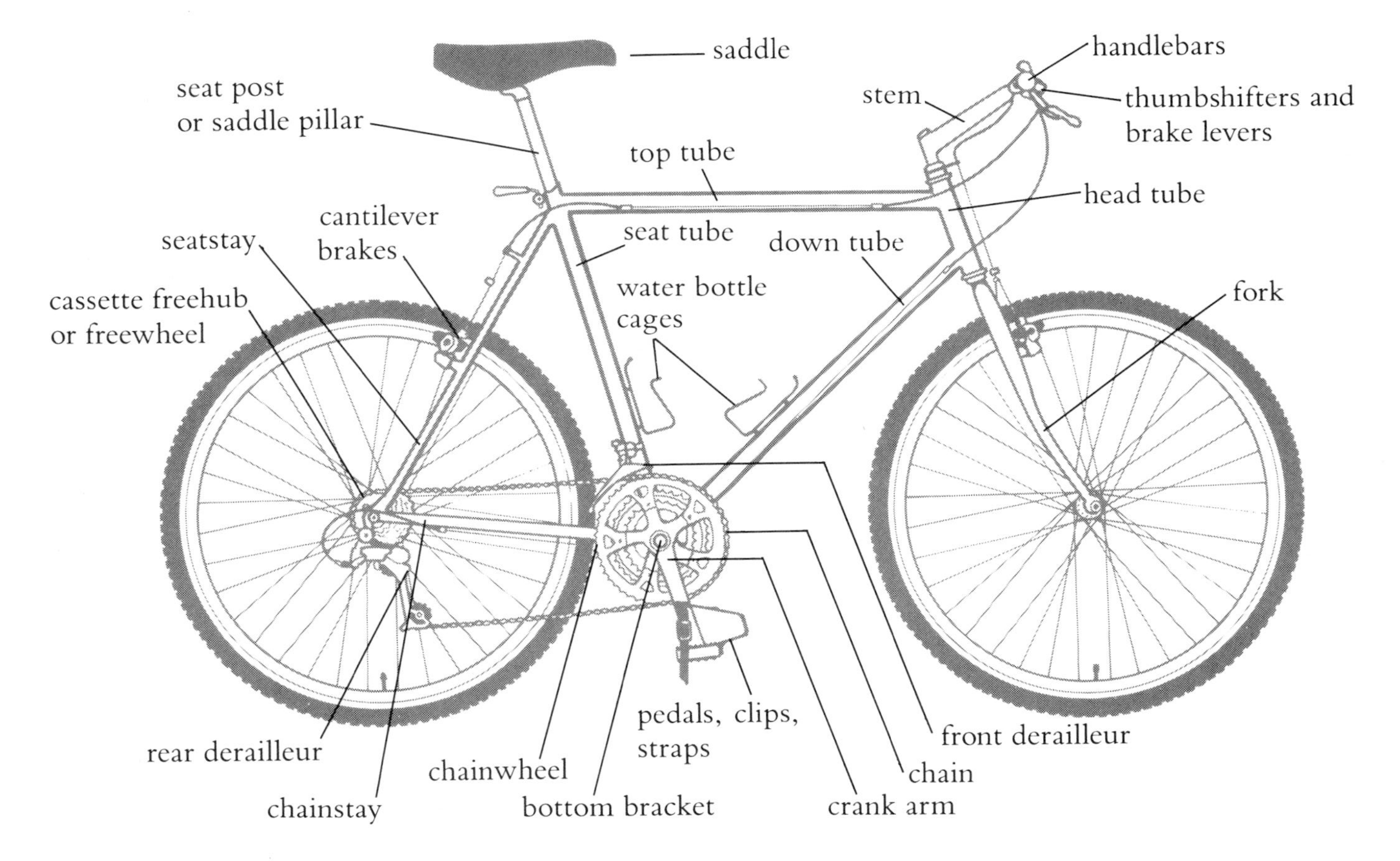

Bicycle Components and Frameset Parts

bearings in the steerer (headset) are loose. More assembly demerits.

Then get off the bike and check the wheels. To judge if the wheels are fairly true, hold each wheel off the ground just enough to spin it. Watch where the wheel rim passes through the brake blocks. The rim shouldn't move up or down, in or out in relation to the brake pads. Grip parallel spokes on the same side of each wheel, all the way around each wheel. There should be even spoke tension all the way around on each side of each wheel.

Get back on the bike and check the shifting of the front and rear gear changers (derailleurs) while riding at moderate speed. Start with the chain in the middle front gear (chainring) and change all the rear gears. Then try the four lowest (innermost) rear cogs with the smallest chainring, and the four highest cogs with the largest chainring. Everything should work fine. Double-check by doing some shifts at slow and fast pedal speeds. Properly adjusted, quality components will function smoothly in all these circumstances.

For the second phase of the test ride, find some dirt. Nothing beats actual dirt riding to find out how a bike's geometry or setup feels to you. Besides verifying shifting and braking performance, see how the bike feels when you stand up and pedal.

Unfortunately, many fine shops just don't have any off-road riding nearby. You can try to arrange to rent the model you're interested in for a short day ride, or try to get out on a group or club ride on a loaner that's similarly equipped. (Neophytes can benefit from having more experienced riders along who can answer any questions.) But if circumstances don't allow this much research, use the pavement testing to verify the service competence of the store and to narrow your model selection.

4. Buy the most bike you can afford. We all work hard for our recreational dollar, so it makes sense to get the highest quality we can afford—the stuff simply works better longer, which saves repair costs, especially if the bike's going to have to last another 20 years. Also, if the high-performance bug bites and you're looking to trade up, you'll get more for your used bike.

When compiling your bike budget, remember that anyone new to cycling will need to spend an additional $75–100 for a hardshell helmet, a pump, and basic tools.

5. Think twice before test riding what you can't afford. Many people can ride the top-of-the-line models, discover that "the best" doesn't feel that much better, and buy lower in the product line with no problem. Others find that riding a more expensive bike spoils the fun of riding what they can afford.

6. Get a bike that fits properly. You're not only the bike's rider, you're its motor. And if the motor isn't mounted on a properly sized frame, your speed, power, and comfort will be adversely affected—that's guaranteed.

Fit guidelines

Proper bicycle fit ensures that the distances between the center of the bottom bracket spindle and the top center of the saddle and between the top center of the saddle and the handlebar/stem joint are adjusted to the geometry of your body. If you don't want to get too technical with numbers and measurements, here's a rule-of-thumb method for determining your bike size.

Go shopping wearing your riding shoes and shorts. Crotch clearance is the easiest thing to check out first. Straddle the bike with your feet flat on the floor, approximately six inches out on either side of the bike's frame. There should be three inches of clearance between the top tube of the bike and the crotch seam of your shorts. Lift the front wheel off the ground until it touches your shorts. There should be approximately four inches of air underneath the front tire.

Next, see if the saddle height can be adjusted properly. Set the pedal crank arms parallel to the seat tube, and put your foot on the lower pedal, the ball of your foot over the pedal shaft.

Set the saddle height so there is just the slightest bend (about 10 degrees) in your knee. Then have someone watch you back-pedal. Your hips should rest evenly and be stable on the saddle, not rock or reach for the pedals. Also, when you set the crank arms parallel to the ground and close your knees together, the top tube should be just below your knees.

Finally, check to see that the stem is set so the handlebars are just a little lower than the saddle. (The top of the bars should be 1.5 to 2.5 inches lower than the top of the saddle.) Look at both the handlebar stem and seat post to see that they are not extended beyond the maximum safe amount as marked by the manufacturer.

Fit Guidelines

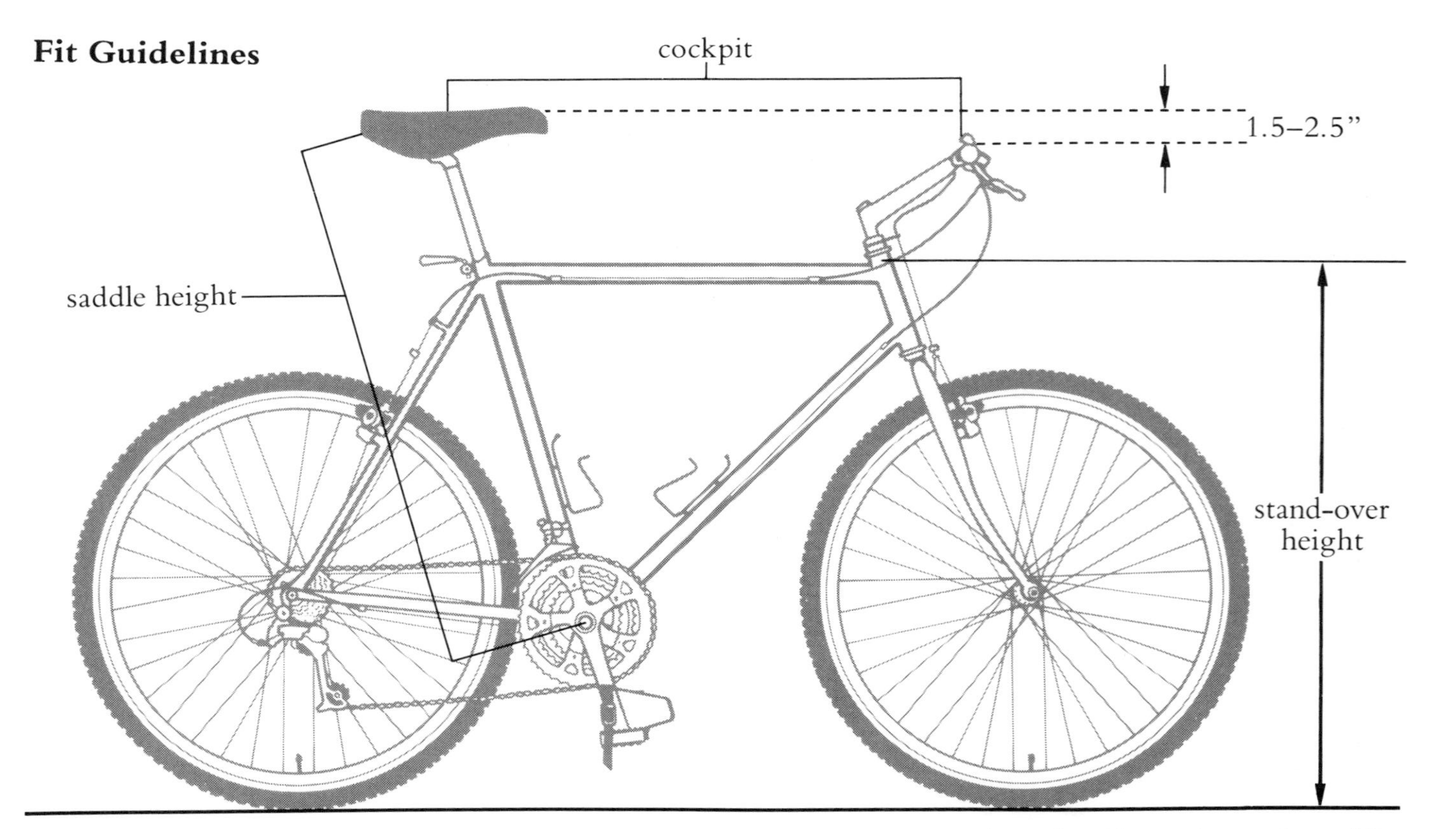

Proper mountain bike sizing includes an efficient saddle height, an ample cockpit, and comfortable stand-over. A good fit allows a small bend in the leg when the pedal is furthest from the saddle, and a comfortable height difference between the saddle and the handlebars.

Shortcut for roadies

If you're an experienced road rider already competent in road bike sizing and know your seat tube and top tube lengths, shop for a bike with 2.5 to 3 inches (7–9 cm) less effective seat tube length (center of bottom bracket to the intersection of seat tube center line with center line of top tube) than your best-fitting road bike. Because different bottom bracket heights will mean different crotch clearances, you'll still want to check straddle clearance the rule-of-thumb way.

The minimum amount of room you need for your upper body can be easily determined if your road bike is properly set up. Place a frame pump across your road bike's brake hoods. Measure the distance from top center of the pump (it will be just in front of the stem) to the center line of the seat post at the top of the cylindrical area below the saddle clamp. Use this measure for the distance from the top center of the mountain bike's handlebars at the stem to the center line of the seat post just below the saddle clamp.

By the numbers

Okay, all you folks who don't know your road bike frame size as well as your shirt-sleeve length but who want to do this right—by golly, here we go:

Grab a flexible, sewing-type measuring tape and arrange for a half-hour with someone you don't mind having near your crotch and chest. It doesn't matter whether you count centimeters or inches, just keep it consistent.

Take off your shoes and stand straight-legged, facing a wall free of obstructions, your feet six to eight inches apart on a level, uncarpeted floor. Take a medium-sized book (.5 to 1 inch thick), place between your legs and push the binding up until it touches your pubis bone. For men, this should push your genitalia up the way the nose of a bike saddle will. Make sure to spread your thighs sufficiently to allow a full level pressing of the book against your bone. Have your friend either measure the height of the book binding from the floor or mark the height of the top edge of the book on the wall with a pencil.

While you're standing there, mark the height of the V-shaped indent in the upper edge of your sternum, or chestbone, on the wall

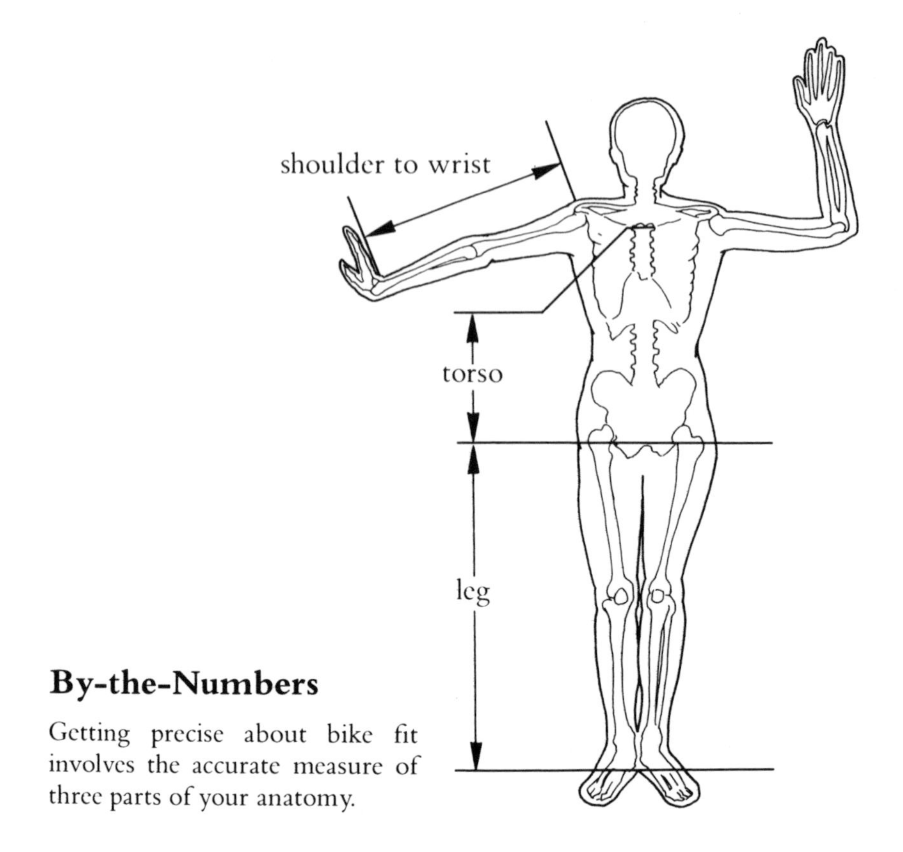

By-the-Numbers

Getting precise about bike fit involves the accurate measure of three parts of your anatomy.

directly above the book mark or measure the vertical distance from the top of the book to the sternal notch directly. Measure the distance from your pubis bone to the valley of the V shape of your sternum and write this down for later use. Also, have your friend measure the distance from your arm/shoulder joint to the wrist at the wrist bone or knob and write this measurement down below the pubis/sternum measurement.

Measure the vertical distance from the book mark on the wall to the floor. Multiply it by .55 and .60. The numbers that result are the upper and lower range of your Effective Seat Tube Length (commonly referred to as the size of the bike), that is, the correct length of the seat tube for you, measured from the center of the bottom bracket up the center line of the seat tube to where it intersects the center line of the top tube. (Many mountain bikes have sloping top tubes. Their seat tube sizing is usually specified relative to the traditional parallel-to-the-ground top tube design. All measurements should use the parallel-to-the-ground tube. If you're not sure where that is, check with a bubble level where a level top tube would meet the bike's seat tube.)

Bikes at the low end of the Effective Seat Tube Length are slightly lighter—there's less material involved—and have more crotch clearance when the bike is bounding over uneven terrain. Bikes on the higher end will have more room for water bottles and a pump, be easier to portage, and have less of a "flagpole effect"—the feeling that you're sitting on top of a swaying flagpole, which comes from the increased distance between the saddle and the rest of the frame.

Sizing Basics

Your Effective Seat Tube Length, left, is the key to a correct size of mountain bike. Right, an accurate establishment of the Effective Saddle Height for your body will maximize your efficiency during the drive portion of crank arm travel.

If you're new to mountain biking, test ride models closer to the middle of your Effective Seat Tube Length range first.

Next, use the same leg-length measurement to find your Effective Saddle Height—the distance between the top of the saddle (above the center line of the seat post) and the center of the bottom bracket spindle. Multiply your leg measurement by .85. The resulting figure establishes a reference point for correct saddle height. We say "reference point" because your anatomy, shoe sole thickness, pedals, and measurement methodology can produce differences of plus-or-minus one millimeter.

Some people may notice the variance between this formula and those recommended for a road bike setup, which use a larger percentage of leg length. Each formula works on the principle that your leg is the driving rod of the crank, whose power points are actually a series of triangles. The percentage of leg length identifies the hypotenuse in the right triangle at the forward portion of the drive stroke—where you begin the peak power transfer to the drivetrain during each pedal revolution. The longer crank arm lengths of mountain bikes and the different power/leverage demands necessitate a different percentage of leg length to identify an appropriate drivetrain hypotenuse.

Our formula was developed by investigating riders' experiences with various bike fit formulas, and then accounting for the differences observed in efficiency and comfort from those formulas. Our theoretical bike fit formula for mountain biking was then checked against a sample of measurements from NORBA Expert and Pro/Elite racers and other experienced riders.

We are assuming 175-mm crank arms as standard. If you have very long thighs or if your mountain bike has a very steep seat angle, you may want to get longer crank arms. But this is fine-tuning once your basic setup is established.

Cockpit length

After you've determined that your bike can be adjusted for Effective Saddle Height, check to see if the top tube and standard stem allow Sufficient Cockpit Length (the distance between the center line of the seat post just below the clamp area and the center line of the top of the handlebars at the stem) for your upper body.

Add the pubis/sternum measurement and arm measurement.

Multiply the total by .625. This distance should be obtainable on a mountain bike with your correct size of seat tube using the above formula and a 125–150-mm stem. Purchase your correct stem size accordingly. (See the seat post and saddles section for further tips.)

With the Effective Seat Tube Length, Effective Saddle Height, and Sufficient Cockpit Length measurements, you can take a tape measure to any bike and establish whether it's your size.

There's one more basic adjustment that will make the bike trail-ready. After setting the saddle to your height, sit on it with your feet on the pedals at 3 and 9 o'clock. Have someone hold a plumb bob from the front of your forward kneecap to check its relation to the pedal axle. Adjust the saddle forward or back in the seat post clamp until the plumb bob is centered over the pedal axle.

As long as you don't need to run the saddle entirely to one end or the other to get this position, you're okay. If you can only get your knee over the pedal axle by jamming the saddle to either end of its rails, you need either longer or shorter cranks.

If you switch crank arm length you will have a slightly higher or lower effective gear ratio for the chainwheel/cog combinations you used previously, and you may need some time to retrain your legs to maintain cadence in each combination. But even this is not a hard-and-fast rule. Some people who have long upper legs (and usually similarly proportioned arms) have found that setting their saddle .5–1.5 cm back from the norm enhances power through the top of the pedal rotation, although it tends to slow the natural cadence a smidgen.

Formulas for sizing have a variance of plus or minus 1 mm in Effective Seat Tube Length and slightly less (± 1.5 mm) in Sufficient Cockpit Length room. This is because personal idiosyncrasies like tendon tightness, postural habits, and center of gravity preferences can affect a measurement that much. True precision sizing takes into account such personal factors and may change as you age, or as your bike use changes.

You may want to adjust both upper- and lower-body-related figures, for example, if the terrain where you ride is very steep, or if your use is very specific, such as downhill racing or hunting.

• • What Matters in a Bike

Shopping Design, Durability, and Price

What matters in a mountain bike?

The crucial facts are how it rides, how well it's made, and how much it costs.

That final item—the price tag—has a habit of intruding on a lot of nice plans and too many experiences. But there's no reason why even a basic mountain bike can't be a good buy and provide plenty of pleasurable trail time.

Here, then, is our version of What Counts 101.

The basic bike

You can get a good, basic mountain bike for $600 (1992 prices). Here are the important qualities:

— ***Durability.*** Anything that's sold under the moniker of mountain or all-terrain bike has to be durable. It doesn't take exotic metals or hours of hand craftsmanship to make a frame that stands up to years of recreational trail riding. It does take strong materials and quality construction.

Most likely we're talking about steel bikes here, but possibly aluminum main frame/steel rear triangle bikes or those made entirely of aluminum. If steel tubing is used it should be chrome-moly, which is short for a steel alloy made primarily from chromium and molybdenum.

Durability also depends on how well the stuff is put together. Look for clean, even welds at the joints of unlugged frames (those without a reinforcement layer of metal at the joints). The joints should be symmetrical and the ripples should be regular. Any gaps, pinholes, or ripples that look like miniature river rapids are signs of hurried or sloppy work and lousy inspection practices. Leave those bikes on the rack.

Similarly, the joints of lugged frames (those with reinforcement sleeves at the joints) should have clean, smooth edges, without any breaks or tiny holes in the thin line of braze filler material.

Tubing diameters should appear consistent as they near joints, and hold a smooth, steady line right into the next tube. You can check this with the naked eye if you look at the joint in good light and against a neutral, uncluttered background.

— ***Alignment.*** Proper alignment, or straightness, is essential for the components to function as they should, and for the bike to be biomechanically neutral. Biomechanical neutrality may be even more important than component function. The human body has literally hundreds of joints that work to accommodate an assortment of postural demands. Unless your bike frame is properly aligned, your body will develop idiosyncratic quirks that may be inefficient or even cause injury when performed thousands of times over a lifetime of cycling.

Unfortunately, the bicycle industry has gotten away with sloppy standards as far as frame straightness is concerned. The two most common techniques for determining alignment—riding with no hands and checking the rear triangle with a string—are holdovers from the days when bikes were not expected to perform under the stress that's the norm for mountain bikes. Both techniques only address tire tracking and chainline. They're virtually worthless when talking about total frame alignment.

A no-hands riding test tells you whether you can easily balance the bike. Any bike whose wheels track fairly closely and whose fork dropouts (which hold the wheels) are reasonably aligned can be ridden that way. The string test (running a taut string from rear dropout to rear dropout around the head tube) tells you how well the rear end is centered relative to the seat tube. Neither test mea-

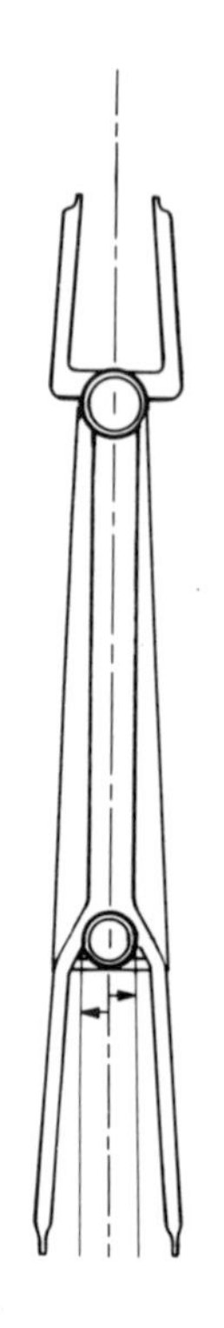

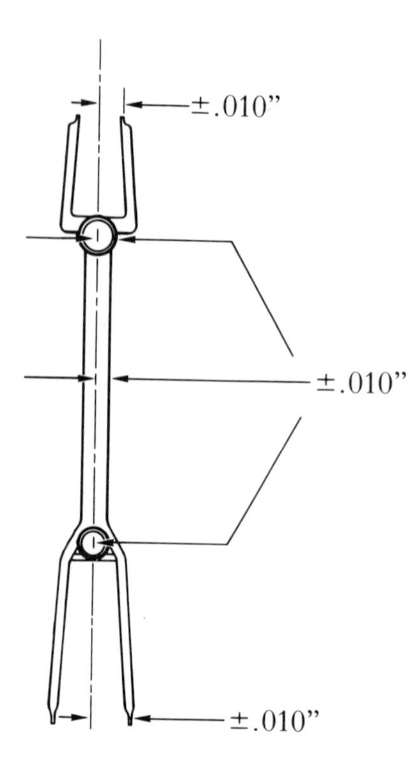

String Test **True Frame Alignment**

The string test, left, only checks the relationship of the rear dropouts to the seat tube, and only at the part of the seat tube near the string. Total frame alignment, right, establishes the relationship of the steering axis, seat tube center line, and both front and rear dropouts to a fore-aft dead center plane, and expresses those relationships in thousandths of an inch.

sures the alignment of the entire frame or any parts against a consistent referent.

True frame alignment means that the center line of the seat tube and the center line of the head tube are verified to be parallel and equally spaced from a referent surface. In addition, the rear triangle and fork dropouts are verified to be parallel and equally spaced from the plane that includes those center lines.

For purposes of measurement, the center line of the head tube should be understood to extend 18 inches below the bottom of the head tube and 3 inches above the top. The center line of the seat tube should be understood to extend 24 inches up from the center of the bottom bracket.

The purpose is to ensure that the steering axis of the bike isn't 1.5" to one side and that subsequently the tire patch you actually steer and ride on excessively cambered, or angled, toward the right or left. Also, that the principal mass of your body is centered, not randomly situated an inch or more left or right depending upon which bike you take home. The wider the tolerances (or larger the tolerance numbers) the more your body will have to be twisted, angled, or offset to make the bike ride neutrally, or straight. And the greater the imbalances of forces may be on your legs, hip joints, and back simply from the act of pedaling.

In the machine-tool and metal-fabrication industries, an acceptable standard of deviation is expressed in terms of plus (+) or minus (−) thousandths of an inch. The (±) means that parts could deviate to the right or left of the center plane up to that amount. (The referent surface is usually a granite or steel plate certified to be dead flat.)

The mountain bike industry avoids this clear expression of alignment, long established in manufacturing, and declines to so warranty the quality of mountain bike construction. It's an ironic situation, because plus or minus ten one-thousandths of an inch (± .010") is a completely realistic and functionally relevant standard for this level of bicycle. Adhering to such standards would enable buyers to properly determine quality and would be a real boon to the sport.

If your mountain bike frameset is guaranteed to be aligned to this uniform standard, or a better one, you're reasonably assured the bike will perform well. To determine what standard of alignment a frame meets, ask for a written warranty or affidavit from the manufacturer. If the dealer doesn't have such a document, ask him to call or fax the company or distributor and get a guaranteed alignment standard.

Such a inquiry can be informative. You'll at least get to see how straight an answer you get from the dealer or that the dealer gets from the bike company. It's an opportunity for each of them to display how much they value your business. If the dealer or company replies with a standard expressed in the terms used above, even if it's much looser than those we discussed, you'll at least have a forthright answer and know how straight or crooked the bike may be.

Wheel dropout alignment can be verified by using Campagnolo-type "cup" tools.

— ***Weight.*** Ah, there, now we've got your attention again. Weight should be under 30 pounds, tops, for a 21-inch frame. That means no more than 30 pounds for the total bike, minus water bottles and racks.

For any bike, you want to be assured about repairability and warranty replacement, particularly of forks, the right rear dropout, and the derailleur hanger.

Find a bike that meets the above criteria and it will be a sound buy for the customer and a fair deal for the bike shop owner.

Details

If you're trying to choose between two mountain bikes with equally valuable frame design, wheels, and components, there are several functional details to look for that can make one a better buy than the other. These details are trickle-down benefits some manufacturers borrow from their higher-end designs. It's worth a little effort to see if these goodies are on a bike within your budget.

- *Slotted cable housing stops.* These are little lumps fastened to the frame where the cables for the brakes or derailleurs go from .250 inch of colorful housing to a thin wire on the other side. Stops that are shaped like little barrels with a slot on them make cable maintenance ridiculously easy compared to the other kinds (unslotted).
- *Seat tube/top tube reinforcement.* This area takes a lot of flex and stress, some from riding, some from working that seat post quick release, so an extra thickness of metal here reflects prudent thinking.
- *Wheel quick releases.* If a quick release makes moving your seat post easy, just think what one does for removing and repairing flats (yes, even you will get some), or storing your bike in a car trunk or on a rack.
- *A place to mount a pump.* Strange as it may seem, even some

expensive bikes made don't accommodate this vital tool. Don't be embarrassed to ask. Make sure you can carry a pump somewhere convenient.

- *Water bottle cages.* Make sure you can carry two large water bottles.
- *Portability.* Make sure you can easily carry your bike over sections of trail that can't be ridden. Small frames and those with elevated chainstays or sloping top tubes are often the victims of flawed design in this respect.
- *Vertical or semihorizontal wheel dropouts.* Wheel dropouts should not be horizontal and should be cast or machined from a single piece. Verticals are lighter and stronger and require more accurate building than horizontals.
- *Good tire or clog clearances.* You should be able to mount the biggest tire in the store (2 to 2.5 inches) and still have room for a bit of mud betwen the tire and the frame. If mud is a serious concern in your neighborhood, look for more than 65 mm of space between the chainstays where the rear tire is widest.

Better bikes

You can buy a better bike ($700 and up) made out of almost anything these days, from steel to composites. If it's steel we already know it had better be chrome-moly, but at this price it should also be butted because that saves weight while maintaining strength.

"Butting" is a manufacturing process that varies the wall thickness of tubing. Butted bicycle tubes are made so that the walls are thicker near frameset joints where greater stresses accumulate, and thinner where the material isn't needed as much.

So how does Josephine Seven-Speed know that the manufacturer put the superlative tubing together properly? Does she rely on a salesman, or advertising? First, look for flaws. (Although some flaws can be hidden with a little cosmetic work.) Then consider these other areas:

— ***Alignment.*** Evidence of quality construction brings us back to frameset alignment. "It should be as straight as possible," is how Michael finally put it. That means upper-end bikes that are straight within five thousandths of an inch (± .005"). If a mountain bike is warrantied to this standard, the extra money you spent on it will pay off in performance. Components will work better and be easier to maintain.

This standard takes into consideration the limitations of the material the manufacturers have to work with (the straightness of the raw tube stock). From experience and researching this book, we know it's not only possible to produce bikes to the standard, but that a large number of high-end custom and mass manufacturers are already doing so. Not surprisingly, bikes made by these manufacturers share a reputation for excellence.

Manufacturers who guarantee alignment within uniform standards tell the public in verifiable terms that they exercise a high degree of care and quality control. Such a guarantee lets you know what quality you're getting for your extra dollars and tells you that you're dealing with disciplined, conscientious businesspeople.

Some shops verify alignment using such tools as surface plates, dial indicators, and vernier scales. They either check each frame as it comes out of the box or institute quality-control "spot checks" by testing every nth frameset before the bike is put together. (It isn't fair though, to ask retail owners to disassemble a bike and check its alignment on whim, or without cause or compensation. Such frivolous and uncompensated alignment checks are too costly for a dealer.)

Your local pro shop (one that deals with top-end equipment and tools, as compared to the mom-and-pop store) should also be able to check or align the dropouts and verify that the front and rear wheels track in line by mounting a pair of reference wheels or using a dummy alignment wheel tool to see that their planes coincide with a tool-and-die-maker's quality straight edge.

— ***Nice ride.*** Okay, so you're looking at bikes that are built strong, out of good stuff, and built straight. What is a "nice ride"? There's no way this can't get a bit subjective; you've got to consider your weight, the kind of riding you do, the terrain in your territory. But better bikes reveal predictability in cornering and handle with reasonably quick (but not hair-trigger) steering. These are not vague or elusive qualities. To get them, a company uses larger-diameter tubes in the front triangle and fork, or at least in the down tube. Steel bikes may have an oval top tube.

You want a wheelbase that can't be measured with a meter stick (at least 40 inches, 38.5 for small riders), and a front center (the distance from the bottom bracket spindle to the front axle) that loads a fair amount of weight on the front wheel (approximately 45% of total rider/bike weight when seated and on a level surface).

When riding, the front wheel should turn when you want it to, but not so fast it scares you, because it will have between 1.625 and 2.10 inches of offset or rake (the amount that the front dropouts are set off from the center line of the head tube). The amount of offset changes with the headset angle. Here are our recommendations for appropriate offset, taking the headset angle into consideration.

Head Angle	69°	69.5°	70°	70.5°	71°	71.5°	72°
Approx. Offset	2.10″	1.92″	1.85″	1.80″	1.74″	1.68″	1.62°

This chart is for reference only; the numbers aren't written in stone. We used a bike with 2.2-inch tires, minus rider, to develop it. The feel of particular offsets will change with different head angles, the tire used, and the amount of the rider's weight on the front wheel.

Fork offset becomes a bizarre question when considering a "leading link" suspension system. The leading link design incorporates a straight or negatively raked main fork pivot-connected to a forward-projecting or leading auxiliary fork to improve handling. A shop that sells a leading link design should be able to tell you the design's handling equivalence in a positively raked fork.

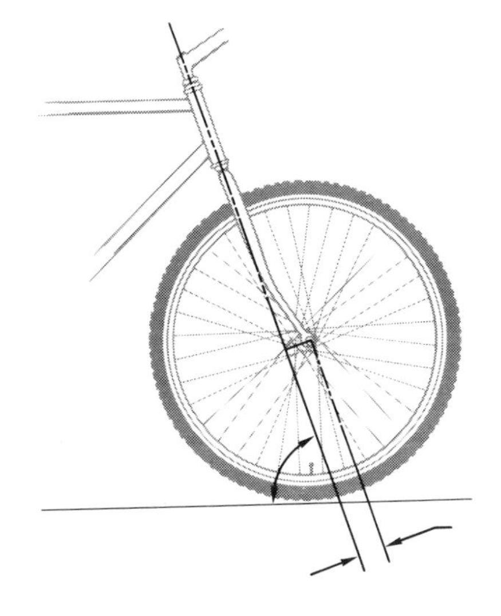

Fork Offset

Fork rake, or offset, and head angle are prime indicators of how the steering of a mountain bike feels.

Most companies list fork offset in their technical literature. Understanding quick yet controllable steering design and determining your preferences is best done with a test ride.

— ***Flex.*** The bottom bracket needs to be rigid. This is an absolute. Without it, you're wasting a lot of energy that's going hither and yon instead of into driving the rear wheel. The most straightforward way to guarantee rigidity is to get a bike with chainstays that join the front triangle at the bottom bracket.

But whereas stiffness or rigidity is desirable in the bottom bracket, you want some vertical flexing in the whole frame for shock dampening. To get—or not get—flex, mountain bike designers alter the design of the chainstay, how the rear triangles are braced, and the type of tubing. Some aluminum bikes, for example, are comfortable and some hammer the rider with shock waves.

— ***Tire clearance.*** The yearning for large tire clearance has resulted in some manufacturers using an elevated-chainstay design. The challenge of a worthwhile elevated-chainstay bike is to avoid the extra weight needed to keep your bottom bracket from wagging like a dog's tail. Some elevated-chainstay bikes also have an insufferably rigid rear triangle, and a too-short wheelbase.

— ***Weight.*** This is the wild-card. Of course lighter is better (given that all else is equal), and any bike that sports one of the top component groups (SunTour XC Comp or Pro, Campagnolo Icarus or Centaur, Shimano XT or XTR, or Mavic) should be closer to 25 pounds than 30. Titanium bikes have recently brought the total much closer to 20 pounds, but well-designed chrome-moly (steel) mountain bikes that weigh less than 24 pounds are also being produced. Builders achieve this by knowing what counts and paying attention to detail. So be sure of durability and quality first, then start counting pounds.

— ***Geometry.*** Many high-end bikes have unusual frame geometry (alterations in the head and seat angle, bottom bracket height, or chainstay lengths). The feel or ride of bikes with such deviations depends in part on the shape, diameter, and gauge of the tubing used, how it was joined, and how well that joining was executed. All other things being equal though, changes in geometry do have functional consequences for the rider.

Increasing the seat angle puts the rider more forward, more over the pedals, which promotes fast, smooth pedaling or spinning. A more reclined seat angle lends itself somewhat to tooling up hills in a

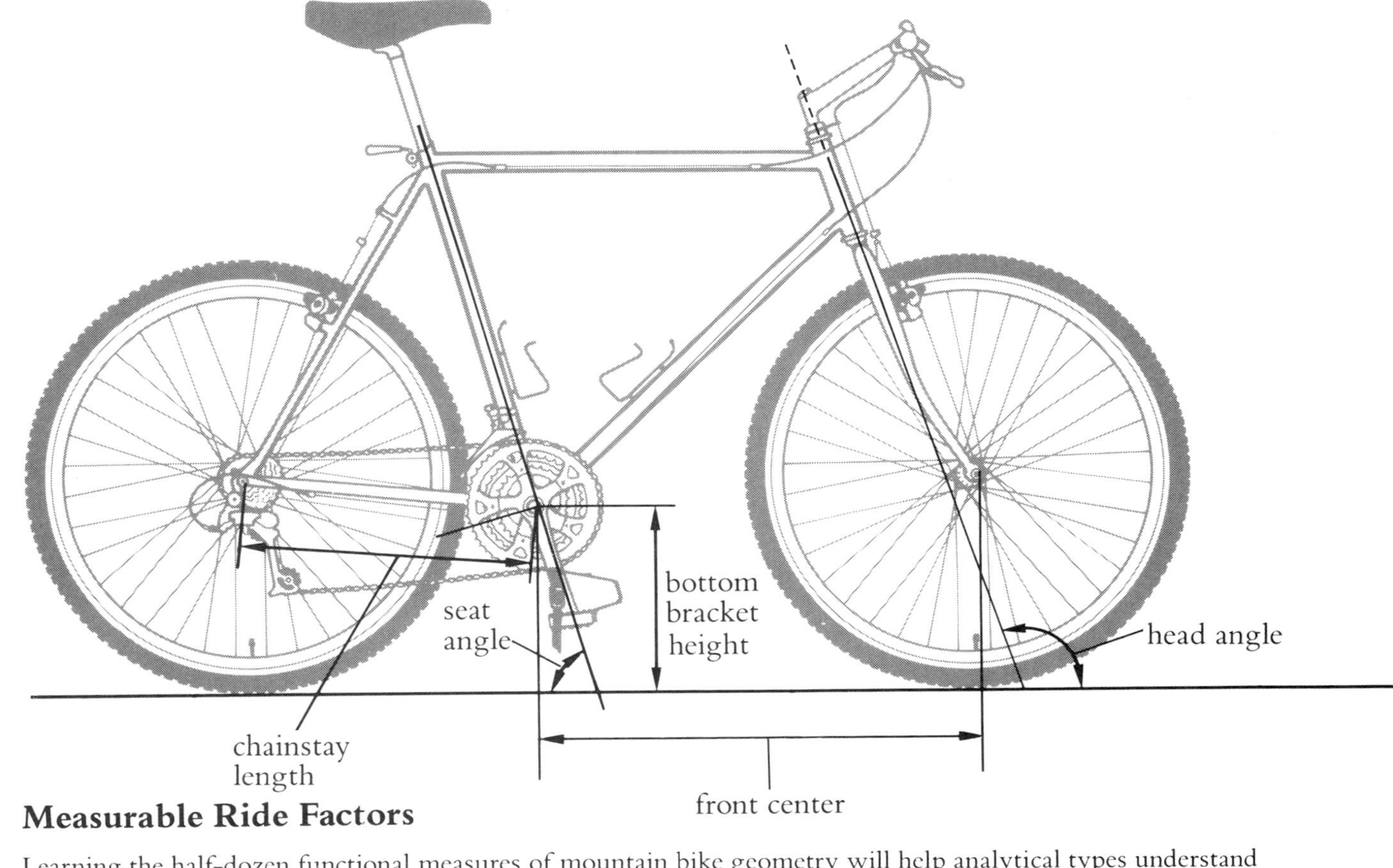

Measurable Ride Factors

Learning the half-dozen functional measures of mountain bike geometry will help analytical types understand how a bike rides.

seated position, especially for those who like the seated, low-gear feel of pushing the pedals on the downstroke.

Steeper head angles bring more riding shock to the rider, but this depends on how much weight is on the front wheel, which is largely a function of cockpit room, which in turn is most appropriately taken care of by correct top tube length.

Higher bottom brackets allow better clearance over felled branches, rocks, and logs. Lower bottom brackets feel more stable because of a lower center of gravity.

Shorter chainstays provide better traction on climbs and more responsive acceleration. Longer chainstays dampen rear-end shock and stabilize downhill runs.

Mountain bike designs break down into two general camps—those for leisure or adventure riding, and those for performance. The angles break down roughly like this:

	leisure	**performance**
Seat	71–73°	72–74°
Head	69–71°	70–72°
BB HT	11.375″+	11.375″+
Chainstays	17–17.5″	16–17.125″

Nothing says that a rider who does one kind of riding may not prefer the feel of a bike with the other category's design, so you may want to ride both to determine your preference.

The figures above are for all-round design bikes. However, there are more and more specialty designs coming out, principally technical, trials, and downhill models. Technical bikes feature ultra-short chainstays (15–15.5″), high bottom brackets, and shorter top tubes for controlled riding through rocky, limb-strewn, steep sections of single track. Trials bikes are perhaps the ultimate technical bikes. These pogo sticks with wheels and a chain are for deft maneuvering across piles of boulders, logjams, dry rocky creek beds, and picnic tables. Downhill bikes are long, super-stable dive bombers for streaking through hundreds of feet of vertical terrain.

— ***Appeal.*** Positive emotional bonding is a key ingredient for mountain biking enjoyment, so follow your instincts. If Bike A and Bike B are pretty much the same but you love Bike B for whatever reason, then get it.

— ***Getting advice.*** If you're a hammerhead who already has a race schedule marked on the calendar, listen to sound advice from experienced riders you respect, but don't get a bike simply because some top rider uses it or does ads for it. Just because Joe Racer rides Brand X doesn't mean that's his dream bike. As a sponsored racer you aren't always riding what you consider optimum equipment, although you do get good at dialing-in to get the most out of what you have.

The perfect bike

Each of the three of us has gone through a series of bikes in search of the Fat-tired Grail. Martha's story is typical of the bike changes a rider can go through.

> *I began by borrowing a friend's bike, then borrowing money for the only one available at the time in my neck of the country—an 18-inch-plus bike with 69- or 70-degree parallel tubes that was too big and too long, but affordable. I had fun with it all that summer. However, a few backaches and a couple of races later, I knew it left things to be desired.*
>
> *A mechanic friend who worked with a framebuilder helped me get a custom bike built that was sized for my leg length and designed to put me more over the pedals. Then racing started to determine everything on the bike. I got one that was lighter and had better mud clearance even with BIG tires. I also discovered positioning that made me part of the bike, not a thing perched on top of it.*
>
> *In 1988 I was able to have a bike built by an experienced mountain bike designer. It seemed perfect: 71/73 head tube/seat tube angles with 17-inch chainstays and a 40-inch wheelbase. A sloping top tube provided plenty of crotch clearance, and it was light—I could flick the rear wheel around a corner or rock just by moving my hips out. But there were still problems.*
>
> *The bike had a harsh ride, and we decided this came from the straight forks and tubing selection. So we put a curve in my forks and made the top tube smaller in diameter. I also felt that the stem was too long to stretch out properly, so we lengthened the top tube by almost an inch.*

> *The goal was closer: optimum race position on a bike that had stable handling on downhills yet was quick and light and didn't beat up my back and neck.*—Martha

Truly great all-around bikes for both performance and leisure riding are scarce, so if that's your goal, be prepared for some research and buying and selling before discovering one that best matches your riding style and handling preferences—and also fits.

The mountain biker in pursuit of that personally significant bike is frequently confronted by the riddle of fadism and innovation. The cycling industry's habits were formed during decades of marginal profits and commercial insignificance, so mountain biking products are often ballyhooed with a lot of personal opinion and advertising rhetoric but little or no impartial testing. Fork blades, chainstays, and brakes come to mind as examples of equipment that has suffered in this regard.

Mountain bikes as they are work pretty well in outrageous conditions from sub–Arctic Alaska to the Chilean desert. It's not as though there's no room for improvement—it's just that given this state of affairs, how's a rider to tell whether something is a true innovation, the mistaken product of overworked minds, or Rube Goldberg's idea of recreational sports marketing?

Testing that would illuminate the merits of most hot new bike products wouldn't be that hard or expensive to conduct. Unfortunately, such a tradition of disciplined verification doesn't exist in the mountain bike industry.

Until it does, here are some suggestions:

- Consider how much hype and how much sound logic is used to discuss a product or design.
- Consider the record of companies making any claims for new products or designs.
- Investigate whether principles of engineering or physics shed any light on the topic.
- Remember that bicycles were the hotbed of experimentation and innovation a hundred years ago. Are there records of similar ideas that were tried and discarded?
- Conduct two or three trail tests in differing terrains with the new device and compare the feel to a standard top-line bike.

If—despite your best efforts to get to the truth about the merits of something—you're at an impasse, if your bike is otherwise fine, and your livelihood doesn't depend on having the top edge of high-tech advantage, you might want to wait for the idea to weather two or three years in the market. That's an era in mountain biking technology. If the equipment holds up you may be the last person on the trail to be super-cool, but the first person to leapfrog to the second generation spin-off that's even better.

Then again, if you have the spare money and consider playing with the latest toys to be half the fun of mountain biking, go ahead and buy it. Just remember, it may be outdated in a year.

• • Brakes

What Makes for Good Stopping Power?

Given the type of terrain mountain bikers travel over, it's both critical and difficult for them to be able to control their speed and to stop at will. That's why all mountain bikes need good brakes.

Beware of salesmen and pundits who dodge this rule with the assertion that most mountain bikes never get off-road. This is simply not true. And fortunately, the demands of off-roaders have stimulated manufacturers' creativity until today there is a wide choice of reliable, effective brake systems.

Most of the stopping power is in the front brakes—they're in a stronger position to dissipate momentum. Unfortunately, too much front braking often results in pitching you like a human projectile over the handlebars. Therefore, it behooves a mountain biker to have a strong rear brake to complement the front brake and to provide better control of the bike.

What makes a good brake? Better brakes get their bragging rights by delivering more strength (mechanical advantage), stiffness (even resistance against the forces from the wheel and their own cables), and modulation (the ability to make minute changes in control).

Brakes generally have three parts: levers, cables, and calipers. However, major progress has been made in the past couple of years on hydraulic brakes similar to those used in cars. A hydraulic unit with the modulation, smoothness, and longevity of automotive hydraulic brakes that could withstand the rigors of mountain biking yet still be light and low-maintenance would be a real boon to cycling. Unfortunately, no such unit has made it into mass production.

Levers

The brake levers are the handles on the handlebars that are squeezed by your fingers. They generally pull on cables that connect them to caliper units, which are mounted on the frame where the wheel rim passes.

In order to function properly, brake levers must be sized and adjusted to your hands. Not surprisingly, most bikes come equipped with medium-sized levers. Better-quality bikes come proportionally sized, which means the manufacturer has taken into account the probable dimensions of the human being that fits each size of bike.

Some medium levers have reach adjustment, which modifies the distance between the lever and the handlebar. This enables you to fine-tune the lever to the length of your finger joints.

> *To keep my fingers from fatiguing too much, I adjust the reach of my brake levers so that when my hands are relaxed on the handlebars and my fingers are resting on top of the levers, the levers fit right behind the first bend from the end of my fingers.*—Martha

If your hands are simply too large or small for medium levers, you can buy properly sized, quality levers.

Brake levers should also be rotated around the handlebar to correspond to your line of grip so that the pulling action of your fingers and the travel of the lever are the same. And they should be secured on the handlebar at a comfortable distance from the bar ends.

Levers are available in long and short versions, sometimes referred to as "two-finger" or "four-finger" levers. The short versions are for those who prefer to use two fingers to squeeze the brake lever, leaving the other fingers on the grips to help steer the bike. The long versions are for people who prefer using three or four fingers on the brakes. (If your bike has four-finger levers, and you want to try operating the two-fingered way, move your brake levers in, swapping places with the thumb shifters. Adjust the reach, and you effectively have a two-finger lever.)

> *For index-and-forefinger braking, a shorter reach and continuous braking action to the grip offers more control and less fatigue. With short levers I most often use one finger on the front brake and two on the rear. If the going gets steep I'll keep two fingers on both.*—Michael

Most levers have a rotating cable-tension adjuster that allows you to fine-tune your brakes. This comes in handy when you get a blipped rim and need to widen the pad spread, or when you want to tighten the spread for wet, gritty conditions.

Cables

The cables pass from the levers to the calipers (the hinged arms that hold the brake pads) through the cable housing. Pulling the cable against the static housing operates the brake calipers. Cables should be made of corrosion-resistant steel (stainless), run in a friction-reducing housing liner, and lubricated with grease when installed (both to reduce friction and to resist corrosion that can cement the parts together).

Cables come in various thicknesses and constructions which have different "feels" or performance sensitivities. Generally, preferences in high-quality cable divide into two camps. Some riders prefer the sureness of large cables with large housing caps (ferrules) to steady the cable run and help transmit force to the calipers. Others prefer the smoothness and increased sensitivity of slightly thinner cables run in housing with a dry lubricant liner.

Both designs work well enough, so if you test ride bikes with both types and honestly can't tell a difference, don't worry about it. Even for most folks, it's a half-point on the decision-making scorecard. Split the hair toward the heavier type if you do a lot of panic stops, toward the thinner gauge if you think your riding style will benefit from more fluid control.

Calipers

When it comes to caliper units, partisans debate braking performance in a big way.

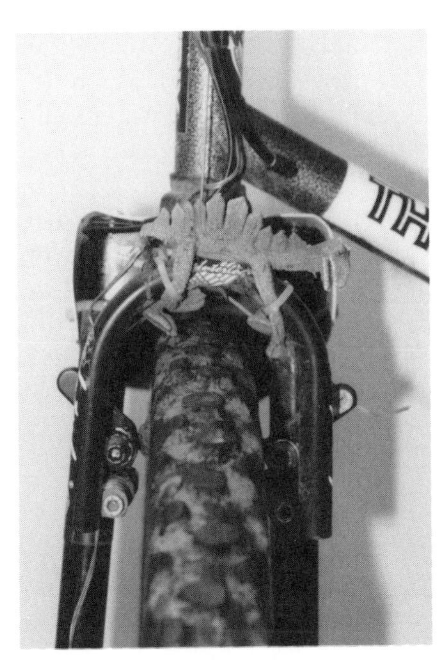

Even the best cantilever brakes can benefit from a stiffener plate or hoop to reduce movement in the mounting post, which helps eliminate rim squeal and fork chatter.

The casual rider can rest assured that most units on the market today are vast improvements over what existed even five years ago. Trailworthy general-purpose mountain bikes come with cantilever, U-brake, roller-cam, or rotary-style calipers. Cantilevers have a distinctive, outward-curving profile. U-brakes also get their name from their shape. Roller-cams have two huge arms, a triangular plate, and pulley wheels, while rotary brakes are distinguished by the round cam in the middle.

Although any kind of calipers can be mounted on the front, most front brakes are cantilevers. This is because the shorter cable run to the front gives that unit sufficient control and sensitivity and cantilevers are relatively inexpensive.

Which style unit should be mounted on the back varies according to frame design, intended use, and terrain considerations. Roller-cam, rotary, and U-brake units are designed to mount underneath the chainstays near the bottom bracket. This is a structurally strong place to mount them. It's also out of the way—there's no cable sticking out behind the seat to scratch your legs on and the rear area is clear for mounting gear, child seats, or trailer hitches. Finally, it's far easier to design vertical suspension for bikes with chainstay-mounted brakes.

On the other hand, seatstay-mounted calipers (usually cantilevers, but also roller-cams or U-brakes) give almost as strong a performance as chainstay brakes with far less risk of getting fouled from mud and debris. They're also less likely to freeze up in wet, slushy conditions.

Those of you who require smaller bikes (less than 17 inches) have additional considerations when it comes to rear brakes. If your brakes are seatstay mounted, make sure your heel and/or calf doesn't hit the rear brakes. If it's a very close call, don't assume you'll learn how to avoid it. Martha Kennedy and Sara Ballantyne are just two of the many sub-compact humans to have gotten major bruises from hitting these brakes. Sometimes it won't reveal itself as a problem until you're on technical terrain, moving your body around a lot. Duplicate these moves with the clothes you'll be wearing (especially shoes) before you hit the trail.

Caliper units all mount directly on internally threaded studs that are brazed or welded to the frame. For a more solid or sure feel, they can be fitted with a semicircular plate washer. These washers are marketed under names like "Brake Booster" and "Flex Fighter." They improve brake performance by preventing the mounting studs from twisting under pressure. You can also make a homemade brake reinforcement plate with a section of an old chainwheel with a bolt circle that matches the brake mounting studs. Secure both the brakes and plate with a longer bolt and a washer between the chainring plate and brake body.

Braking can also be improved by replacing your brake pads with higher-quality ones.

Road bikes are commonly set up with the pads .00625″–.0125″ from the rim. But the variety of situations encountered by a mountain bike suggest a mountain bike's brake pads be adjusted .0125″–.01875″ (some would even say .250″) away from the rim.

Keep in mind

If you're considering upgrading your brakes or deciding between bicycles with different brake setups, here are some things to keep in mind:

— ***Consider what you're going to do with your bike*** and what kind of terrain you'll be riding when deciding whether to use seatstay- or chainstay-mounted rear brakes.

— ***Roller-cam and rotary brakes*** offer superior mechanical advantage in the amount of pressure exerted on the wheel rim (stopping power). This is especially important in rear brakes. Roller-cams also offer solid modulation. However, they need constant adjustment as the pads wear, and require extremely accurate alignment between braze-on mounts and cable runs, which makes them torture devices for the moderately technical. They are also notorious mud collectors.

Rotary brakes are relatively new units and are still very expensive. More significantly, they have a completely different lever feel from all other brakes, which requires some operator re-education.

— ***U-brakes*** have more mechanical advantage than cantilevers, but less than roller-cam or rotary brakes. They offer better mud clearance than the stronger brakes, and stick out less than cantilevers.

— ***Cantilevers*** are economical, light, and sufficient for most mountain biking, and maintaining rear seatstay-mounted units is much easier than chainstay-mounted brakes. On the other hand, the resulting vertical flex in the frame's rear triangle compromises braking performance. A brake bridge reinforcer is almost mandatory.

— ***SE or self-energizing brakes*** are cantilever brakes mounted on a two-barrel body. The inner body has a helical path machined into it so the brake uses the forward momentum of the rim to increase braking power. (SEs are great on the front wheel of tandems.) Mechanically, there are a couple things to note about them: First, they require heavy-duty, braze-on studs. The standard square-base, riveted brake stud will be torn by the braking (that's how much power the helix generates). And second, the shell of the brake that encloses the spring and helix collects water, so if you ride in even moderately damp conditions, you'll have to conscientiously purge and relube them.

— ***If you use high ear cantilevers,*** such as Grafton Speed Controllers and IRD Switchbacks, which have a very high mechanical advantage, you'll have a limited pull-back of the pad from the rim. You must also allow for the mechanical advantage of your brake lever, which varies according to the distance between the pivot point and the cable ferrule, and the length of the arc of travel of the lever itself.

Combining high mechanical advantage calipers with high mechanical advantage levers can result in minimal mud clearance, low modulation, and many headers.

— ***Brakes work by applying pressure*** on the rims. If the rims are wet or coated with dirt or mud, the brake pad has to clean the rim before it begins to slow the bike. Development of a precision disk brake unit for mountain bikes would be a real plus.

— ***A cable-controlled, hydraulic disk brake*** for both front and rear wheels is now available and seems particularly useful for tandems, which need much more braking force than singles. A disk brake is especially good in wet weather, when rim brakes lose half their power or more.

• • Wheels

Making or Breaking Bike Performance

A mountain bike is composed of three equipment packages: the frameset, the wheels, and the components. All three are vital to good value. And, although the frameset and components (drivetrain, brakes, and bearings) get most of the attention, it's the wheels that most often establish the true worth of a particular bike.

This is because the entire experience of cycling rests on the two hubs and, through them, the spokes and rims. They are the part of the bike through which you feel the trail. They're simultaneously the primary means of suspension, the foundation for the frameset, and they carry out the bike's driving force and stopping action. A mediocre set of wheels can limit the performance of an otherwise exemplary bike, whereas a good pair of wheels allows an average bike to ride to the fullest of its design capabilities.

For a quick and easy check of the wheels on a bike you're considering, look at the technical specifications of the hubs. Substituting cheap hubs is a common practice with some manufacturers to lower cost and make a few more dollars. Check the specification graphs you can find in most bike catalogs. The hubs should match or exceed in quality the derailleur and brake units that come on the bike, not be some flashy off-brand of mysterious origins. If you can't find the information you need, don't be shy. Ask the salesperson for details.

After considering the hubs, look for stainless-steel spokes and chamber-profile (not simple U-shape), aluminum alloy rims that weigh under 600 grams each. Better bikes should have rims weighing 450 grams or less.

Whether you're buying wheels for a stock bike or a custom build-up, you'll be using the same basic criteria: durability, weight, tire-changing ease, and braking performance.

The main job of every bicycle wheel is to remain round and true. Assuming proper air pressure in the tire, how it will hold up depends upon the merits of the rim and the method used to tension the spokes. (That's why checking the evenness of spoke tension on a new bike is important.)

Rims

Assuming proper wheel lacing and tensioning, wheel durability relies on the rim.

A rim can be made strong by adding material, by using a better metal recipe, or by incorporating a stronger cross-sectional design. To determine the quality of various rims, ask if the shop has cross-sectionally cut sample pieces. Rims that display internal chamber designs in their cross-section view can be stronger and lighter than simple U-configured rims or rims with small tubular channels on the inside corners.

Two other things you'll want to see are an increase of material around spoke nipple holes (either with a reinforcing ferrule or thicker rim material) and plenty of tire bead (the hooked edge that holds the tire on the rim).

Mountain bike rims are either narrow (19–23 mm) or wide (25–32 mm). Improvements in chamber and tire-mounting design have brought the weight of performance rims down. The necessary weight of reliable, mid-priced, heavy-duty rims has dropped from 575 to 480 grams. The use of slightly more expensive 32-hole rims (instead of 36-hole) with strong cross-sectional design can bring the rim weight down below 400 grams per wheel, saving on spoke weight and improving aerodynamics.

Weight saved in the rim magnifies in advantage because the rotation of the wheels multiplies the rim weight and its effect on handling, braking, and acceleration power.

If you decide to go with sub-400-gram rims, the question is

whether to go with a slightly wider, box-rim design or a V-profile "aero" rim. On the plus side, aero rims are lighter, tend to shed dirt, mud, and snow better, and have a deeper cross-section. But they require inner tubes with an extra-long Presta valve, and some rim/tire combinations produce a squirrelly, floppy feel in corners.

Box rims provide wider support under the tire, make for easier brake setup (especially with mass-produced bikes suffering from poor brake post alignment), and allow the use of heavier rim tape for inner-tube protection. Yet tire changing is still relatively easy.

Spokes

Spokes are sized in wire gauge on a reverse numerical scale, similar to the way electrical wire is sized. Bicycle spokes suitable for mountain biking run in gauge sizes 14 (largest) to 17. Which gauge you'll use depends on your weight and your performance needs.

The only spokes worth talking about are stainless steel or titanium. But at six times the cost of high-quality stainless steel, and with a failure rate almost as high, titanium is, at this point, technical esoterica.

Stainless-steel spokes come in straight gauge and butted forms, butted spokes being thicker at the ends than at the middle. Butted spokes are identified by the two gauges used, for example, 14/15.

Straight 14-gauge spokes are the workhorses of cycling. They're economical, strong, easier to work with than butted spokes, and hold a wheel straighter when individual spokes break. Wheels built with them are not necessarily sluggish, and are usually significantly longer-lived than wheels with lighter gauge or butted types (especially for loads over 175 pounds). If you weigh less than 175 pounds and want the benefits of straight-gauge spokes, you can build fine performance wheels with 15-gauge stainless spokes.

Butted spokes offer strength where you want it, at the ends, and suspension elasticity overall, which helps the wheel withstand minor impacts. Using butted spokes can also save you several ounces per wheel and reduce aerodynamic drag. Their elasticity, however, makes them much more difficult to work with, so you'll want to find a skillful wheel builder.

Racers under 175 pounds can safely opt for three-cross pattern, 14/15 butted-spoke front wheels. Using 15/16 butted spokes on your rear wheel will save you some weight and improve suspension.

You can also have wheels built with shorter spokes that cross each other fewer times between hub and rim. This saves weight and cuts down on spoke frontal surface, which improves aerodynamics. But a two-cross wheel will be stiffer from the shorter, more direct spoke run, and will have less torsional strength from the decreased weave of the spokes. All of which may translate to increased spoke breakage in rough terrain.

Riders under 150 pounds can successfully ride unloaded bikes with a two-cross 14/15 front, and a two-cross left side/three-cross right side 15/16 rear. Riders in this weight class should have no problems using 28-spoke front wheels, but folks over 150 pounds should stick to 32 or more spokes per wheel.

Ultralight riders (under 130 pounds) are in the enviable position of being able to use three-cross 15/16 front, 15/17 rear on sub-400-gram rims and expect reasonable longevity despite the gossamer weight.

If you want to save some grams where it really counts—where centrifugal force exponentially increases the ounce value of savings—use aluminum-alloy nipples instead of brass. And if you want to spend money on pizazz, you can get the nipples in colors, too.

Hubs

Worthwhile mountain bike hubs are generally either traditional cup-and-cone designs with labyrinth outer seals, or cartridge units. Either type can deliver excellent performance.

You won't have to choose between the two until you reach the intermediate and upper end of bikes and componentry because less expensive bikes don't feature such bearings. If you like working on your bike, including semi-annual bearing overhauls, then traditional cups and cones might be for you. They also allow for on-site repairs when you find yourself 500 miles from a bike shop.

Cartridge bearings last longer, and are, for the most part, easier for a competent mechanic with the proper tools to deal with than cups and cones. If you're willing to pay for the tools, or just have the pro do your bearing replacements, then this might be the hub type for you.

Another option for top-quality hub bearings is to get one of the quick-purging lubricating systems that are becoming available.

These allow two-minute lube jobs on bearings, which means that riders with grease guns can inject fresh grease into their bearings immediately following a ride through water. With quick-purge systems, mountain bikers with a minute amount of mechanical ability can extend the life and performance of their bearing units dramatically.

Spare pair

Besides adding a rear rack, the one purchase you can make that will really extend the range of your mountain biking is a second set of wheels. The most common variation on the dual wheels plan is to have a pair of around-town or commuter wheels with slicks or treadless tires and a pair with heavier tread for trail use. Racers might have a pair of crash-and-trash or training wheels and a pair of race-day wheels.

Once you find out how much fun it is to ride in the dirt on weekends, you might get motivated to ride during the week so that you're in better condition on the weekend rides. Or you just might find cycling so much fun that you start doing more and more of it—including running errands or maybe even commuting to work.

But good off-road tires aren't really good road tires. The large knobs that give you traction on dirt make a distinct buzzing sound on pavement (known as "swarming" when a pack gets going). Their lower air pressure means they're harder to pedal and don't corner as well, and pavement eats your tire tread like cheese puffs.

Changing tires every time you want to go from road to dirt is not only a nuisance, but tough on tire sidewalls. By having a pair of sturdy wheels with minimal tread, your bike can be transformed from road to trail worthiness (or vice versa) in minutes.

But make sure the rims of both sets of wheels match so the brake setting is the same. Rear hub spacing, dish, and drivetrain componentry must also match.

Weekend racers can benefit from saving their premium-quality wheels for races and using sturdier, if heavier, wheels for training. Again, make sure rim widths match or you're going to be spending valuable training time doing brake adjustments each time you switch wheels.

Slightly heavier training wheels actually help the rider by giving a slightly increased training workout, which, all other things being equal, translates into increased speed on lighter race wheels. This is like swimming competitors who don't shave until the day of an important meet.

What about getting a pair of ultimate wheels? Well, interestingly enough, the field-proven criteria for ultimate mountain bike wheels are almost the same for racing as for adventure riding. In either situation you want durability, easy tube changing, and as little rotating weight on the rim as possible.

For most folks, the only difference in such a pair of 32-spoke wonders would be in the spoke gauge and lacing. Use the previously mentioned weight guidelines for spoke gauge and patterns (but bump yourself up a 20-pound class if you expect to go on loaded expeditions). Racers can use the sparser cross patterns mentioned, while others should stick to three-cross reinforcement throughout.

Rubber

The type of terrain you'll be riding will determine which tires to mount on your wheels. Tire size refers to the width, or diameter (in inches), of the tire. You can get 1.5, 1.75, 1.9, 1.92, 2.0, 2.1, 2.2, 2.5, and 2.6 tires.

Strictly street use? Then 1.5–1.9 is all you'll need. Consider treadless tires (slicks). They handle great, roll easier, and hold up surprisingly well.

For off-road use, keep these points in mind:

- Larger tires provide more cushioning and more knobs on the dirt for improved traction, but they're heavier.
- Kevlar-bead tires are foldable, which makes them nice for spare carry-alongs. They also mount more easily on some rims and weigh less than other tires. They have a more flexible sidewall, so are more workable in loose sand or snow where you run extremely low tire pressures for better tooth. But beware. Some brands of Kevlar tires are significantly lighter than their standard siblings, so much so that they get flats more often and wear out in weeks instead of months.
- Using a slightly larger-sized tire on your front wheel can improve control, particularly on rolling hills and winding downhills. Run an aggressively treaded larger tire on the front (the 202 Fattrax,

Ritchey Z-Max, and Joe Murray Equilibrium are good examples) and use a slightly smaller rear with a good cornering lug pattern (like the Specialized Extreme, Ground Control, or Michelin Hi-Lite Hot).

Many tire companies produce different tread patterns for all the variety of terrain on the planet. Generally speaking, tighter tread patterns work better in harder packed soils, while treads with larger gaps or open, obtuse angles between the knobs work better in muck and loose stuff. Tread patterns that wrap over the edge onto the sidewall will steer more surely through corners in gravel and sand.

Remember that rubber compound and casing quality are less mentioned but vital aspects of good tires. Soft tires may have superior tactile foot but wear out significantly quicker. Casing quality is important to a tire's ability to resist cuts from stones and rim pinches.

Rubber selection boils down to performance versus protection. If you're like us, you want to spend your recreation time riding the bike, not repairing flats. That's why we think "bullet-proof." If you're a recreational rider who wants maximum protection and durability from one set of good all-around tires, then get a pair of K4 Ground Controls or Kevlar Fattrax tires, stuff them with Mr. Tuffy tire liners and thorn-resistant inner tubes, and hit the dusty trail.

Mountain bike tubes come in Presta and Schrader valves, just like road tires. Make sure your pump matches your valve stems! We recommend Presta valves: they're mechanically superior, take a smaller rim hole, and can use either type of pump fitting as long as you have an inexpensive adapter.

● ● Drivetrain

Choosing Derailleurs, Controls, and Gearing

A drivetrain is only as good as how well it transmits the force exerted by your legs to the rear wheel, how well it holds up, and how easily it matches your conditioning to the terrain you're riding. Your personal habits will largely determine which system is best for you.

Do you race? (This can refer to general riding style as well as actual participation in licensed, officiated, and sanctioned events.) Does having the most recent technical wizardry count in terms of your livelihood, self-esteem, or satisfaction to the extent that you replace your bike every year, or at least replace your components every two years?

If so, you're a classic Type A rider and you want the advanced functional nuances offered by the larger companies' top two or three component groups, and only the top-of-the-line component group of the smaller manufacturers.

You're also interested in the components' weight (odds are, you're a gram counter). But even though weight is an absolute, quantifiable quality, there's not too much to excise from bike components at the top of the line. Reliability, smoothness of operation, stiffness, and surface hardness of parts are just as important. And your components should match any physical or operational idiosyncrasies you have.

Type A riders should consider these two things when evaluating the true merit of lighter component weight:

- Lower rotating weight (rims and tires, your shoes, pedals, crank arms, hubs) is more significant than having lighter static parts.
- The closer to the center of gravity a static component is (generally lower, closer to the bottom bracket), the less difference its weight makes.

A good example of the rule that weight should not override function is found in pedals and crank arms, which rotate but are about as close as a component gets to a bike's center of gravity. Ease of entry and exit for your feet can very well offset the 100-gram difference between two very good pairs of pedals. The value of a lighter pair of crank arms can be negligible if the bottom bracket bearings don't hold up to average lateral pedal pressure, or if the chainrings are soft and deform easily, causing shifting interference or mishap (that is to say, chainsuck).

On the other hand, an excessive jump in weight or reliability may be a tip-off that the latest hotly promoted component product is more engineering fadism than hi-tech advancement.

Five-year plan

Plenty of dedicated enthusiasts who demand as much or more from their bikes as Type A riders only trade in or up every three to five years. They've found out what works for them and they're not about to abandon it just for the sake of owning the latest hot ticket.

Those with this kind of controlled enthusiasm for component technology point out that truly significant technological improvements in performance only become established after three to four years anyway. (It takes that long to get all the bugs worked out.) To them it makes a lot more sense to get the dollar value out of your major appliance purchase and modify it here and there as need be.

If this sounds like your game plan, then durability becomes even more relevant. You want components that are going to hold up throughout your ownership and that still have some resale value when you're ready to update.

Since things might get bashed or busted here and there during the time you own a bike, piecemeal compatibility of a brand's components is important. Otherwise, someday you might find yourself spending money for an entire new system when all you need is one part. Ask mechanics about a component brand's average span of utility before you invest $700. If rear derailleurs or shift levers available today work with that company's product from two or three years ago, you're probably safe.

For people who buy a new bike once every decade or so, maximal functional lifetime are the watchwords. These folks got 15 or 20 years out of their last bike purchase, and there's really no reason why they shouldn't be able to match that with a relatively equal real-dollar investment in one of today's mountain bikes.

To these people, the ongoing availability of small parts becomes just as important as durability or a brand's component compatibility. The only way to find out is to ask at the service desk.

Crankset

The core of a drivetrain is its crankset, which includes the bottom bracket, crank arms, and chainrings. To do a quick check of bottom bracket quality, look at how the crank arms are fastened to the bottom bracket spindle. Better brackets use bolts. Some lesser units use nuts, with the end of the spindle itself being turned and threaded. If you imagine doing a regular amount of trail riding, you want the bolted type.

Bottom brackets as well as hubs come in cartridge, or cup and cone semisealed designs. If you plan to do your own overhauls, the cup and cone design is probably best. On the other hand, top-of-the-line cartridge bearings offer superprecision and exceptional load capacity. The ultimate is to get a zirk-fitted cartridge bearing bottom bracket assembly, or have such a system retrofitted to your bike. For regular trail riders and water hazard devotees, such quick-purge lubrication systems are instruments of the gods.

Chainring value can be determined with straightforward industrial standards—are the ring's teeth stamped or machine cut, and how hard are they? Machine cut is superior to stamping, and harder tooth metal wears longer. Product literature usually mentions machining as a plus if that's how the chainrings were made. Occasionally there's mention of the Rockwell C scale, a numerical scale of hardness (a value of 40 is minimum). If you're spending more than $500, chainring wear isn't going to be an immediate problem, unless you're racing and training almost daily in a place where it's rainy throughout the race season, in which case you might be replacing rings once a month.

Every manufacturer has claimed superior chainring tooth shape at one time or another, and the only way to find out about any product line's performance is, again, to ask around.

Mountain bikes come with three chainrings bolted to the crank arms. Most mountain bikers can get a sufficient gear spread for their needs with available stock rings. You can, for example, downsize your "Granny" ring to 24 teeth for steeps and put on a 50- or 52-tooth big ring for downhills.

Those who ride on exceptionally steep terrain may want to resort to adding a fourth, even smaller, chainring known as a quad ring. Installation involves the fourth sprocket, an adapter that allows the sprocket to thread onto your third chainring, and often, a replacement spindle (longer). Parts cost around $70, and shop labor is about $15.

SunTour recently introduced a matched downsized system of chainwheels and freewheel cogs called Micro-Drive. It's the commercial version of an old gram-counting, custom retrofit in which smaller cogs and chainwheels supply the same effective range of standard gears but with weight savings.

The functional price of this downsizing has always been increased wear and tear resulting from the same amount of force being transmitted through less surface area. Whether SunTour has engineered a tougher or harder set of components to withstand the increased wear remains to be seen.

Optimal chainring tooth count is something we get into at the end of this drivetrain discussion when we talk about gearing (oh boy!).

Readily available crank arms come from 165 mm to 180 mm in length, although generally only 170 mm or 175 mm are on stock bikes. A really good shop will substitute longer or shorter crank arms at no extra charge. The standard 175s will be no problem to sell later.

Ideally, crank arms should be proportional to your upper leg length, as well as inseam length. That's because on a bike, the rider is the motor. His or her legs and the crank arms make up the motor's multiple-hinged crank shaft. For best efficiency, its parts should be proportionally sized, and since people's legs are variable, it's the cranks that should be adjusted to fit. Otherwise, the rider's muscles will never function to their potential.

Check pedal axle and kneecap alignment as mentioned earlier. If you can't get proper alignment with your correct seat height and cockpit room without moving the saddle either completely forward or rearward on the rails, you need to move up or down in crank arm length.

Attached to both your feet and the cranks are the pedals. Bearing and axle quality are the mechanical concerns here. You want no friction and no slop. Look at pedal cage width, and strap and clip allowance for easy entry, exit, and strap snugging. Try them out with the shoes you'll be riding in.

The chain of a mountain bike takes more abuse than anything else and gets replaced more than any other component part. How well a drivetrain functions is largely dependent on the chain. But even the most exemplary system can be worthless if replacement or repair of the chain is a hassle. Find out if the drivetrain of the bike you're interested in works well with commonly available chains and whether repair is possible with standard tools or whether it takes an expensive dedicated tool.

Derailleurs

Derailleurs move the chain between cogs or chainrings, providing multiple gear choices. They simply lift the chain and knock it over to the desired neighboring cog or ring.

Front derailleurs should provide a clean, crisp action across the entire range of chainrings. Today's derailleurs all have the required range, and, at most, take only a little tweaking to give crisp shifts.

In the few years mountain bikes have been around, a handful of builders have experimented with top-tube routing of derailleur cables. It's a great idea except for those who like to bundle things to the top tube. The cables are away from mud and flying debris. Now manufacturers are even making top-pull front derailleurs to accommodate the design. Not necessary, but as we said, a nice touch.

For years many mountain bikers have been waiting for final development and deployment of the BEAST—the Browning Electronic Accushift Transmission. It's an electronically controlled (no cables!) front changer that works with hinging quarter sections, much like a railroad track switch. Its advantage lies in being able to shift gears up front under pedal pressure, because the chain is always engaged. But recurrent kinks (including problems with mud) seem to forestall mass production and development of kits for existing bikes. Retrofit kits probably won't come along until mountain bike design parameters settle down, or until SunTour, owners of the rights, decides they can specify frame geometry and alignment standards for which they'll guarantee the system.

At the other end of your chain is the rear derailleur—the widget that does the bulk of gear-change work. Midline and higher models work so well that you have to get into particulars like pulley or "jockey wheel" design to decide which is better. Jockey wheels are the pair of stacked 1.5-inch diameter wheels the chain snakes around before arcing over the rear cog and going back to the crankset. (Some indexing rear derailleurs depend on built-in slop in the upper pulley mount as part of their cog/chain alignment mechanism. If you want to try to improve drivetrain performance in these derailleurs, replace only the lower pulley wheel with a bearing-mounted pulley.)

The pulley wheels are held in what's known as a cage, which

Today's mountain bike components are remarkably functional in the most extreme environments imaginable. This is Martha Kennedy's rear derailleur halfway through the inaugural Iditabike race.

comes either long or short. Shifting action is quicker with shorter cages and you save 20–70 grams, but you either lose tooth-count capacity (how large a rear cog the derailleur will handle) or have to settle for a narrower range of chainrings. A shorter cage might make designing an adequate gear spread for your needs tricky, but generally this type can handle a 28- or 30-tooth rear cog.

Freewheels

Which brings us to the freewheel, that cluster of toothed wheels bundled on the right side of the rear hub. They look like little circular saw blades, and there are six, no, make that seven or even eight of them.

Bicycle component designers began burning candles before the image of Still More Cogs in the mid '80s, the idea being to provide more gear choice. Theoretically, with more gears the rider can more often have the one that best matches his/her output ability with the terrain. Well, theory can go on forever, and product managers from the cog-count cult have. There has been some success to the higher-cog-count systems, which were instituted at the same time as easier-shifting tooth profiles. But there is one practical problem that comes up—mud.

If you live in a muddy place such as the Pacific Northwest, you might find it worthwhile to make sure the derailleur system on your bike can index shift six- as well as seven- or eight-speed clusters. The wider spaces between six-speed cogs don't clog and skip gears as easily as seven or eight speeds (although the shorter Hyperglide teeth still clog up). If you go with seven or eight, be sure to carry a small straight-bladed screwdriver in your jersey or jacket pocket so you can reach back and scrape out your cluster.

That cluster of gear cogs mounts on either a freehub or hub and freewheel. With the hub-and-freewheel design, the cluster of gear cogs mounts on a body that itself screws onto a threaded flange on the right side of the rear hub. You can change the entire gear cluster using a freewheel remover tool and a vise or pocket vise, and the design allows retrofitting quick-grease purging ports for the bearings. (The same freewheel removal operation is the first step in replacing broken spokes.)

Freehubs integrate the body of the freewheel into the hub. The gear cogs mount directly onto the hub. Freehub fans like the freehub's wider placement of the rear wheel's bearings, and the simplicity of changing cogs without a vise. Whether you use a freehub or hub-and-freewheel design, be sure your drivetrain can be reset to index between different cog-count clusters.

Controls

One of the early user-friendly triumphs of mountain bikes was the placement of gear shifters, known as thumb-shifters, on the handlebars right by the handlebar grips. People loved the fact that they didn't have to let go of the bars and reach down between their legs to shift gears. But as mountain biking got adventurous, riders discovered an operational problem—sore thumbs. Various solutions have been brought forward to remedy this nuisance.

In the early days of mountain bikes it was considered a significant achievement when designers eliminated the protruding parts below the handlebars where you banged and too often tore your knee. That line of development has led to the introduction of Grip Shift brand rotating gear shift controls (similar to the same brand of controls that have been successful on road bikes).

These shifters mount between the four-finger brake levers and the hand grips, and you change gears by twisting the shifter grip around the handlebar. Those who like them cite ease of operation (especially in winter), minimum of moving parts, and unobtrusive structure. Others dislike the different movement it takes to use them, as compared to standard shifters.

Campagnolo has also introduced a twist-shift mechanism, the Bullet system, which works well when used with a Rhuloff chain, a very expensive proposition.

SunTour and Shimano have both introduced double-push controls. Taking a cue from racers who mounted reversed thumb-shifters underneath their handlebars for better operation, these models mount a pair of levers to a body underneath the handlebars. Whether upshifting or downshifting, gears are changed by the thumb pushing on a lever.

Double-push levers are easy to operate, but there are numerous serious disadvantages to the system. Most importantly, there's no friction mode for when the rear derailleur and/or its mounting dropout hanger get bashed many miles into a ride and can no longer index well. Other problems are that the shifters' body size turns back the clock of handlebar improvement by virtually guaranteeing knee-banging sessions, and the levers' size makes them marginal or worse for smaller-handed riders. Also, both weight and replacement cost are almost twice as much as the other shifter systems. And you can still get sore thumbs from them, and since they mount under the bars, you no longer have the option of shifting with your entire hand.

Another control arrangement is to use road-style drop handlebars or flat handlebars with fore-aft extensions on the ends that allow the mounting of indexed bar-end shifters. (Just be sure that the extension ends flare a bit outward to ward off undesired knee-shifts.)

You can also mount a pair of Moots Road Bars, forward-pointing grip-length sections of tubing, between your brake levers and thumb-shifters. The thumb-shifters can then be activated with either the traditional action, or with the base of the thumbs with the hands resting on the extensions.

If your thumbs get really sore using the shifters on your particular bike, and you don't want to use any of the options outlined above, you could just try another model of thumb-shifter with less friction or lever action. Otherwise, strengthen your hands and thumbs, and learn to massage pressure points in the area to relieve pain and strain.

Gearing

That only leaves gearing itself, that wonderful yet basic mechanical discovery around which all the above equipment is based.

Multiple gears allow mountain bikers to pedal as though they had several sizes of wheels—from very large to very small diameter—all on the same bike. Gearing's avantage is twofold: you can make the bike go faster for the same number of pedal strokes or you can keep the same pedal speed despite a change in the terrain. Gearing is the primary reason why bicycles are the most efficient transportation method ever invented. (By converting calories burned riding a bike to British Thermal Units (BTUs), and comparing those to BTUs in gasoline for automobiles, researchers discovered that bicycles get about 1,500 miles per gallon.) Understanding proper use of a mountain bike's gearing is vital to its fullest functioning and enjoyment.

The number of teeth on each of the front chainrings and the number of teeth on each of the rear cogs combine to form your bike's gearing. With all those tooth counts and possible combinations of front chainrings and rear cogs, the entire thing can be confusing, but fortunately you don't have to deal with the numbers at all to begin to get a handle on it. Here's a simple way to look at it.

High gears help you move the bike faster because you go farther with each turn of the pedals, but you have to put out more effort to turn the crank arms. Your gears get higher as you move the chain farther away from the bike frame to either the outside chainring or outer freewheel cogs.

Low gears help you ride up steeper terrain because it's easier to turn the crank arms, even though the bike covers less ground for each turn of the pedals. Your gears get lower when you move the chain closer to the bike frame by moving it to an inner chainring or freewheel cog.

You use middle gears for flat or relatively flat terrrain, shifting up or down as needed to maintain your preferred rate of pedal speed.

Which front chainring you use with which rear cogs is a function of gear spacing and chainline. You want to avoid chain crossover, a front-chainring–rear-cog combination that creates a sharp chain angle. Such placement wears the components excessively, which ultimately costs you repair money. (If you have a short-cage rear derailleur and short chain setup, it can cause chain jamming and really screw up your day.)

For those who want to keep things simple, use the middle chainring up front with the middle four rear cogs. Use the smallest (most inward) front chainring with the largest three or four rear cogs for your lowest, hill-climbing gears. Use the largest (outwardmost) chainring with your smallest three or four cogs. Learn whether to shift the front or rear derailleur by judging how much of change is coming up in the terrain just ahead. Large changes will usually mean a shift of chainrings.

For novices, most gear-changing panic arises in downshifting for surprising uphills. If you can't remember where the chain is, and are too concerned about crashing to look at the rear hub, first check to be sure that the chain's on the front middle ring, then downshift to the inner rear cogs. If you downshift the rear all you can and it's still not enough, then bail out to the smallest ring up front.

It all sounds more complicated than it is. The more you do it, the more automatic it'll become until soon you won't even have to think about it. You'll already have shifted automatically to meet the demands of the terrain you just scanned.

The most efficient use of this marvelous gearing system depends upon knowing the sequence of gears from lowest to highest. There are three principle factors: spread, spacing, and count. Fortunately, the entire mess can be rendered in a single scale of numbers known as gear inches. The higher the number in gear inches, the larger the gear (harder to turn but faster, if you can do it).

To deal with that easy, single scale of gear inches you need to know the number of teeth on each of your bike's chainrings and gear cogs. Happily enough, sometimes this information comes in printed form with your bicycle. If not, count them. (Another easy way out: often you can read the count of teeth on the front chainrings by looking closely at the chainrings themselves, where the number is sometimes stamped.)

Now set up a chart with the number of teeth on the chainrings across the top, and the number of teeth on the gear cogs along the left side (smallest cog's count at top to largest cog's count at the bottom). See below:

	24	36	48
13	X	( )	
15	X		
18			
21			
25			X
30		( )	X

Each number represents a chainring or gear cog. Notice that we've put big Xs in some spots. These are the "crossover" gears that wear down your drivetrain parts and which you shouldn't use. Parentheses mean it's okay in dire circumstances, but not advisable as a regular shift.

Now fill in the other spots with the appropriate gear inch from the chart in the back of this book. Those of you who want to do the math yourself can measure the diameter of your wheels, with tire mounted, in inches. Then divide the number of chainring teeth by the number of rear cog teeth and multiply that number by the wheel diameter. This will give you the gear inches.

You now have a gear chart that should look something like this:

	24	**36**	**48**
13	X	(72)	96
15	X	62	83
18	35	52	69
21	30	45	59
25	25	37	X
30	21	(31)	X

Your gearing spread is important. It's the total range of your gearing, from your lowest wall-clinging wrap to your high speed overdrive. In our sample it's from 21 to 96 gear inches, which is reasonable. You want a bottom bail-out gear that's 24 gear inches or lower, and an overdrive high gear in the 90s or low 100s.

Gearing count is the actual number of usable gears you get after discounting crossovers, gearing duplication, and extreme double-shift problems. Taking a look at the chart, you'll notice that there's virtual duplication of two chain arrangements (30 and 31), giving us 13 actual gears.

"Double shifting" refers to gear changes during which you have to shift both derailleurs. As a rule, you don't want to change more than two rear cogs at once.

Gear spacing is the jump between any two gears in your usable sequence. Some people consider the ideal to be nice even jumps between all gears. And on the bike, your middle gears should have pretty even spacing, but there should be slightly tighter jumps between your higher gears, and deeper jumps into your low gears.

You want the maximum number of even increments possible so you can keep up your pedal spin under varying circumstances, but when you have to downshift for steep climbs, you usually appreciate lower lows in the granny-gear range.

Some people like to structure their gears so they have one giant overdrive gear on top. Our sample has that, but is a little lacking in increments in the higher end.

A handy way to learn your gearing is to make a single-spaced chart like the one above and tape in on the top of your handlebar stem. It'll help you learn what each gear in the sequence feels like, what different gear inches are like as far as power requirements go, and what your shift sequence is. By the time you're comfortable with those things, you'll probably be ready to get rid of the chart if the elements haven't destroyed it already.

Here are some of our gearing preferences.

6 Speed

	24	34	46
12	X	74	100
14	X	63	85
16	39	55	75
19	33	47	63
22	28	40	54
26	24	34	X

	24	36	48
12	X	78	104
14	X	67	89
17	37	55	73
20	31	47	62
24	26	39	52
28	22	33	X

	24	34	48
13	X	68	96
15	X	59	83
18	35	49	69
21	30	42	59
25	25	35	50
30	21	30	X

	24	36	48
13	X	72	96
15	X	62	83
16	39	59	78
19	33	49	66
22	26	43	57
26	24	36	X

7 Speed

	26	**36**	**48**
13	X	72	96
15	X	62	83
17	40	55	69
20	34	47	62
23	29	41	54
26	26	36	48
30	22	31	X

	26	**34**	**48**
13	X	68	96
15	X	59	83
17	40	52	69
20	34	44	62
23	29	38	54
26	26	34	48
30	22	30	X

	26	**34**	**48**
13	X	68	96
14	X	63	89
16	42	55	78
18	38	49	69
22	31	40	57
26	26	34	48
30/32	23/21	30/28	42/39

	24	**36**	**48**
13	X	72	96
15	X	62	83
17	37	55	73
20	31	47	62
23	27	41	54
26	24	36	48
30	21	31	42

	26	**34/36**	**48**
12	X	74/78	104
14	X	63/67	89
16	39	55/59	78
18	35	49/52	69
21	30	42/45	59
24	26	37/39	52
28	22	31/33	X

8 Speed

	24	34	46
12	X	74	100
14	X	63	85
16	39	55	75
18	35	49	66
21	30	42	57
24	26	37	50
26	24	34	46
30	21	29.5	X

	24	38	48
13	X	76	96
14	X	71	89
16	39	62	78
18	35	55	69
20	30	47	59
23	27	43	54
26	26	38	48
30	21	31	X

	24	34	48
13	X	68	96
14	X	63	89
15	42	59	83
17	37	52	73
19	33	46.5	65
22	28	40	56
24	26	37	52
28	22	32	45

	24	34	48
13	X	68	96
14	X	63	89
16	39	55	78
18	35	49	69
21	30	42	59
24	26	37	52
28	22	32	45
32	19.5	28	X

• • Fine-tuning

Custom-fitting Saddle, Seat Post, Handlebars, and Stem

The saddle, seat post, handlebars, and stem are where you fine-tune and custom-fit your bike. How well you choose and size these pieces of equipment can have a major impact on how much fun you have riding your bike.

These are places for gram counters to save a pinch here and a smidgen there, but before you start looking for the lightest, be sure the parts are safe, correctly sized, and durable.

The seat post is an easy place to save weight. Seat posts now come in hi-tech mineral-compound materials, with lightweight, butted tubing. Just be sure the seat post is long enough to leave three inches in the seat tube at its highest extension.

Most seat posts provide for fore-aft as well as up-and-down adjustment. These adjustments are secured with a lockdown device that has either one or two bolts. Both bolt types work. More important than bolt count is how the lockdown device grips the saddle. It should have a broad four-point rail grip and enough material to counter the rocking and torsional forces on the saddle rails.

Bicycles replaced horses, not cars, and that's why what sits upon the seat post is known as a saddle, not a seat. (It's also why the drivetrain gear is on the right side of the bike frame. That way you won't spook the bike by getting on from the wrong side!)

Your saddle is not the place to try to save $5 or a few grams of metal weight, because you'll end up with big losses in durability and comfort. But don't just assume that you're going to need a wide, cushy seat. Most people find they ride best on a fairly firm saddle. If you're really new to cycling, you're going to have to allow time for your posterior to toughen, which doesn't take long if you ride regularly.

Try different saddles in the store by asking to use different bikes on an indoor trainer. Women should try both the wider women's saddles with shorter noses or horns, as well as those with less padding on the horn, and regular narrow ones. Many female racers prefer the the narrower saddles, both because their hips may not be especially wide, and because riding a wide saddle off-road for a few hours can be uncomfortable. That's because you're not really "sitting" on a bicycle saddle, you're balanced or perched upon it and have to accommodate an exceptional amount of leg movement and riding vibration. Plenty of saddles come with gel pad cushioning material for friction dampening, and a narrow gel saddle can be just the ticket, especially on tandems, which tend to ride a little rougher than singles.

If you're a veteran roadie used to a turbo saddle, you should get a similar model on your mountain bike. That way you'll experience less discomfort switching from road to off-road riding.

Get a saddle with steel rails. The couple of grams saved by aluminum alloy are not worth the inconvenience or the replacement cost when they break (and they will break).

Saddles can be adjusted for nose angle as well as for fore-aft position. Try to avoid pushing the saddle all the way forward on the rails. If you have to do so for comfortable, correct leg/pedal placement, you probably need shorter crankarms. Keeping the saddle back keeps weight on the rear wheel for climbing. Angle adjustment usually involves raising the nose of the saddle for a tilt of up to 10 degrees. Don't be afraid to play with saddle adjustment if you're uncomfortable. Just do it in tiny increments, and don't change anything else while you're trying different settings.

Many mountain bikes come with a Hite-Rite height-adjustment spring connecting saddle and seat post. This is a nifty device that allows you to preset your flat-ground and uphill saddle height, and then to quickly switch between that and a lower saddle height for downhills on which you want the freedom to move your posterior farther back over the rear wheel. It also acts as a saddle and seat post theft deterrent, forcing aspiring thieves to work with wrenches instead of simply undoing your quick-release seat post lever. Many racers, though, consider Hite-Rites unnecessary weight and bother, and choose instead to work on improving their downhill technique.

Cockpit room

Once you have proper saddle height, etch a mark on the seat post to make repositioning easier after removal. Then you're ready to establish the right amount of operator cockpit. This involves the drop between saddle height and stem height as much as forward reach.

Women might consider setting up their bikes with a little less drop than on their male friends' bikes. Many female mountain bikers ride well with such a setup, although whether this is due to proportions or adjusting for different pressure points is unknown. Just make sure to keep two inches of stem length below the headset locknut for safety's sake. (On very small frames this may be a challenge.)

If you're getting a stem with a built-in brake cable pulley, make sure it's of good quality. Inexpensive "imitation quality" models

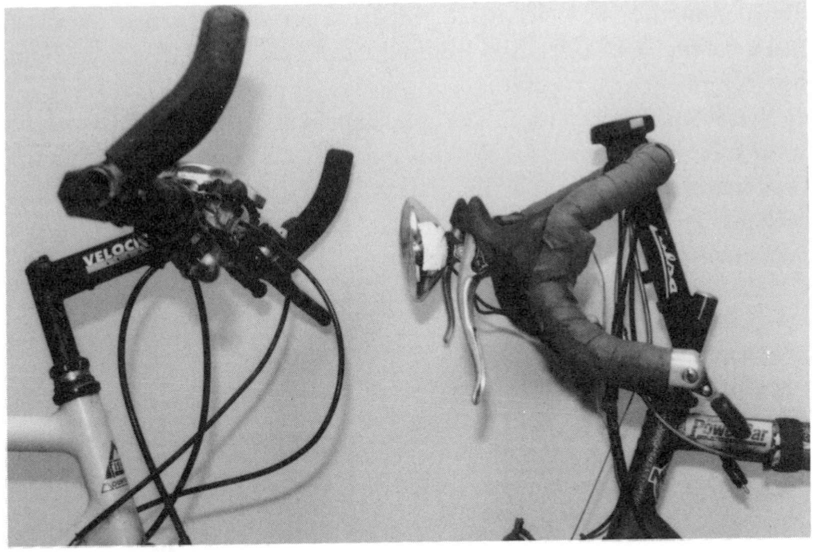

Stems, handlebars, and bar ends are available in a range of lengths and angles, to fit your body proportions and your riding preferences.

actually increase cable resistance and hinder front brake performance.

Proper stem length and height (rise) are essential to proper, enjoyable riding position. It's also a nice place to "trick-out" a high-end bike with a better functioning setup. You should be able to build up any intermediate to high-end bike with a stem of correct length to achieve your required upper body room. To assure accurate fit and comfortable setup you may want to deal with a shop that has a Cunningham stem-fitting device. It's a tool that allows you to try different reaches and rises until you dial-in what seems best for you.

Handlebars should be sized to your shoulder width, from 20 to 23 inches. Don't be afraid to cut the bars down. (Just be sure to cut equal amounts from each end).

Many lower-priced bikes come with double-bent, uprising bars. Such bars greatly restrict your ability to adjust your handlebars to your most comfortable riding position. A much better, more versatile setup includes so-called flat bars, which actually have between zero and 20 degrees of sweep resulting from a single angle with its apex at the stem. Even these don't necessarily line up flat when properly installed. A slight turning of these bars has afforded many riders a more comfortable and less-fatiguing position, because the strongest wrist-forearm position is one in which there is little or no "break" in the wrist joint. If you have wrist problems, you may want to try bars with a different degree of bend. Even a couple degrees can make a difference.

You'll find your ideal bar position with the combination of proper handlebar width, downward roll, and degree of bend that best matches your forearms as they reach down toward the handlebars. Before you spend a chunk of bucks on ultralight, super-resilient bars, make sure they meet those criteria.

• • Tools

Hardware to Take on the Road

Go mountain biking without a basic tool kit and you can easily find yourself up a trail with a long and not very thrilling walk home. So, although tools are commonly referred to as "accessories," the prudent mountain biker knows that a basic tool kit (and knowing how to use it) is essential.

A basic repair kit should go with you on every ride. That way you know you have it, and you're not at a total loss if something goes awry. For longer day rides, exploratory rides, overnighters, and extended touring and expeditions, build larger tool collections around the basic kit.

A minimum, and perhaps dangerously bare, tool set includes:

- A spare inner tube sized for your tires with the appropriate valve stem for your rim and pump.
- Two tire "irons" or levers for removing the tire from the rim.
- A patch kit, because sometime you're going to get more than one leak.
- A pump for inflating the replaced or repaired tube.
- A chain tool (rivet press) for repairing broken, stiff, or otherwise mysteriously malfunctioning chains.
- Duct tape or cloth first-aid tape about 1 inch wide, wound around

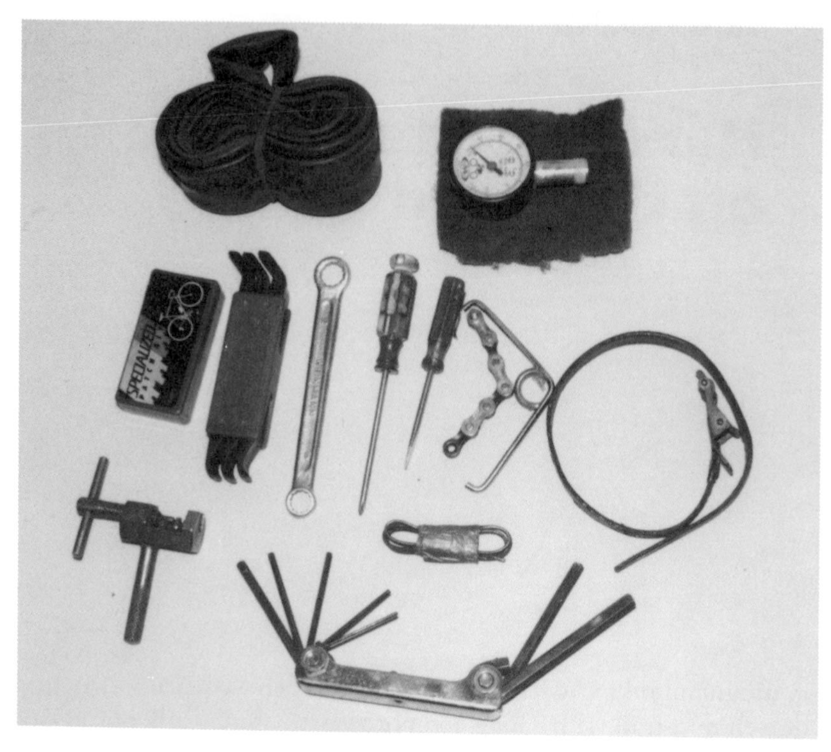

This basic saddle-bag repair kit includes (from left to right, starting with top row): spare inner tube, scuff pad, pressure gauge; patch kit, tire levers, 8mm/10mm wrench, Phillips-head screwdriver, flat blade screwdriver, three chain links, Quick Link tool, old toe strap; chain rivet tool, multiple Allen wrench, baling wire with duct tape.

an 8- to 12-inch length of baling wire, folded down to 3 inches long. (When Murphy's Law strikes this will enable you to keep your rig ridable.)

- Four chain links that match your drivetrain's chain.

Those items comprise the minimum that should go with you on every ride. A more reasonable and prudent tool package would also have:

- Chain lube, SynLube, Finish Line, or Sachs brand stuff in the handy small bottle, or some other specific chain lube product of your choice, or a vial of 20- or 30-weight oil.

- 4-, 5-, and 6-mm Allen keys.
- 8-, 9-, and 10-mm wrenches or a 4- or 6-inch adjustable wrench.
- Needlenose pliers with side-cutters or a universal plier tool.
- A spoke wrench, "T" or hoop type, that fits your wheels' gauge of spoke nipples (or nuts).
- Brake and gear cables, one each. In a pinch you can fabricate a brake yoke cable from the gear cable.

Other tool options you may want to consider are:

- A tire gauge, if you're the type who likes to make sure things are accurate, including air pressure.
- A synthetic dish-scraper pad to clean the gunk off parts and tools. It also makes a jingle-quieting wrap for your tools. Bind it with a couple rubber bands (which can be made by cutting old inner tubes into 3/8-inch-wide strips).
- A freewheel comb to keep you running in severe muck. These handy 6–8" plastic claws are a godsend. If you want to keep the good one clean at your home work bench, you can make handy trail-grade copies from .125″ tempered masonite.
- Talcum powder in a sample-sized bottle to sprinkle on the inside of the tire prior to loading the inner tube. It acts as a dry lubricant, reducing friction and helping the tire seat itself.
- Bicycle grease, carried in a 35-mm film canister, can keep things functioning and should be smeared onto brake or gear cables before they're inserted through the cable housing.
- A packet of hand cleaner pads can do a lot to keep your hands, gloves, clothes, and handlebars clean, as well as reduce the risk of getting toxins in your food.

During races, you can prune the basic kit according to the length of the race and what your experience tells you. You may want to augment the tire pump with compressed air cartridges for faster inner-tube inflation or in case your pump gets broken.

When Martha races, she counts on her well-maintained bike and lightens the tool kit load down to two quick-fill cartridges, a spare tube, tire irons, and a chain tool. She includes a pump in longer events.

Mike takes a spare tube, 2 quick-fill cartridges with adapter, 1 or 2 plastic tire irons, a chain tool, some 3–6-mm Allen keys (short versions), a spoke wrench, and a 5-inch pair of mini-Channellock pliers.

On any sort of extended ride you have to be able to get by on your own. Spoke breakage is more likely on loaded tours, and if it happens in the rear wheel, it's more likely to happen on the freewheel side, which means you must be able to remove the freewheel cogs. That adds spokes, of the proper length and gauge, to your tool kit, along with a freewheel remover and pocket vise or a cassette-cracker freehub tool.

A straightedge, stubby screwdriver will come in handy for various items, including many neo-sealed bearing covers, although you should check to see if the company that produces your bearings makes a specific tool for lifting the seals. A travel-size pin tool, in conjunction with the stubby screwdriver, lets you make a trail-side adjustment of standard bottom bracket bearings. A pair of spare brake shoes can help you get back home safely.

Of all the bearings on the bike, the headset bearings take the hardest beating. Repeated shocks combined with infiltration by water and grime frequently loosen headset adjustment. But carrying a standard set of headset wrenches is too much like bringing along the kitchen sink for most people. An alternative is to make tracings of your headset wrenches' working ends on eighth-inch aluminum plate, cut them out with a saber saw, file the edges smooth and carry them on long day trips. You can also purchase a commercially produced mini-headset wrench set which just became available and which attaches to water bottle bosses.

The minimum and reasonable tool kits can fit in a "wedge bag" that hangs behind and beneath your saddle. Put the inner tube, lube, grease, cables, and chain links in first, followed by the tools wrapped in the dish scraper.

> *I put the inner tube inside a thick plastic bag to prevent the tube from being worn through at the creases, because if that happens you end up with a spare with a lot of holes in it.*
>
> —Michael

Some people prefer to save the space beneath their saddle for a quick-access jacket or windbreaker. If you like that idea, you can get a bag that goes under the seat tube/top tube joint or one that attaches to the handlebar/stem area.

Another option is to carry your tools in a canister in one of your water bottle cages. You can make a canister by cutting the tops off a pair of water bottles and putting the two bottom sections together. A piece of foam or a rag will keep things from being too noisy on the trail. This is particularly handy if your bike has three sets of water bottle cage mounts.

When going out on extended day trips, exploratory rides, or overnight ventures, you should include some or all of the following:

- a light, one of the newer mini flashlights or Tekna lights for seeing in the dark
- a compass and topographic map of the area, for knowing where you're going
- some high-energy food bars for emergency rations
- aspirin, acetaminophen, or ibuprofen
- antiseptic, first-aid tape, and gauze bandages
- matches in a waterproof container
- a 12-hour tube light, a little green lamp about 4 inches long that glows for 12 hours when snapped
- a "space blanket" for emergency shelter

All this may seem like a lot, but remember the Murphy's Law of mountain biking. Whatever tool you must have to fix something so you won't have to walk for hours will be the one tool you didn't bring along.

• • Riding Essentials

Don't Leave Home without These

Besides the tools that can keep the party rolling, there's also a short list of items so handy or so vital it's difficult to call them "accessories."

The most important of these items mounts on your head—an ANSI Z90 or Snell Foundation certified helmet. It's not difficult for any of us to imagine even our most proficient riding buddies getting whupped on the head at 15 mph or faster, which is all it takes for serious brain damage. Compound such injury with where you might be on a mountain bike when it happens (that is, how far or long it might be until you can get medical assistance) and you can see that wearing a helmet is essential.

When you select a helmet, the most important thing is proper fit. There should be no slop when you move it side to side or forward and back, and it shouldn't easily spill or rotate off your head. And when you wear it, make sure the straps are adjusted so that the helmet covers your forehead, not the back of your neck. Be sure it has a label certifying that it meets the drop test standards of either the American National Standards Institute (ANSI) or the Snell Foundation. Many helmets meet these criteria. Which one you choose is a matter of your wallet and your taste.

Water bottles

Almost every mountain bike these days comes with mounts for two water bottle holders (known as cages). Bottles come in 21-ounce and 28-ounce sizes. Some riders find the larger bottles difficult to manage while riding, others consider them handy for taking that vital extra allotment of replacement fluids. Whichever bottle you get, get the cages that are designated for mountain bikes. They're a little thicker than road bike ones and retain their tension longer, so they hold the bottles securely in rough going and don't break as soon.

A viable alternative to the traditional water bottle is the Camelbak water bag. The vinyl sack holds 70 ounces of water in a small backpack-like sack. You sip on a quarter-inch hose that clips to your shirt or helmet strap. If you use this on long rides, one water bottle can hold carbohydrate drink. That still leaves one bottle cage to hold a lamp battery on night rides.

Toe clips

Once you're riding regularly and want to improve your performance, you'll probably want to get toe clips and straps. Get mountain bike toe clips (those with two sections for the strap to pass through), not the narrow ones intended for road riding. Clips and straps help hold your foot in the correct position on the pedal, and you get improved power transmission. They also keep your feet from flying off the pedals on rough downhills, possibly sparing you from a close encounter with your top tube. Because the shoes or boots used with mountain bikes are generally bulkier than road racing shoes, you should get the longest straps available. Take the time and spend the extra couple dollars to get straps with well-designed, heavy-gauge buckles. Strap buckles get banged about a lot. The thinner-metal, save-a-couple-dollar brands simply break too quickly.

> *A double set of toe strap buttons will make it both easier to grip the strap for tensioning and to control how large a loop it will make when let out—ensuring that you have strap to grip.*
>
> —Michael

Racks

More than any other single piece of equipment, a rear rack will increase the range of activities possible with your bike. It'll carry extra clothes, your lunch, or complete expedition supplies. The best rack mounts are braze- or welded-on threaded mounts about 15 inches up the seatstays from the rear dropouts. These are much stronger than those with a single mounting point for the rack, because the single mount acts as a pivot point for the rack (and your gear) as it tosses and sways as you ride. Also, a rack made with a solid center panel running the length of the rack makes an excellent fender for rear-wheel spray.

Fenders

Riding wet dirt roads on two-inch tires can quickly make a mess of your face. Those who don't want to let a little (or a lot of) inclement weather get in the way of their cycling may want to install a pair of fenders to prevent the slop from splattering up.

On the other hand, much rough and rugged riding can make quite a mess of your plastic and metal fenders, which may result in a lot of noise. Or your fenders may get gunked up with 10 pounds of crud and stop your wheels, which some find quite distracting. Clip-on half-fenders that snap on and off quickly may be the answer.

Cycle computers

If you're mounting a serious training regimen, or just want to know how far you've ridden, a cycle computer is a great device. A computer can be a big help when you're exploring new routes. For example, if you know that a turnoff is two miles ahead, you can pinpoint exactly where it is. Besides telling your mileage ridden, pedaling speed (revolutions per minute or rpm), and average speed, many computers also feature 24-hour clock functions, which means you can leave the wristwatch at home.

Be aware that with a mountain bike, mileage on a cycle computer can be low due to wheel slippage, time spent airborne, and tire softness. Or seem low because it feels like you've ridden much

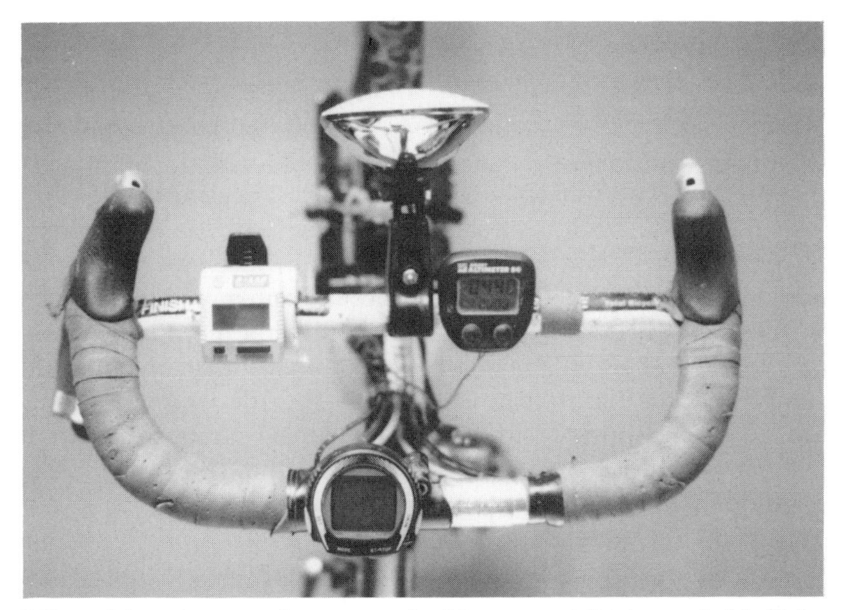

Off-road drop bars can be mounted with a second flat bar to hold all the electronic gear you may desire.

more. When guesstimating the amount of time you need to get home, it's always a good idea to fudge toward the longer side. Eventually you'll get an honest sense of your average speed on dirt.

Packs

A fanny pack makes going into the outback totally prepared an easy proposition, especially when combined with a rear bolt-on rack. Because your body acts as a suspended mount, a fanny pack allows you to carry vibration-sensitive items like cameras (wrapped in clothing or foam) much better than on a bolt-on rack. Fanny packs also let you get to clothing, food, and maps without dismounting (most of the time), and some models even come with built-in water bottles.

Besides quality of construction, important considerations in fanny pack design are how the belt and buckle sit relative to your abdomen and diaphragm, how well the load is carried against your back (not hanging out uncomfortably), whether the pack has cinch straps to adjust various loads for the most comfort and most secure holding, ease of entry, and waterproofness.

Lights

Much of the time that's available to hard-working folks for enjoying their mountain bikes comes during periods of darkness or near enough to darkness that it's essential to have a dependable lighting system.

Lights come in both bicycle-mount and helmet-mount designs. Both have their advantages and the ideal system would incorporate both kinds. A helmet-mount system directs a beam of light wherever you're looking. (However, most helmet manufacturers make a point of noting that they can't warranty the effectiveness of their helmets when outfitted with lights.) But a bicycle-mounted system can give you a lot more illumination. With a little bit of work, the beams of two such systems can be adjusted to meet at a spot comfortably in front you.

Both types of lights are available in rechargeable packages, with different power and recharge options. The trade-offs one makes in settling for any particular system usually involve weight for time of power charge, and quality of light for amount of wattage.

A helmet-mount light should be exceptionally lightweight (six ounces or less), with a sufficiently long and stable cable running to its power pack, which is usually carried in a fanny pack.

A bicycle-mount light can be either a self-contained battery-powered unit, or a lamp wired to a power pack that hangs under the rear of the saddle, at the seat joint, or in a bottle cage. Look for easy mounting and unmounting, weather-resistant cables that make clean runs, and for easy replacement of electrical parts.

• • Softwear

Clothing and Accessories to Increase Safety and Fun

Clothes can do a lot to improve the fun factor of any ride, although they won't make you a gnarly dude. Cycling shorts, gloves, and shoes (in that order) provide the largest boost in comfort.

Cycling shorts come with a one-piece liner or chamois sewn into the crotch area, and are designed so that there are no seams running down the middle of the crotch. Though chamois were traditionally made of leather, now they're usually constructed of synthetic super-wicking material, including polypropylene, pile, and artificial leather.

The chamois pad should be shaped so that it reduces friction given your various positions on the bike, your leg movement, and the bumps of off-road riding. Secondly, the pad should absorb and wick moisture away from the crotch area. And, since it should be washed after every ride, you want it easy to care for. Because women tend to be more moist than men, females should look for very absorbent chamois.

More than one former road rider has discovered that good road shorts don't necessarily translate into good mountain biking shorts (or vice versa). That's because your positions are slightly different on the two bikes, resulting in different contact areas between your body and the saddle. That changes pressure points and areas of friction. If your combination of fat- and skinny-tire riding is plagued by irritation from these factors, some of the problems can be eliminated by riding identical saddles on both your road and mountain bike. If you still have trouble, flip your shorts inside out and line them up against each other. Use those with a wider rear chamois pad on the mountain bike.

Wool knit was once the predominant material for cycling shorts, but it passed to the wayside with the advent of Lycra-Spandex shorts. Although it doesn't possess the insulating or wicking properties of wool, Lycra-Spandex is lightweight, quick drying, and holds its shape.

Shorts are usually pocketless and skin-conforming with an elastic band waist and elasticated thigh-hugger hems. They are sewn in patterns requiring two to eight pieces. The best fit is usually found with shorts made of six or eight panels. To get good, durable shorts, you'll need to spend in the $35-$50 range. In our experience, Avocet, Hind, J.T. Actif, Giordana, Louis Garneau, Pearl Izumi, Top Performance, and Baleno are brands that have provided consistent quality for reasonable price.

Touring shorts are chamois-lined shorts that resemble hiking shorts. Usually constructed of knit or twill fabric, they are made for short rides and situations where the wearer may not be comfortable in black, saran-wrapped thighs. Touring shorts should have a minimum three-inch inseam to prevent seat rub while pedaling, be made so there's no fabric bunched at the peak of the inseams when you sit on the saddle, and preferably have side-mounted pockets rather than traditional front and rear ones. Better side-mounted pockets have closure flaps on them so that everything doesn't fall out when you sit down.

Gloves

Cycling gloves insulate the ulna nerve in the hand from some of the constant shock transmitted up the front fork and handlebars. Padding materials vary from maker to maker. The best manufacturers use material called visco-elastic polymer. It's deceptively thin material, but it works.

Durability reveals itself in construction details like double stitching on important seams, individual panels for each side of each finger, colorfast dyes (be leery of black and intense colors—they tend to bleed), and no holes on the inside when you turn them inside out. Try gloves on in the store before you buy them. The padding should conform to the crimps your hand makes when gripping the bars, and the finger holes should be snug but not tight.

Shoes

Stiff-soled shoes or boots will transmit power from your legs into the pedals more efficiently. They'll also support your arch, saving you from foot cramps (an awesome nuisance 10 miles out). Off-road cycling shoes are available with leather as well as nylon-mesh uppers, and in low-cut, high-top, and two-thirds high-top styles. How high a style you'll be happiest with depends on the amount of ankling you do (exaggerated flexing of the ankle as the foot goes around the circle of pedal travel), and how often you take your bike on terrain where you have to get off and walk. In such times the ankle support of a two-thirds or full high-top is a plus, although mid-top shoes sometimes seem to collect gravel pebbles more than others.

Hammerheads will want to duplicate the pedal power of road riding. The only way to do that is to use cleated cyclocross shoes, or a pair of the new generation of cleated or clipless high-performance mountain bike shoes.

Most mountain bike shoes fit nicely with wide toe clips and straps. But in many situations, toe clips and straps are not essential and may even be a hindrance. Birding and outdoor wildlife photography both require quick and quiet dismounts coupled with periods of slow cadence, which benefit from an unencumbered pedal platform. For example, L.L. Bean Maine Hunting Boots with steel insole stiffeners work fine in these situations, but not with clips.

Most hunting and hiking boots also work well as mountain bike shoes if they're laced just ankle high. In fact they work quite well when coupled with Power Grips, a nifty diagonal strap that wedges the foot to the pedal.

Many field boots are now made with Gore-Tex liners or Thinsulate lining to keep feet warm and dry in bad weather. Since the foot is the most exposed area on a cyclist, such boots can be just the thing to extend the cycling season. Those who already own slightly roomy mountain bike shoes can use Gore-Tex and Thinsulate-lined socks, available from Cabela's, a mail-order hunting and fishing supplier in Sydney, NE.

In good weather conditions, though, the feet are usually best served by a thin polypropylene liner and thin wool ankle sock. The liner wicks sweat away, the double layering reduces friction, and the wool insulates and wicks.

Extras

For cooler-weather thigh protection or for very technical terrain, many mountain bikers have found knickers to be just the thing. Polyester baseball/football pants sold in sporting goods stores—usually around $15 a pair—fit the bill perfectly. In 40- to 55-degree weather wear the knickers with high, thick, wool field socks instead of ankle socks.

Periodically spraying the knickers with water repellent makes them surprisingly effective in drizzles and showers. And if you sew a panel of water-repellent ripstop nylon to the leg fronts, your legs will be comfortable in anything but a deluge.

This brings us to the topic of layering, a mandatory practice in all outdoor sports that reaches new levels of sophistication with mountain biking. On a mountain bike you switch frequently from periods of intense work (like climbing) that produce heat and sweat to cooling downhills or level spins. It's a heating, air-conditioning house of horrors. You need to be able to adjust your clothing to suit your heat level.

In nice weather with a cool breeze, you can get by with a pair of battered cotton T-shirts. Tearing off the sleeves doesn't just look macho, it introduces ventilation, while the double layering offers a surprising range of comfort. But cotton has its limitations. It doesn't dry quickly, so if you're sweaty and it gets cool, you get cold. And if you're wearing armless shirts, you expose your shoulders to scrapes if you fall.

Fine-mesh knit cycling jerseys conform to your body, dry quickly, ventilate well, and have practical pockets in the small of the back for food, maps, and other things. Knit tops made from polypropylene, Pro-Core, Capilene, or wool all work well in moderate to warm weather. Synthetics are preferable in warmer temperatures, not only because they're cooler but because it's easier to clean mud spray off them.

In cool temperatures, a long-sleeved T-shirt is the perfect outer garment for mountain biking. With a super-wick synthetic or silk T underneath, you get a modicum of brush protection, along with thermal regulation and sweat-wicking. Of course, a long-sleeved jersey will keep you comfortable in cooler situations, but you won't see your investment disappear in dirt if you wear an outer long-sleeved T.

As the weather gets colder, a mid-weight layer of super-wick synthetic knit in a long-sleeved, zip-neck style will increase your ventilation/insulation options.

> *In cold, damp weather, like a foggy, drizzly day, the only thing that keeps me warm is a super-wick underlayer over a bra or similar breast-protector, and a wool jersey.*—Martha

Wet weather gear

Rain introduces a whole new ball of wax—nothing seems to be able to keep you thoroughly vented from sweat yet dry from precipitation. But with the right combination of clothes, you can stay pretty comfortable.

Pack a change of layering to switch to after any stop when your surface temperature will drop and the moisture in your layered garments turn from an insulating wetsuit to a damp heat sink that drains your body of its warmth and energy.

A number of companies make stretch waterproof helmet covers, and they seem sufficient except in the heaviest of downpours, at which time you should have a hood. Rain shells or jackets are available in many different materials. Ideally yours should have both a zippered and storm-flapped front, underarm zippers, and an under-the-yoke vent in the back. Arms and rear panels need to be long enough to cover all of you when you're bent over the bars. A stand-up "Nehru" collar is the best.

Burley makes a cycling shoe overboot that will cover mountain bike shoes quite well, although walking traction is not the greatest. If traction is a concern, put the rain-proofing in the boot or sock, or make yourself a pair of toe covers that protect the front of your shoes by snapping over your toe clips.

Truly functional full-length rain pants feature snug ankle closures. Those made with zippered ankle pleats are far easier to get on and off. Sectioned construction increases seam leakage possibilities, but assuming proper seam sealing, improves fit and function.

Any rain pant I've tried is more comfortable with suspenders. But the arrangement can make quick-relief stops a hassle. Guys, make sure there's plenty of waist cinched with that elastic, then you won't have to disrobe and get soaked just to void your bladder.—Yuri

Women, sorry, there isn't much you can do except pull 'em down, unless you have a "female funnel," a handy little plastic device that allows you to stand up and write your name in the snow just like your male riding companions.—Martha

If the weather is that wet, though, it may be better not to ride off-road at all. Rain destabilizes soil, accentuating erosion with any use. Consider riding on the road, training indoors, or cross-training. If you do ride off-road, try a shorter session.

Few articles of outdoor clothing have proven themselves like a chamois shirt, and that old standby is handy on a mountain bike as well. It can serve as a light-rain garment for a few minutes, provide fairly warm insulation, and even save you from hordes of mosquitoes.

Does the sweat of good, hard cycling get in your eyes? If you've felt the stinging of salt once, you know what we mean. The cure to that malady is the RaceAid, a half-inch polyvinyl trough that makes terry-cloth sweatbands history.

Anyone who rides consistently needs eyeshields. More commonly known as sunglasses or goggles, cycling-dedicated eyewear protects your eyes from bugs, branches, and the dirt and mud thrown up by your front tire, as well as from ultra-violet radiation.

You'll get more for your money if the eyeshields you buy have interchangeable lenses for different lighting conditions, and you'll save yourself many headaches if the earlobe rods (or "temples" to use the industry jargon) don't fall off with every twitch or flick of a branch.

Those of you wearing prescription lenses don't have many options. You can wear contacts. They allow you to wear eyeshields that wrap around your face and give much better protection than glasses.

I'm using Suspension Eyewear. They're like regular eyeglasses but the temples are fishline material attached to a hooked

earpiece. They don't fall down on your face, even in the roughest terrain. My glasses jumped all over even when I wore various types of behind-the-head retainer straps.—Martha

People have tried using eyewear that darkens and lightens but we've heard complaints that it doesn't change quickly enough, resulting in reduced vision at crucial times.

• • Mechanics

Maintaining an Even Machine

Mountain biking is one of those things where there's simply no escaping some mechanical details. And quite a few of them can get quite frustrating. "Tools. Grease. Parts. How does this go? Ah, the heck with it!" can be a tempting response to the bundle of recreational technology you've invested in. After all, this is supposed to be fun. But if you don't devote a minimal amount of attention to your bike, you'll get stuck sometime, somewhere when there's little help and a long bike push home.

The truth is, mountain bike mechanics aren't really all that difficult. And almost every community has a bike shop, recreation program, community center, or college extension program that offers a class in bicycle repair. We recommend you try one, because bike mechanics is one of those things that's best learned in a hands-on situation, not from a book.

Which is not to say we're going to dodge the topic entirely. We're going to discuss basic things every off-road rider should know, outline a quick routine you should do after every major ride, and then describe the tools you need for the no-frills, home pit stop for those who want to do more.

An emergency pit-stop primer

Self-reliance on a mountain bike begins with knowing how to change and patch an inner tube, replace a tire, and use a pump. This means being adept at using a pair of tire levers or "irons," finding where the puncture occurred, and identifying what type of puncture it was: a rim cut ("snake bite") in which the tube was pinched between rim and ground, or a puncture from an object (in which case be sure the object isn't still stuck in the tire or it'll just puncture the next tube you put in.)

Once you find the hole in the inner tube, repair the hole with a patch, pump in just enough air to make the tube round and help seat it properly, and then put the tube in the tire. (When you put the tire back on, make sure the brand name on the tire sidewall is at the valve. This provides a good reference for checking tire puncture spots in the future. The next time you get a flat, find the hole in the inner tube and then measure the distance from the puncture to the valve. Then measure that same distance on the tire from the brand name to look for a cut or object in the tire.) Be careful to seat the tube in the middle of the tire, and center the valve in the valve hole so that it sticks out straight and perpendicular to the rim.

Clasp the edge of the sidewalls on either side of the valve area to begin putting the tire back on the rim. Work both ways from the valve as you reinstall the tire bead on the rim. After tucking the last section of tire onto the rim, pump a little air into the tube, then work your way around the wheel, adjusting and centering the tire. Complete the reinflation of the tube and tire, and remount the wheel on the bike. (Don't forget to lock down the bolts or quick-release levers, and reset your brakes.)

You also should know how to:

- Replace a chain link, or your entire chain, and remove a stiff link with a chain-rivet press tool.
- Clean your brakes—both arms and pads—and rims and adjust your brakes.
- Clean and lube your derailleurs and pulley wheels, and clean the space between your freewheel cogs.
- Replace or relube brake and gear cables.
- Remove your freewheel or cassette cogs. (If you can do that you

can handle cleaning and relubing your freewheel, which will be well worth the effort.)

- Replace a spoke, and touch-up true your wheels.
- Check the headset (the bearings between your handlebar stem and fork) and adjust if necessary.

If you don't know how to do these procedures, ask at your local bike shop or check into one of the classes mentioned above.

The home routine

Since most of the mechanical parts of a mountain bike are exposed, they need consistent care if they are going to be functional. Wipe your bike with a big rag, or if it's dirty enough, wash it with half a bucket of warm soapy water, using a long-handled soft-bristled scrub brush, after every major ride. Rinse and then dry wipe with a rag.

While wiping the bike, keep an eye out for any cracks, chips, or buckles in the tubing. It's better to discover a crack at this time than on a gnarly downhill.

Hold each wheel off the ground and spin the rims. Lightly clean debris off the rim and sidewall while it turns. Wipe the brake pads and arms, then spin once again and check for rim deformation (up and down or left/right). Note any movement of the rim relative to the brake pad to determine if the wheel needs truing.

If you washed your bike, you'll need to clean and relube the chain and the jockey wheels on the rear derailleur. Do this by using one of the chain cleaner systems on the market, by squirting some solvent on an old toothbrush and scrubbing with it, or by spinning the cranks and holding a wire brush to the chain and the jockey wheels. Afterward, relube the chain and jockey wheels.

There are a number of good products out there, including some marketed for motorcycle chains. When you use them, be sure you have plenty of cross ventilation that not only moves clean air by your face, but also removes toxic mists and fumes from your living area.

You'll also want to lube your cables. Nonaerosol molybdenum dysulfide-based lubricants work great for cables, and often come with a handy needle-nozzle feeder. Feed a couple squeezes of lubricant at the uphill end of the cable housings for both brakes and gears. Also squeeze a couple dabs at seams of the brake armature mounts, and at pivot points on the derailleurs.

Once in a while, pull your seat post, stem, and quick-release skewers, and wipe and regrease them. If you ride in a wet environment and don't take this precaution, there's a strong possibility of discovering one day that you can't remove them.

If you crossed any streams that put any bearing unit under water (most likely bottom bracket or hubs, but maybe your headset too if you fell over), then that bearing unit must be overhauled, or regreased at the minimum.

Timely service cues

We've all occasionally slipped into the "happily we roll along" routine. Everything works fine and we're lucky enough to fit regular rides into our schedules, let alone bike maintenance. So we try getting by with extended rides and stretched return times while not providing ample time at home to do basic maintenance. Suddenly, the chain breaks, jams on shifting, or worse. Or, as happened with a friend of ours, the front-brake mount pops off, along with the entire half of the front brake, in the midst of a steep single-track descent.

The point is, routine checks and a regular maintenance schedule get you into a habit that makes maintenance less of a burden and keeps things tight and right for maximum riding enjoyment.

We've just discussed what to do when you get back from a ride, especially a rainy or muddy one. Now we'll list a regular maintenance schedule.

Every two weeks, or if it's easier for you to remember, the 1st and 15th of each riding month (or after every 20–30 hours of riding):

- Check headset and bottom bracket adjustments.
- Clean and lube brake and derailleur controls, cables, and mechanisms.
- Clean and relube your chain if it hasn't been done on a daily basis.
- Lube your derailleur pulleys.
- Check your brake adjustment.
- Check your tire sidewalls for cuts.
- Remove any rust from scrapes and paint with antirust primer or touch-up paint.

Bimonthly (June 1, August 1, October 1) or every 80–100 hours of riding:

- Overhaul your pulley wheels.
- True your wheels.
- Grease-gun overhaul your freewheel and pedals.
- Relube your seat post.

Semiannually (every April 1st and Thanksgiving weekend):

- Overhaul the entire rig. Replace all ball bearings except press-in cartridge units and freehubs which aren't made to be taken apart regularly. Soak your brake units and derailleurs in solvent. Relube, and/or replace control cables as needed, and replace brake blocks, as needed.
- Replace your chain every 500 miles of off-road riding. Check freewheel cogs for wear.

The home repair kit

Nothing makes bike maintenance an easier habit to acquire than having a sanctioned area for bike work. If you can establish an actual workbench and stand area in your garage or basement then terrific, but you can also set up a work area that's easily tucked away after use.

You can find a number of stands made for home bike repair. Get one with enough base weight (or distribution of weight) to stabilize the bike during work. You should be able to easily mount your bike on the stand without causing cosmetic (or worse) damage, and the mounted bike (or bikes) should be at a height convenient for you.

If you don't have the bucks for one of these things (or don't have storage room for one) but you do have some exposed wood beams into which you could thread a couple of lag bolts, you can devise a perfectly workable repair stand. Use 3/8" rope, cut and tied so it goes through the bolt eyelets and then hooks over the saddle/seat post and handlebar/stem areas of your bike. A similar setup is possible in the woods, hanging the rope from tree branches. Cut the rope so that the bike hangs at a convenient height and is easily leveled.

Tooling

Tool acquisition can become an obsession. Nothing like having the right one, you know. We attempted to put together a fairly complete master list without getting too carried away. A well-stocked tool bench is something that evolves or builds over time, unless, of course, you just happen to have a few hundred dollars to spare and can get everything at once. To help in the orderly evolution of your bike station, we've prioritized the tools (1 is highest, 5 lowest).

Your first need is cleaning supplies, including bucket, soap, car-wash sponge, and brush. Get a brush with an 8″ handle and a 5″ by 5″ square of 1.75″-deep bristles or a 3″ paintbrush for getting into tight areas. Old toothbrushes are great basic cleaners for the small hardware on a mountain bike.

Hand tools should include:

- Allen keys, 2 mm to 8 mm. Buy good quality keys so their corners won't round off. Those with ball-handle ends are excellent for getting into tucked-in bolt ends. (1)
- Chain rivet-pin tool. Get two, one for home and one for the road. (1)
- Quick Link Chain Compressor, a bike-specific tool that will relieve many chain assembly headaches. (3)
- Tourese Chain Holder (optional) for making wheel repairs (i.e. flats) less messy on your hands. (5)
- Campagnolo 15-mm "peanut-butter" wrench, or high-quality 14-mm or 15-mm socket and handle, for the mounting bolt that holds your crank arms onto the bottom bracket spindle. Better socket brands have higher-quality metal and thinner walls to fit the recessed hole in which the bolt head fits. (2)
- Breaker-bar handle for above socket so you can apply adequate torque to mount the bolt tightly and to remove it from the bike. (4)
- Torque wrench for accurately measuring the amount of force with which a nut or bolt is hand-fastened. (4)
- Cotterless crank puller to pull crank arms off bottom bracket spindle. Get the universal type so it will fit both your current and your next bike, your friend's and your mate's. (2)

- Bottom bracket C-spanner and universal pin spanner for adjusting traditional bottom bracket bearings. (2)
- Headset wrenches (often found built-in on one end of bottom bracket tools) for headset maintenance. Unless you do a lot of stream crossings, headsets will require much more adjustment than bottom brackets. (1)
- Freewheel/cassette remover for changing cogs and cleaning and lubricating freewheel. Besides the chain and control cables, the freewheel is the component most often in need of cleaning and lubrication. Use a rag to get dirt out from between cogs or use an Allsop cog cleaner. (1)
- Bench vise, the preferred tool to use for removing a freewheel from a rear wheel. The freewheel remover mounts in the vise, and you use the wheel for leverage to loosen the freewheel from its threaded mount on the hub. If you don't have a bench vise, you can use a 12-inch adjustable wrench by cautiously bearing down on the wrench from about a 120-degree angle from the floor (wheel off the bike). Not recommended for anyone with previous back injury, however. (2)
- Straight-blade screwdrivers in tiny (electrician's size), small, and medium. (1)
- Phillips-head screwdrivers in 0, No. 1, and No. 2 sizes. (1)
- Cone wrenches or sealed bearing tools for your wheel hubs. (2)
- Side cutters or high-quality cable cutters for cutting control cables. (2)
- Third-hand tool for properly tensioning control cables without fraying the ends. (2)
- Needlenose pliers for those spots where third-hands just won't fit. (3)
- Fourth-hand tool, mountain bike tire size, for adjusting your brakes. (A toe strap works in a pinch.) (2)
- Spoke wrench—hoop type—for truing wheels. (1)
- Rubber mallet for loosening stem bolts, seat posts, and relieving frustration. (3)
- Freewheel vise to hold the freewheel for cleaning and cog changing. (2)
- Freewheel chain tool for changing cogs on your freewheel. (4)
- Floor pump with gauge for easier, more accurate tire inflation than a hand pump provides. (2)

Other tools that come in handy are:

- Metric wrenches (8-mm to 12-mm box-end wrenches) or a set of 6 bicycle brake wrenches that have all these sizes. (2)
- Metric and English tape or ruler to measure bolt sizes, clearances, handlebar or saddle setup, etc. (3)
- 6″ half-round bastard file. (4)
- 8″ (long) round file, approximately 1/4″ diameter. (4)
- 10″ half-round smooth file. (4)
- 8″ flat smooth file. (4)
- Wire brush, 6–12″ with 4″ bristles. (Some gunk needs strong encouragement to dislodge from bike parts.) (2)
- Grease gun and grease injectors for built-in grease injection systems. These injection systems, which have been used in automotive and machine tooling for generations, are just getting applied to mountain bikes. They're terrific because they make grease purging and bearing relubing many times easier than the heretofore required disassembly method. The system makes the prompt maintenance of bearings no more hassle than your post-ride wipe-down, and greatly enhances the life expectancy of the bearing components. (2–5, depending on your equipment)

As this goes to press, highest grade components from two manufacturers come with grease-injection engineering. We can only hope it trickles down to other grades of componentry. In the meantime, after-market grease injectors exist for your pedals and freewheels and are worth their price. You can have your bottom bracket retrofitted for such maintenance, but the cost is high.

Solvent work

Removing grease and grime from mechanical contrivances demands specialized cleaning and utensils.

— ***Chain cleaners.*** There are a number of systems on the market which purport to improve on the old toothbrush-scrub method. Their value lies in the speed, ease, and tidiness they bring to daily postride chain maintenance. Your drivetrain will function better and last longer with a couple minutes of cleaning and lubing each time the chain gets fouled. Chain cleaners make the chore so easy there's no longer any excuse for poor chain maintenance. But they don't replace the thoroughness possible with serious monthly scrubs the old-fashioned way.

— ***Solvent soak tank.*** This doesn't have to be real fancy. A three-pound coffee can with a lid, a five-gallon plastic bucket with a lid, or a large rectangular food-storage-type container with a snap lid will work fine. You can soak components and parts in solvent and keep them covered for fume control. A basting brush or paintbrush helps clean parts. Air drying is best. Swing the dripped-off part sharply—outdoors—to remove excess solvent, or better yet, use compressed air.

— ***Solvents.*** You have several options when it comes to cleaning solvents. Old-timers often used kerosene for soaking parts, which is infinitely safer than gasoline. Most hardware stores and auto parts stores sell strong parts cleaners, but petroleum-based agents have toxic fumes and are carcinogens.

We recommend using disposable gloves, aprons, and long-sleeved shirts when degreasing your bike. Surgical-type gloves, which are sold at many paint stores, detract little from hand dexterity. If you work bare-handed, minimize the use of solvents to clean grease and gunk from your hands, and rinse copiously with water as soon as possible to minimize absorption by the skin. (Shampoo makes an excellent hand soap for bike gunk. The formulas for cleaning oily hair work almost as well on bike messes.)

Good air flow that moves fumes from the work area to the outdoors is essential, even when you're using the small aerosol cans of solvents. The rule is, if you can smell fumes, they're getting into your lung linings. A $2 fumes-and-mists respirator, available from any large hardware store, is a practical safeguard.

We can hear some old bench-buddies scoffing as they read that. And we don't always take the precaution, but as toxin dangers to health become more clear, it's odd that many people prudent about protecting their clothes from staining (wearing aprons) don't provide as much protection to their lungs.

A number of water and citrus rind extract degreasers are now available. Even though they're less toxic than petroleum distillates, it's still worth remembering that anything strong enough to dissolve grease off your bike should be washed off your body quickly, with copious amounts of water.

Also remember, you still need to filter and dispose of the gunk safely. (Most of the ground-water pollution in the U.S. is from home mechanics, not industry.) Many mechanics say they get great results with Spic and Span household cleaner, but don't let parts soak in it.

Tricks of the trade

In cycling, as with any pastime, everyone builds a bag of tricks for dealing with little particulars. Here's some we felt worth passing along:

- You can tape wheel rims with .75″ fiber-reinforced strapping tape a lot cheaper than with imported rim tape.
- If you sprinkle some talc inside the tire before inserting a new tube, the talc will act as a dry lubricant and help seat the tube properly.
- Rim and/or brake pad performance can be helped by a little surface preparation. Riding up and down your driveway with pieces of synthetic mesh pad (sold in auto body shops) between your brakes pads and rims will remove surface glaze. Immediately following that, wipe the rim and pad with a clean rag, then place a foot-long strip of coarse abrasive (40–80 grit) between the pads and rim. Rotate the wheel forward (with brake pressure on) so that the strip is drawn into the brake area. Then reverse rotate the wheel back to the starting point. Rewipe and you're all set. Repeat the abrasive-pad treatment whenever you suspect you may have substance build-up on your rims or on your pads (glazing). It can also stop brakes from squealing and squeaking.
- Puncture-deterrent tire-liner strips and heavy thorn-resistant inner tubes add weight, lessen cornering performance, and make acceleration more work, but may be worth it if you're in a no-hurry ride through wickedly vegetated (thorny) territory, or out training for racing. (In which case you get a boost when you switch to lighter rubber for race events. Just be sure to use the same tires, so you're used to their cornering quality.) If you're racing in thorny country, pink latex tubes work great without sacrificing weight on your wheels.
- A slotted pump holder (that bolts to the chainstay bridge behind the bottom bracket) doubles as a mild mud guard for chainstay-mounted brakes.

- Square, dice-type valve caps for Schrader valves are much handier to work with in mucky situations than factory valve caps. They're easier to grasp and their corner points are handy to use for lowering tire pressure for more traction. Besides they're fun and cool. Unless of course you are in deadly earnest about rotating weight on your high-performance wheels, in which case you've forsaken Schrader valves long ago, and probably don't even ride with valve caps at all (to save weight).

  Then again a pair of Presta-Schrader adapters threaded on your Presta valves come in handy if you're ever in hard luck for air at a service station. Those who are more fashion mongers than gram counters might want to check out the valve caps shaped like shoes, fire hydrants, cartoon characters . . .
- An old toe strap makes a great carry-along third-hand tool for trail-side brake adjustments. Michael once cracked a carbon-fiber seat post at the top where it's bonded to the aluminum rail clamp. He wrapped a toe strap around it a couple times and rode 15 miles back home.
- Duct tape will hold a tire with a torn sidewall together, although you'll feel the bump every time the wheel goes around.
- Practicing inner-tube changes at home will shorten time lost for flats in races.
- A pump comes in handy if your quick-fill cartridges get bashed or fall off during a race, or you just get fed up with contributing to the mess being left behind by our disposable culture.
- Baling wire can hold a bashed derailleur in place, allowing you to ride home.

Once I found a 12-foot strand of 3/8-inch rope on a logging road. I picked it up just out of anti-litter sentiment, and it just stayed on the rear rack for a while. Not too many rides later, a severe bashing necessitated drivetrain work on the trail, and voila, *I had a repair stand by slinging the rope over a tree branch. Now that rope goes on all long rides.*—Yuri

• • Shock Absorption

Curbing Shake, Rattle, and Roll

Dissipating shock from rugged terrain is one of the great conundrums in mountain biking. Effective vibration damping improves traction and control and reduces fatigue, all of which increase enjoyment and speed. But mechanical suspension materials can add unwanted weight and reduce handling capability.

Frame materials, gauges of tubing, tubing diameters, and frame geometry (lengths of tubing sections and joint angles) all have an impact on what a frame will feel like to ride, and manufacturers often tout their particular materials or designs, but there's no independent testing to verify any manufacturers' claims. The only thing you can do is ride various bikes with similar wheels and tires on the same trails and be aware of any differences. Keep in mind as you do this that how you ride is still the most important factor in shock absorption.

Given the similar geometries of many bikes, the biggest difference in shock absorption is in the wheels and tires. The larger the tire, the smoother the ride. A lighter rim, if it has the same resistance to impacts as a heavier unit, is also better. The lighter rim also allows the use of lighter gauge or butted spokes, which can increase wheel elasticity a great deal. (See guidelines in wheel chapter.) Rims with box and triangular cross sections handle the forces of mountain biking better than simple U-shaped designs.

Active suspension hardware has flooded the mountain bike market in the past few years, and some of the equipment has many merits. But none are as cost-effective as better riding technique. Your body has a great deal of shock absorption capability.

By keeping your elbows bent you can use your arms as shock absorbers. Your hands will fatigue less quickly if you avoid riding with a death grip on the bars. Ride with a soft fist, one that uses only the necessary amount of tension to hold the bars. You can practice this by grabbing a piece of one-inch-diameter wood dowel (or a broom handle) with one hand. Try pulling the dowel out sideways with your other hand. Begin by holding the dowel tightly, then loosen your grip until it's just a pinch difficult to tug the bar out. Next, try to find the same amount of grip on your bike. Begin with a handhold that amounts to little more than laying your fingers around the bar, then gradually increase tension.

Upper-body suspension is improved if you don't hold your shoulders tight. When sitting on your bike, check to see if your shoulders are tense, hunched up, or rolled forward. Relax the muscles between your arms and neck and see if you can feel your shoulders drop. That's where they should be. Also, a rigidly held back (either pulled straight or compacted into a curve) will tire quickly and may be more susceptible to injury.

Another set of major anatomical shock absorbers are your thighs, which come into proper play only with correct saddle height. Their most obvious absorber function comes when you're coasting over rough terrain, a feat best accomplished with the pedal cranks parallel to the ground (at the 3 o'clock and 9 o'clock positions). By raising your weight ever so slightly off the saddle you can maneuver around obstacles, increase or decrease traction, or prevent front wheel washout, all with slight shifts of your suspended body weight. Yet you can also quickly make yourself and the bike a single unit by squeezing your upper legs together on the horn of the saddle.

Since your thighs are also the primary pedaling muscles, it stands to reason that they are what will be tired toward the end of a ride or race. If they've been acting as suspension units for a lot of rough terrain they'll tire more or sooner than otherwise. The best way to prevent that, besides working on riding form, is to build deep strength and endurance in your thighs and lower torso.

Unless you're riding tricky terrain, your weight should be pretty evenly divided between your right and left legs. All riders tend to favor one side or the other, so be sure you practice this off-the-saddle stuff with both right and left leg forward. (Naturally, you'll tend to go to your stronger side when tackling terrain at the edge of your capabilities.) Keep the inside leg forward (at 3 o'clock) during any turns.

Tips on suspension

If you're interested in retrofitting your bike with suspension hardware or buying a "suspended bike," here are some guidelines. (See the glossary for mechanical terms regarding suspension.)

Suspension stems can take the edge off a lot of the rough trail hits coming up from the front wheel, but the experience takes some adjustment in your sense of security. Because the handlebars bob with the stem action, your upper body tends to move. Because this includes your head, it can be disconcerting. Relaxed arms and shoulders that allow the upper body to float in relation to the stem movement minimize the head bob action and complement the suspension.

Telescopic (2–3″ travel) suspension forks add 1–2 pounds of weight to a bike—almost 8% on some models. So you want to get optimal performance out of any such retrofit. The heaviness seems inevitable, because very light suspension forks with small diameter tubes suffer from torsional twisting, in which each fork blade acts somewhat independently instead of in concert with the other. This can make handling sketchy instead of more stable. Some companies are redesigning front axles with 10mm diameters to reduce these problems, but there is also the matter of damping.

Damping refers to the rate of quickness of compaction and extension in the shock absorber unit. A stiff unit (lots of damping) keeps the unit from bottoming out at the end of its travel, but doesn't activate on small bumps. A unit with minimal damping responds too quickly.

When an ultra-light telescopic fork compounds light blade torsion with minimal damping the fork changes the line of travel haphazardly as the front wheel twists between the independently acting blades in undulating single track. This is an eye-opening experience at speed.

Using an active front suspension also involves some modification of riding technique. The most important thing to remember is that as your front wheel comes up when it hits a bump, say a water bar, it also moves under the front triangle of the frame, shortening the wheelbase of the bike. As the wheel comes in you need to adjust your weight back a tad, then adjust it again forward as the fork lets out on the downhill side of the bump. Otherwise you may find you have too much weight over the front of the bike and take a header.

If you retrofit a bike with a suspension fork, ride with the largest tire your rear triangle can accommodate until you get fairly sophisticated with your riding technique on the new unit. This may save you the expense of a new rear wheel, which takes more abuse as the front suspension leads you into a more aggressive riding style.

A third way to add mechanical suspension to the front end of a mountain bike is a "leading link" fork, in which the front axle is held by a strut or duplicate fork that links with the main fork through a toggle linkage or pivot mount. The wheel rises and falls on the hinge of the linkage between the forks. Shock is dissipated by a cushion or rebound damper at the bridge of the auxiliary fork. These are sometimes often paired with an "anti-dive" brake unit, which actually lifts the front wheel a bit upon application, rather than augering it into the ground.

If you're examining complete suspension bikes—those with a suspended rear triangle and front end—keep in mind that active suspension compounds the task of the bike designer, not simplifies it. Rather than eliminating the problem of large impacts and thrust forces, the new mountain bike must be an even finer balance of design fore and aft. Lateral stability is more important than on a static frame bike, and the suspension units must complement each other not only on rough terrain, but while climbing slowly on relatively mild uphills and through twisting single track.

Keep in mind that the primary goals of suspension hardware are improved traction, improved control, and reduced shock impact on the operator. Increased average speed is a secondary benefit, because a well-designed and skillfully ridden suspension bike provides more accurate tracking in the correct line of travel and more contact between the rear wheel's lug faces and the ground.

Finally, if active suspension hardware has opened revealing doors of experience anywhere, it's on the mountain bike tandem. A strong, stable, long-travel fork combined with suspending the stoker saddle and the largest tires imaginable allow a tandem to crank over anything the boom tube and stoker bottom bracket will clear.

A tandem captain is already partially suspended by the tandem. The stoker usually takes the abuse. But with suspension they are comfortable to keep supplying power. And as long as there's power on the cranks, a tandem seems able to keep on going.

If this gets you interested in riding off-road on a tandem, look for a lateral-strengthening tube from beneath the captain's seat tube/top tube joint to a set of mid-stays or an uptube from the captain's bottom bracket to the stoker's seat tube/top tube joint, a high stoker bottom bracket (approach hub axle height), and clog clearance between the chainstays of at least 65 mm.

• • Handling

Honing Bike Skills

You can learn how to handle a mountain bike through tutoring, by observing others, or by trial and error. Trial and error can be painful to your ego and your body on occasion, so any opportunities to use the first two methods are recommended. Then again, don't be intimidated about striking out on your own to expand your abilities.

> *When approaching new territory—whether all-time high speeds or a technical section I've never cleaned—I try to see it as another challenge. Turn that determination on. I might watch someone else do it, try to see what they do. Then once I commit, I try to squelch the fear and use the excitement for the adrenalin rush, not let it overtake and freeze my reactions.*
>
> *I've often gone flying through a boulder field or a gnarly single track not realizing the difficulty until I'm through. Then I'll stop, my whole body shaking, and just wonder as I look back at it.*
>
> *It seems that it's often not basic skills that are lacking, but letting the body act in its best interest even at times when the mind doesn't believe it's possible.*—Martha

When it comes to bike handling, the first rule is to pay attention to where you're going—particularly the best line of travel for you and your bike. You need to look far enough ahead to give yourself time to react to obstacles and changes in terrain.

There's an adage in skiing about focusing on where you want to go, not where you don't want to go. It also holds true in mountain biking. Nine times out of ten, if you see a rock and allow it to preoccupy your concentration ("Oh no, I don't want to hit that"), you'll hit it.

> *I was downhill skiing several years ago and got into some tricky snow. I made exactly that mistake with an eight-inch-diameter aspen tree. Fortunately I only received bruises for my mistake.*—Michael

Sight the object, then set your focus on where you want to go, keeping the obstacle in your peripheral consciousness, and you'll make it through okay.

Mountain bike frames can take a lot compared to road bikes, but you can't just go through and over every obstacle without exacting a penalty. The challenge is to pick the good line of travel, not to survive blind forays through rough terrain. Sometimes you do end up making blind forays, racing through fog or water, but if you know how to be light on your bike you'll survive these times better than your crash-and-bash buddies.

Simple tricks like unweighting your front wheel and moving your body around not only make a smoother, more comfortable ride, but also lower the attrition rate on bike parts. Riders who boast about how many frames and forks they've cracked are really underlining their poor skill level.

Learn to ride "with" your bike not "on" it, or, to put it another way, ride with a bit of finesse. You want to hone a feeling of dynamic unity with your bike, using your combined structure (yours and your bike's) to move across the terrain. Your actions and reactions should be smooth even if the ride is rough and jarring. Relaxed, ready responsiveness is the key—be prepared to hop, jump, brake, or lean as the trail dictates.

Overreacting can be a problem. Go out on rides and try using as subtle body language as possible. Lean into a corner with just your body. Next time maybe stick out the inside knee. How much? Try it and see. Or you might try flicking your back end to avoid hitting a rock with the rear wheel. Put more weight on the right or left grip, feel the tire dig in, get traction. Watch what happens to steering. Think "lightness" and "floating" next time you enter a rocky section.

In a technical section, make sure your toe straps are loose enough for quick foot exits. If you're not using clips, consider doing so. You can handle the bike much better when you can also manipulate it with the pedals, and with toe clips your feet won't go flying off the pedals on bumpy terrain.

Learning how to read the terrain you're about to encounter takes time and experience. Most of us get used to our own areas. Then when something new shows up in front of our wheels, it can be a rude encounter.

Finally, appropriate gear choice is key to handling any kind of terrain. Your gearing should suit both your abilities and the ground you're riding. The grade of the trail isn't the only consideration: surface texture also dictates gear selection. And try to anticipate shifts. Contemporary components will bear a greater stress than models made just a couple years ago, but even today's stuff lasts longer if you don't repeatedly stress it to the maximum.

Specific skills

— ***Ground obstacles.*** Get around obstacles on the trail by hurtling the bike to the side while counteracting with your body in the opposite direction. Start the bike throw by driving the outside pedal down in the direction you want to move the bike. This can be done by pedaling forward or backward. This maneuver gives the pedal nearest the obstacle a better chance of clearing it.

— ***Hanging things.*** Above-ground obstacles can be avoided with just the opposite technique. For example, take a branch that's suddenly in your face. Hurl your body away from the branch while leaning the opposite way with the bike. Depending upon your bike's crank length and top tube design, you might not want to try putting your "outside" foot down, since doing so limits how far away from the bike you can move your upper body.

> *If the branch is real low I often slip forward off the saddle and rest one hamstring across the top tube, ducking my body over the handlebars and sometimes off to the side of the handlebars if necessary.*—Michael

— ***Rocky sections.*** Technical, rocky climbs or descents have their own set of problems. The first order of business is to get your front wheel over obstacles. To do this, shift your weight back and lift the front end, junior-wheelie fashion. Then shift your weight forward, using a twisting, lifting motion on the handlebars. This will lift you over the obstacle. When leaning forward try to lift on the toe clips

Clearing the front tire and correct weight placement are important on rocky terrain.

but make it a pedaling motion rather than a vertical hop-lift with the feet.

When riding over sharp rocks, watch where you have your weight as your rear wheel crests the rock. Too far forward and you'll just spin the rear wheel and slam your knees into your handlebar stem. Too far back and you won't crest, or your front end will come up.

— ***Stairs.*** Descending stairs is comparable to riding off a succession of curbs, really no more difficult than a bumpy hillside. Approach slowly using much more rear than front braking. Let the bike roll over the step edges, using your arms and legs as shock absorbers each time the bike lands. Have your butt slightly off the saddle, loosely holding the bike with your inner thighs, but be ready to put your weight back down as needed.

As you get more proficient at this, the combination of bike/rider unity, weight shifting, and arm and leg suspension will carry you down stairs quicker and smoother, although the experience will be just as exhilarating as when first approached.

Once you become accustomed to descending stairs you can go quickly enough to lift slightly as you go down them. Then all you'll feel is a slightly bumpy vibration under the wheels.

Remember that although riding down steps is preferable to cutting ruts alongside them, pedestrians aren't accustomed to cyclists on stairs. Don't take on blind-turn steps without shouting or warning (ring that bell and use voice communication), and always ride within your ability. You can't blame anyone for not taking kindly to reckless riding.

— ***Turns.*** Cornering technique varies incredibly, depending on the situation. Your objective may be simply to get through alive or to do it comfortably or in the most efficient manner or the quickest way. The way to accomplish any of those goals will depend on the condition of the terrain you are riding.

Even a nice, wide logging road can present a peculiar combination of technical requirements if there's, say, a hump of gravel between tire ruts, a sudden series of large potholes, and a ten-foot drop in the apex of the turn. Plus, you usually ride faster on logging roads than on single track, and speed changes everything.

Because the circumstances you may find yourself in are endlessly varied, you'll need to rely on a battery of control principles and technical skills that you can combine in momentary recipes to meet each situation.

Also, you want to be able to change tactics quickly whenever your initial stab at something begins to prove erroneous. We've all been there—a third of the way through a technical turn at whatever speed you dare attempt, you realize "I shouldn't be doing A, I should be doing B." Usually there's not even enough time to think the entire thought. (If you do, you're usually picking yourself up off the ground by the time you finish the sentence.) The thought/reaction needs to be "Not that, this," or even "No, that."

— ***Picking a line.*** You can ride a bike through a smooth, even turn with greater control and at higher speeds when you set up on the outside edge heading into the corner, pass through the inside line of the corner at its tightest point, and then move on to the outer edge again when exiting. In effect you're making a larger arc of the turn than the midline of the trail does. The less-acute geometry affords you more control and more speed.

This is all fine and dandy on all-weather roads, but can be a technical challenge on unvarnished earth. Still, the principle of setting up for the corner and tracking through the apex of the turn (as much as it is technically feasible) is a habit worth developing.

— ***Calculated countersteering.*** Most corners can be taken more smoothly if you turn the front wheel in the direction away from the turn a moment before heading into the corner. It's like a musical half-beat leading into the phrase of the turn ("and-one"), or a graceful major league power hitter's swirl of shifting weight as he initiates the swing of the bat. The extent of that front wheel swing, its timing, speed, and degree of punctuation or smoothness, depend on the terrain and the arc of travel you want to execute.

— ***Weight balance.*** You want enough weight on the front wheel for stability and proper tracking, and enough weight on the rear wheel for traction, especially during turns that you're pedaling through. On uphills this means putting a little more weight over the front wheel, while getting to the back of the bus on downhills.

Evenly graded downhill turns allow greater speed and let you lean into the turn with your entire body, using your gyroscopic forces for stability. Turns with a marked lateral pitch that require pedaling are best handled with low vertical body placement relative to the frame. Lean your torso over the top tube to maximize tracking and traction.

When coasting down hills that resemble the inner sides of a mixing bowl, moderate your speed and lean your upper body inside the travel arc while leaning your bike the other way. Keeping the pedals at a 2 o'clock (front) and 8 o'clock (rear) allows even weight distribution.

— ***Speed control.*** Develop feathering skills with both brakes, taking care not to overdo the front brake, which can produce fork flutter. For turns, slow down before you enter, then release the brakes just as you initiate the countersteer sweep that hooks into your line of travel through the bend.

Practice

It's important to practice the skills laid out in this section, even if you're not into gonzo rock-hopping, gully-descending, high-speed craziness. Even the quietest trails sometimes erupt with obstacles: rocks, trees, pedestrians, even motorbikes. If you're versed in even the basic techniques, then you can react instinctively and very likely avoid crashing.

Just don't get frustrated—it takes time. Start small and go from there. Soon enough you'll be doubly surprised—first at what comes up, and secondly at how well you handle it.

• • Falling

Getting Comfy with Gravity

Mountain biking and falling down are not synonymous, although it may sometimes seem that way. Common causes of falling are fear-induced hesitation, poor reaction habits, and physical rigidity.

Often a new rider attempts to follow the moves of a more experienced friend, thinking, "If she can do it, so can I." Then, halfway through an obstacle section or downhill, fear begins to catch up. The beginner starts to think about what he's gotten himself into and tightens up, losing his instinctive abilities. Instead of simply reacting, executing, and going on, he pauses to think about it, reacts too late, and falls.

Yes, in order to improve your skill level you need to edge into the zone of what you've never done before. But heavens, take it on gradually. If you allow your confidence to grow at the same rate as your skill, you won't really have to worry too much about falls, and you'll learn from the falls you do make, instead of being further intimidated.

There's a theory about auto accidents involving drunk drivers that it's often the sober victims who are more injured because the drunk is oblivious to the danger, stays loose, and flops about. The drunk's body dissipates the shock forces more easily than the terrified sober person's body. This illustrates the importance of staying

Learning to tuck and roll can save you from many injuries.

loose, even when going down. Don't panic. Yeah, easier said than done, we know. But if you want to minimize the risks of getting injured you need to train your body to react instinctively so your mind can stay relaxed. This often involves retraining primary reactions such as reaching out your arm to break a fall. The resulting broken or sprained wrist is far too common in off-road riding. There's just too much pressure on the wrist, and snap—no more riding for a while. Likewise, when taking a header, people twist to save their heads, landing instead on a fully exposed shoulder and breaking a collarbone.

The chances of both of these types of injuries are minimized by learning to tuck and roll. That's a falling technique that attempts to turn the human body into a wheel. You'll still lose skin, get bruised, or tear clothing, but you may avoid more serious injury.

A great way to learn how to do this is to get together with a group of friends and someone who knows tumbling (as in gymnastics). Meet on a soft stretch of grass wearing your bike helmet, a long-sleeved T-shirt, and any padding you might ride with. Have the instructor teach the group the basics of a tuck-and-roll tumble from the standing position.

After getting the basics you can progress to a running tumble, and eventually, a tumble from your mountain bike. The tuck and roll has to become second nature to be really effective, so have someone there who knows how to teach you, and practice under controlled circumstances. Finally, go out for a "spill session" on soft, wide trails wearing your most protective riding outfit.

It looks a lot less foolish, and you feel less foolish, if there's a group of five or six of you falling off your bikes (like laughing alone versus laughing with others) than if you were to practice this alone. If you don't have access to such a group, or if you don't know anyone versed in tumbling, or if you just prefer a more formal approach, you can take Akido lessons. Akido is a form of martial arts that utilizes tumbling techniques.

There are, of course, some situations where you may not want to do a tuck and roll, such as if you're descending a steep, rutted, twisting single track or a bench on a sheer cliff face. You may want to bail out to the rear (uphill), pointing the bike toward where you would like it to crash while hopping out of the pedals and back over the saddle and rear wheel. Or you may just want to lay the bike sideways, in which case you simply need to be able to direct the fall.

Some riders have developed a leap-frog, over-the-handlebar bail-out for downhill situations. With this technique, you exit the pedals and spread your legs to clear the bars just as the bike takes the ominous tip forward. (Then again you may just want to carry a giant bungee chord, a grapple hook tied to its loose end and the other end tied to your rear rack, and when you need it, you hurl it toward the nearest tree!)

Seriously though, when presented with a quick bailout or tuck-and-roll situation, it's all too easy to get hung up about clearing your feet out of the pedals and straps. But the problem is more fiction than reality—90% of the time your feet will take care of themselves. Just let go of the bike and worry about its injuries later.

Many people are intimidated by the thought of using toe clips and straps, especially off-road. But there are a lot of ways to get used to them and minimize your potential "down" time. When you get your first set of toe straps and clips, don't cinch yourself in so a bear couldn't pull you out. Ride with loose straps at first. Then move to slightly snug straps. Finally add cleats and tighter strap adjustments. Judge strap tension by the type of riding you do (aggressive, easy, etc.), as well as the terrain.

Another thing you can do the first time you install straps and clips is run the strap through the forward side-plate slot on the outside of the pedal instead of the slot behind the end of the pedal axle. This gives your foot a little more room to exit quickly. When you get comfortable with clips and straps, rerun the strap through the normal posterior side-plate slot.

If you're new to clips and straps and have slightly larger-than-average feet, you may want to try using a clip one size larger than your true size. This will give you a bit more room to center the ball of your foot over the pedal axle. Once that position is habitual, mount your true-size clip, and train yourself to loosen your straps a tad after cresting a climb or other situations where you cinched them down for greater power.

In the past few years several companies have tried, with varying amounts of success, to design a "clipless" shoe/pedal binding system for mountain bikes that duplicates the pedal efficiency of clipless road bike pedals.

There are several advantages to the clipless systems, generally speaking. They do, indeed, increase propulsion efficiency. Engaging the pedal with the shoe after dabbing is much simpler and quicker than with a clip and strap arrangement (especially with a double-sided pedal such as Shimano or Grafton). And since clipless pedals don't have a flip tang, your shins are bound to be spared gouges and scars from the inevitable banging about of legs and pedals on falls.

The disadvantages are the expense and the short lifetime of the present generation of shoes (whose uppers seem wholly inadequate to withstand the stresses of mountain biking for even a complete season). Another problem is the quick wear of some cleats, which then begin randomly disengaging in the midst of a very jarring, gnarly downhill. Some of the pedals are also almost unridable with anything but a system-dedicated shoe, which greatly reduces the versatility of your bike.

The problems that exist today will undoubtedly be resolved by designers in the near future, but these aspects of component value bear investigation before plunking down $200.

• • Hill Climbing

Getting Up without Blowing Up

"We grow weary of those things which we most desire," said Samuel Butler. Although the 19th-century writer never had a mountain bike to help him tend sheep in the hills of New Zealand, his pithy observation relates particularly well to our beloved pastime. You almost can't enjoy mountain biking without having a positive attitude about hills, but nothing grows old more completely than an extended, grueling climb.

Getting up hills is labor-intensive mountain biking no matter what the gear spread on your bike. At some point it's just intense effort. Yet for anyone with a solid training base, the problem isn't lack of aerobic ability. While undertaking the intense effort, you need to place your center of gravity correctly and ride with a smooth, sustainable pedal speed.

The fine points of hill climbing differ from slope to slope because of changes in grade and terrain, but generally, if your rear wheel slips or spins instead of propelling you forward, you need to move more weight over the rear wheel. You do this by changing the lean of your upper body and/or shifting your hips back. You must try to position your weight so that you keep your front wheel down but provide traction for the rear driving wheel.

If numerous experiments with weight shifting seem all for

naught, you might want to monitor your tire pressure. You might need to let a little air out to get more "tooth." Or maybe you need to change the tire. (It could be worn out or the tread not adequate for the conditions.)

Once you start getting a sense of body positioning and a knowledge of which gears you can manage on different types of climbs, work to develop a smooth, sustainable stroke rhythm. Keeping the cadence smooth saves energy, probably the number one athletic concern in climbing. And it helps you relax, which in turn makes tracking the bike easier when your heart rate nears maximum.

Sometimes developing a smoother and more sustainable climbing technique is just a matter of using a lower gear—maybe a 34-tooth middle chainring instead of a 36 or 38, or a 30- or 32-tooth freewheel cog instead of a 28. But switching hardware can only do so much—if you're undergoing extraordinary suffering when pedaling against gravity it's possible that you're tackling too difficult a climb for your fitness level. If you find yourself stuck halfway up a hill when this thought comes to mind, catch your breath, drink some water, and try it again. Pace the attack so you can make sure you're maintaining efficient style.

As we said, you want to conserve energy, which means sitting as much as possible. This is especially true when racing, because in that situation it's important never to let up when cresting the top.

During a seated climb, lean forward or sit back in response to changes in slope or surface texture. As your upper body shifts its angle, remember to keep your elbows down. With standard horizontal handlebars your pull on the bars should feel as if a master puppeteer is yanking cables that run from your hands out the back of your elbows. Although your triceps are working like the dickens, your biceps are relatively relaxed. The downward cast of your forearm makes your fingers into grapple hooks that leverage the front wheel down into the ground.

Occasionally, you'll have to stand on the pedals to get up a climb, but "standing" on a mountain bike is so different from the move on a road bike that a roadie might consider it a misnomer. Traction and tracking considerations are such that standing mountain bikers stick their hips out and back much more than roadies. Such hip shifting allows mountain bikers to stand and deliver on slopes with up to a 25% grade.

Gradual climbs are best conquered with a strong, steady rhythm and powerful hip and leg actions rather than by pulling with the upper body. On smooth surfaces, try moving your hands to the center of the handlebars near the stem (if there's room) to lessen the need for travel line corrections from oversteering. However, this position may restrict breathing. If it makes you feel like it's harder to get air, forget it.

To charge slopes, get your cadence up at the base then stay in the saddle as long as possible. Near the top, lift out of the saddle, using your body weight to keep cadence up without downshifting. If you get good at this, try shifting up a gear just as you stand to put more power to the pedals. Many people slow down when they stand because cadence goes down. The idea is to speed up.

For short, standing charges, shift into a larger gear on the flat to get momentum up. Shift down as you begin the climb, using the resulting high cadence to maintain your momentum.

Short, steep sections (interval ramps) in a longer climb can be handled with an aggressive attack in which you lift your posterior just an inch or so off the saddle. You might even feel the saddle between your thighs as they pump, scraping the nose leather a little.

Conserve energy on long, difficult ascents by staying seated. If there are short walls along the way, raise your body off the saddle in coordination with the upward and forward portion of crank-arm travel to maintain momentum. If it seems that making it to the top while maintaining any reasonable cadence is an iffy proposition, try to avoid grinding gears, downshifting before your cadence slows too much. Shifting will be easier if you increase the cadence just beforehand, then ease up slightly on pedal pressure.

If you find yourself already bottomed out gear-wise or on too steep a slope to consider downshifting, try the lift-off-the-saddle, power-burst maneuver described above.

On super-steep wailing walls, power becomes secondary to stroke smoothness if you're going to stay in the saddle for any distance. Too high a cadence, even in a properly low gear ratio, can have you walking just as surely as poor body position or line errors from overpowered pulls on the handlebars.

Sometimes on a climb it helps to think "forward" instead of "up," especially in terms of foot action and the feel of power transfer through the shoes. This forward "feel" in the feet is particularly useful with cleated shoes. Forward pressure on the cleat surface helps rotate the cranks quicker than just using downward pressure in the power portion of the pedal stroke. Cleats also enable you to pull back rather than up, further smoothing the strokes. This isn't quite possible with uncleated shoes, although an accentuated heel drop when rounding the top of the crank-arm circle helps.

• • Downhills

Going Down with Confidence

Going downhill on a mountain bike can be either the most enjoyable or the most terrifying aspect of your ride. Which it will be is a matter of confidence, relaxation, and experience.

Remind yourself that the pleasure of having gravity pull you down that wonderful hillside is the payoff for the climb you just sweated up. And you need to relax enough to permit a certain amount of speed to develop—more than shy starters are absolutely confident about. That speed helps you roll over minor objects and bumps and makes tracking a line more manageable than creeping caution does. Going n-i-c-e a-n-d s-l-o-w mostly serves to give you time to be fearful, rather than allow you just enough time to figure out what to do.

No matter how skilled you become, occasionally there will be a downhill that seems intimidating. If it's a group ride or race situation where you can watch compatriots of similar abilities try the course, that may be all you need to understand how to do it.

> *That's what happened to me at the World Championships in Durango, CO. I went down to the waterbars section (construction to control runoff) of the downhill/cross-country course and watched Greg Herbald, Paul Thomasberg, and*

> *John Tomac come through. They were going through pretty well, which told me there was no reason I couldn't, too.*
>
> *I probably picked up 10 to 15 seconds just over that water-bar section by knowing, from watching those guys, that it was possible with a slight technique change and with plenty of bend in the knees.*—Michael

One relatively safe way to get used to the feeling of higher speeds is to practice on a local BMX course. Another method is to ride with a slightly faster, but responsible, cyclist. Play follow-the-leader. Then have your buddy ride on your tail as you lead and maybe talk things over later.

On downhills, keep your weight low and to the rear of the bike by shifting off the saddle and keeping plenty of bend in your knees. The steeper the grade you're riding, the more you'll want to keep your center of gravity down and back for better control.

Most mountain bikes come equipped with quick-release seat-post binder bolts. These allow you to raise and lower your saddle quickly and without tools. Lowering the saddle lets you move your weight down and back more easily. (In emergency bailouts on descents, remember to exit to the rear as well, or at least to the side and back. Otherwise you may experience an unpleasant meeting of your private parts and the top of your stem or bike frame.)

You want to keep traction on the back wheel and avoid being pitched over the handlebars. But you don't have to lower your saddle to do it. During racing, saddle lowering wastes time and breaks your concentration. As you get more comfortable dancing with your bike, you'll discover that you only need to use saddle height adjustment for extremely steep and technical sections.

> *I think the Hite-Rite's a great idea, but I only lower the saddle an inch or so for a specific downhill event like the Kamikaze or a dual slalom.*—Michael

If the situation calls for extreme weight adjustment, simply bring your hips behind the saddle and lower your abdomen over the leather. It may feel uncomfortable at first, or even dangerous, but it's a quicker and easier method for controlling the bike in steep descents.

It's not often that we even do this—when you're descending fast you just don't need to be that far back.—Martha

If you simply can't get secure going downhill without lowering the saddle but want to be as quick about it as possible, you might want to install an IRD handlebar remote control for the Hite-Rite.

When coasting downhill, keep your weight back and the pedals at 3 and 9 o'clock.

When coasting, keep the pedals at 3 o'clock and 9 o'clock (roughly parallel to the ground), your weight balanced between both legs. This allows you to control your bike with quick shifts of your weight. Also, this pedal position provides improved ground clearance, and the bent knees give you better suspension. Coupled with slightly bent, relaxed arms, this position will allow you to pitch and yaw as needed. Keeping your weight off the saddle also helps prevent pinch flats (caused by the tire bottoming out on the walls of your wheel rim and cutting the tube) and reduces the probability of being thrown off the bike when you hit a surprise ditch or bump.

Practice the balanced downhill position with either leg in the forward position, so you're comfortable both ways. Then when you're ready to try sweeping downhill turns at speed, you'll be comfortable placing your weight on the rear pedal, whichever it is.

But long before that exhilarating moment, most of us have to learn to use the brakes to control descent acceleration. If you're just beginning, head out to a small hill with smooth surfaces, maybe a graveled or all-weather road or a jeep trail. Find one with some mild descents and take them using both brakes to control your speed. You want to depend on the rear brake to slow you down, and feather or flutter the front brake as needed. The front brake has a lot of power and is essential in downhill situations. You just have to learn how to use it. Even though you're probably not going fast enough to take a header over the handlebars, too much front braking can cause front wheel skidding and loss of steering control.

You'll find that you do have to use your front brake on downhills. Often it's the only way to slow down to a manageable speed. Just don't ever slam it on, locking the front brake and wheel. If you want to know what happens if you do, ask your local track-and-field coach to let you try the maneuver on the pole vaulting path just before the pile of foam. The pole vaulting path is also the place to see what happens when you make sudden, sharp front-wheel turns at speed.

Get comfortable letting go of both brakes slightly to increase acceleration in various amounts. When you have a feel for how the bike handles and how tapering the brake works, go out on a dirt road (not a trail, because of possible erosion) and intentionally lock the rear brake, causing the tire to skid. This lets you experience what it feels like in an unexpected situation when you panic and slam on the rear brake.

People often find their rear tire skidding in corners when they increase their pace on loose terrain. Some get hooked on the technique in tight corners because it helps bring the rear tire around quicker. But the method can backfire on you by bringing the tire around too quickly and sliding the bike out from underneath you. Whether or not you go down, you lose momentum and time having to start again. The technique also contributes to rapid trail erosion and tire wear. Learn to release the brake lever while going into the turn to stop the tire from skidding.

Always keep two fingers wrapped around each handlebar grip. Some riders keep their pinky and ring finger on the bar grips, others their pinky and index finger. Overlap the fingers on the underside of the grip with your thumb if you can. These positions give a strong controlling grip while keeping two stronger fingers on the brake levers. Most brake levers will accommodate such grips.

> *Four years ago while warming up for the Kamikaze Downhill at Mammoth Lakes I hit a waterbar I didn't see and lost control because I had relaxed my hand grip too much. I literally tore my shorts apart and had to go back to the condominium, shower, change, and rush back to make my slot in the race order. I learned forever to keep two fingers wrapped and two fingers on the brakes at all times.*—Michael

Your hands and arms may become tired on long descents. A secure but relaxed grip can lessen the problem and make the descent that much more pleasurable. Forearm and shoulder workouts with weights will help, too.

You also want to minimize shock to your wrists, elbows, and shoulders. If your bike has flat bars, whatever their degree of bend, your wrists will survive the shake and bake of downhilling better if the bars are rotated downward a little. How much depends on your anatomy and upper-body bend preference. Rotate the bars to the point where they take out the acute lateral bend or break in the wrist without changing your upper body position forward or down too much.

The rougher the terrain and the longer the downhills, the more shock absorption you may want from your bike. The easiest way to increase shock absorption, assuming correct body position, is to install larger tires on your wheels. Installing the largest tires your frameset will accommodate and running them at slightly lower pressures (say, 30–40 PSI) will help on smaller and moderate bumps. Hardpacked trails with sharp, rocky edges require more air pressure to prevent flatting, but you'll get jarred. Keep in mind that, generally, the bigger the tire, the more it will weigh, and although it may improve traction, it'll mean more effort to pedal the bike.

Another tire trick is to mount the largest aggressively treaded tire you can on the front, and a slightly narrower, quicker-rolling tire in the rear. The larger contact patch and stability of the front tire helps prevent front-tire washout and brings the less roll-resistant rear wheel around in turns. Both tires should have large edge tread for engaging the earth while leaning the bike and should clear gunk from their treads with nothing more than gyroscopic force and riding vibration. You should also be sure that the rear tire has good climbing bite.

On even the gnarliest, longest downhills, you'll occasionally experience those moments when speed, braking, tire pressure, body positioning, suspension, and line of travel combine in a graceful dance between you, the bike rider being, and the hill. Your track disturbs minimal vegetation and soil, your wheels are swinging arcs on the turns, and your body floats over the bumps as the air brushes your cheeks. We hope you find such moments often.

• • Jumping

"Getting Air" over Obstacles

For those who graduated from BMX bikes, "getting air" is what life on a bike is all about. For them, avoiding a downed tree limb or taking a better line by executing a deft hop is as natural as a dog wagging its tail.

For many of the rest of us, the notion of intentionally tossing ourselves, on top of a bike, over a log, is a matter of "well, er, uh, do I *have* to?"

In a sport that already requires combining judicious use of the brakes with proper weight distribution to avoid mashing your face into the ground at high speed, it's not difficult to understand some people's discomfort with introducing more potential mayhem into the equation.

If you're in this camp, you might want to first get comfortable doing minor, slow wheelies over small objects. All jumps are basically developments of the weight-shifting steps you do in such maneuvers.

Remember that your wheels and tires are suspension units with quite a bit of elasticity. As long as you maintain enough air pressure and keep your flight plans within reasonable bounds, your wheels will act as springboard and landing cushion to a hop or jump.

The main points to remember are: keep enough air in your tires, land with the bike centered and as vertical as possible beneath you, keep the front wheel straight, and keep the crank arms roughly parallel to the earth with your legs acting as suspension springs. Also, get comfortable with toe clips and straps, so that you can more effectively direct the bike with your legs.

To begin, with your posterior just enough off the saddle to easily move it forward and back, approach a 6- to 12-inch-high obstacle at a roll that's just quick enough to easily coast over it. Just before your front wheel hits the thing, shift your weight back. As your wheel tops the object, shift your weight forward, letting your rear wheel ride over more easily.

Next, instead of merely shifting back as the front wheel nears the object, drive the crank arms hard and pull up and back on the handlebars momentarily, almost like a spurt of hill-climbing power. Your front wheel should lift over the object. As the front tops the object, surge your weight forward, giving the bike added momentum.

When you increase your object-topping ambitions to things 18 inches in diameter or larger, you need a little more approach speed. Pull up to a wheelie just before making contact and boost drive force to the rear wheel. As soon as the front wheel touches the object's top surface (hopefully just before its top center) spring your body off the saddle and pull the rear end up and forward.

As the rear rolls over the top of the object, the front end begins to fall, so move your weight back over the saddle to help control the landing. With the front wheel on the ground and the rear wheel rolling off the object, move your weight forward once more to lighten the load on the landing rear rim.

Specific skills

Every mountain biker needs to know how to bunny hop. Beginners should start in a large area free of obstacles. Load yourself like a spring by crouching on the bike with extremely bent elbows, knees, and hips, rolling slowly along, pedals parallel to the ground. From the crouch, explode straight upward, keeping pressure on both pedals and pulling upward on the handlebars with a forward twisting motion (reverse to that of a motorcycle throttle). The twisting motion helps bring the rear end up.

In the beginning don't worry about which crank arm is forward and which is back. Just do whatever comes naturally. Then, after you get comfortable with the basic lifting, make sure to practice with either crank arm forward, and learn to direct the handlebar twisting motion so it turns the front wheel slightly left or right. On the trail you'll want to be able to hop with either side forward, depending upon which side an obstacle is on, and you'll need to be able to turn the wheel toward the best trail line.

Once you can get over six-inch obstacles on a regular basis on flat terrain, you're ready to do the maneuver on a slope, hopping as you traverse across it. Start near the bottom of a gentle, preferably grassy, slope. Do a series of slightly upward and downward traverses, hopping forward, right and left as you go. (Note that on a slope, you want to keep your weight to the uphill side to keep the frame upright, and to keep from tumbling down the hill sideways.)

Once this becomes comfortable, you're ready to use the gravitational pull of a slightly downhill traverse to begin mastering standing bunny hops. Rolling across the slope with the uphill crank arm forward, touch the brakes, bringing the bike to a quick momentary halt. Play with this maneuver until you are at ease holding the bike still for a couple seconds without tottering.

Next, get in a mild crouch, and just when the bike stops moving forward, make a small sideways hop downhill, keeping the front wheel pointed forward or ever so slightly downhill. Release the brakes as you begin the twisting/pulling jump motion on the handlebars. After a landing/rolling exit becomes routine, begin pedaling forward as soon as your wheels touch the ground and straighten the bars to maintain your line on the slope. Once you get that move down, expand the length of your standstill until you are no longer using the momentum of your traverse to hop. Then try hopping the bike upslope.

If you ever feel yourself tottering, try to fall uphill. With luck, you've picked a spot clear of obstacles, maybe even one with grass on either side of the trail for a soft landing. Large institutional lawns are great places to practice bunny hopping.

Track stands

Once you're hopping uphill and downhill with glee, roll on down to the flats and begin practicing the standstill maneuver, known as a track stand, on level ground. The intent here is to stay up as long as possible, without tottering, and with as little front wheel movement as possible. Try to keep the front wheel cocked uphill. (On a roadway this is usually toward the center of the pavement.) Keep your crank arms at 2 o'clock and 8 o'clock, with the downhill side forward.

You stay upright by applying crank pressure against brake-engaged wheels, constantly shifting your weight as needed to keep the bike vertical. Sometimes you'll twitch the front wheel in reaction to a body weight shift. Then you have to either twitch it back or change pedal positions. You can also cheat a little by letting up a fraction on the brakes, allowing the bike to creep forward.

There are myriad places to practice stands, including between the lines of a pedestrian crosswalk, the grid lines on a football field, and the lane on an asphalt basketball court.

> *I find it helps me to balance to pick a focus point—a street sign, stoplight, tree, whatever.*—Michael

Small jumps

Having mastered bunny hops and track stands, you're ready to begin jumping over small obstacles such as curbs, small holes, small branches, or trees.

These jumps require nothing more than application of the same moves you already know, just in a slightly different mix. Practice by approaching a curb or small tree-type obstacle in a quick roll with the crank arms cocked as for a track stand. Lift the front end just before contact, just like in the bunny hop exercises. As the front wheel clears the obstacle, pedal again to drive the rest of the bike over the object.

Once this begins to get boring because it's so-o-o easy, go at it again with a little more speed. Follow the front-end lift with a definitive lift to the toe straps and a jolt of your upper body upward, as if someone just goosed you by surprise, and begin pedaling as soon as you feel your rear wheel touch the obstacle.

For flying jumps, pick a flat surface one- to two-feet wide to practice over. Approach at trail speed (8–12 mph) and do the crouch-spring, release-jump move learned for bunny hopping. Keep the front wheel straight and target the throwing action forward and upward.

Once you can clear 18-inch target patches (such as puddles and manhole covers) with both tires, you're ready to begin flying over

Jumping is just an extension of the crouch-spring, release-jump movements used in bunny hopping.

obstacles. (Be aware that wet manhole covers are particularly nefarious. Your rear is likely to slide out from under you if it lands on one.) Flying jumps take momentum and a bit more upward-lifting energy. The amount of lift-off force and momentum depends on the object you're trying to clear, the amount of gear and sludge build-up on your bike, and terrain softness.

First, try to consciously apply front lift a fraction of a second before rear lift. Then jump again with simultaneous total bike lift-off to see which suits you. Either can work for forward jumping of objects, but only the simultaneous works for sideways jumps while moving at speed.

Don't rush, progress from the basics, and remember that you're on a mountain bike not a moto-cross bike, and you'll do okay.

• • Water

Knowing What You're Riding Into

Nothing can relieve a hard, hot summer mountain bike ride like a splash of cool stream water. You can spend hours at a water crossing taking turns to see who can "clean it" first, then ride home feeling refreshed and like a kid again. (Okay, so you'll have some hub and bottom bracket bearing work to do.) Then again, a poorly conceived or unprepared water encounter can result in a bone-chilling, teeth-rattling time trial home to get warm.

The overriding rule for entering water with your mountain bike is to make sure you know what you're getting into.

Determining water depth is a good starting point, but there are other important considerations as well. What is the stream bed surface condition? Is it even or potholed or trenched? Is it rock, firm soil, or muck? Are there any submerged obstacles? How fast is the current? You may even want to take air temperature into consideration—submerge your rear derailleur during a stream crossing when it's below 33 degrees Fahrenheit, and you might find yourself frozen into one freewheel cog position for the remainder of the ride.

Never attempt a nonstop, uninspected entry into a muddy creek. Watch the water surface for signs of current speed and direction, even if the current isn't strong enough to cause ripples. Grab a stick, if available, and check the water for obstacles and bottom-surface condition. Prod the bottom to check firmness. Inspect the banks for animal tracks that may indicate easier fording. If you are still in doubt about how to proceed, a walk through might be safest.

Visually check the bottom of clear streams. Look for lines of travel with flat rocks or stones smaller than four inches in diameter. If a rocky bottom isn't too mossy it's probably worth attempting.

Fine points of crossing vary with the width, depth and current of the water. Here are some pointers that we've been able to agree on.

Small streams (three to five feet wide, four to nine inches deep). Enter with the quickest speed you can maintain given the bizarre feel and resistance of water, but one that causes minimal splashing. Put your weight back almost to the point of doing a wheelie to prevent the front wheel from sucking in and pulling you into an "endo" position.

Medium creeks (5–20 feet wide, less than bottom-bracket height deep). Be sure to keep your weight back at the start of your entry drive. Be in a gear you could pedal at 100 rpm in your sleep but that has some resistance, using smooth steady strokes and handlebar control. Pick a line where there are no current ripples in the water—indications of rocks or debris on the bottom.

Narrow but deep streams (deeper than bottom-bracket height). Check out the stream banks—there's a good chance they are steep. Can you easily hop over the stream? If not, consider dismounting and practicing your bike toss or your steeplechase portaging technique.

Remember, if your bottom bracket or hubs go under water (or your headset for that matter), then you've got a bearing overhaul job to do as soon as you get home, or a regreasing job at the minimum.

There will be times when you have to portage the bike. Carrying a mountain bike through water is a bit different from hillclimb portaging. In a hillclimb you can get by with a firm grasp of the top tube or a quick hook of the top tube/seat tube joint on a shoulder. Moving-water crossings demand a more solid and relaxed carrying of the bike's weight and floppy mass. The more evenly distributed the load of the bike is on your back, and the more relaxed your muscles, the better you'll manage to cope with difficulties such as water current, treacherous stream bottoms, or even a gust of wind while you're mid-stream.

Hooking your entire arm through the bike's main triangle and

Portaging keeps your bottom bracket and hubs out of the water, but it takes skill to navigate the current and avoid underwater hazards.

holding the front wheel steady helps stability. But on small bikes the configurations of tubing, along with with bottles and a pump, make such stances impossible. Martha often solves the dilemma by hooking the saddle nose over her shoulder and grabbing a chainstay.

Keeping your feet about shoulder width apart works well in mildly moving streams. In faster currents a wide walk—almost as if you're straddling something—helps prevent the current from pushing you around.

In races, aggressive stepping with a pronounced, high knee action can make for quicker crossing, especially in over-the-knee-deep water in which you can use use the water for balance. But the more you disturb the water, the less you'll be able to see what's next for footing, and you have to be alert for mossy rocks.

Some of the trickiest water though, is not in stream beds at all. It's the medium to huge puddles that collect in the ruts and depressions motorized off-road vehicles can make in heavy clay soils. Long, skinny puddles are most likely shelved and rutted, if not disguising mysterious sinkholes.

> *I've seen numerous endos and whole mountain bikes swallowed into these.*—Michael

Even medium-sized ovals can have two-foot-deep bogs for bottoms. In general, if puddles are long and thin (over a bike length long) or in rutted, trenched soil, it's better to go around them.

If you're on a trail that goes through a puddle and the only way past is off the trail, use extreme care, even walking and carrying the bike around. We've all encountered areas where a beautiful narrow track suddenly becomes a huge blob of rutted mud because of alternate trails made around a seasonal puddle.

And although shallow, wide puddles are usually easy to spin through, keep a mental note if you know about any downhills just ahead. Your rims will need some clearing and drying before you can brake again.

• • Fuel

Eating, Drinking, and Being a Buff Biker

Next to air (or oxygen, to be specific), water is the most vital substance for human well-being. Water carries nutrients, keeps your engine from overheating, and dispenses the exhaust that builds up in exercising muscles. So people who make a point of exercising vigorously away from sources of clean, pure water are likely to have problems.

You want to make sure to have plenty of potable water on the trail—hence the popularity of extra-large water bottles and 70-ounce-capacity Camelback water bags. If you're planning an outing longer than two or three hours, you might want to figure out a way to carry even more. Although water is about the densest material to carry on a ride, it's not the thing to get weight conscious about. Remember, it only gets lighter. (Because you're drinking regularly, right?)

Unfortunately, the days when you could count on using stream water are history. Pollutants are routinely dumped renegade fashion into seemingly remote watersheds, and decades of industrial activity have left tailings in many watersheds. If that isn't enough to make you cautious of drinking untreated stream water, there's the Giardia parasite. This teensy-weensy bug gets cozy in human intestines and wreaks havoc. Symptoms can vary from a nagging, vague illness that repeats itself monthly or weekly, to chronic diarrhea, indigestion, and malaise.

If you can't pack water in with you, carry a quality hand-pumped water filter. The models that are durable and that strain small enough particles to block Giardia cost a bit more but are essential if you're going to use water from streams.

A maxim for water consumption during moderate exercise in moderate temperatures (68–78 degrees) is to drink 2–3 ounces every 15 minutes. Vigorous biking increases the water ante dramatically. If you're riding near race intensity, you should consume a large bottle of water for every hour on the bike.

Your particular needs may vary, of course. Generally, if you don't ever need to pee on long rides, you're not drinking enough. If you're stopping every 30 minutes, try cutting back.

Temperatures above 70 degrees demand more replenishment, but don't let cooler temperatures fool you into thinking you don't need to drink that much. The fact is, those who like to make fat tracks in the snow have the same hydration concerns as those who prefer hot, semi-arid conditions. That's because between the heat of exercise and the effort to maintain body temperature, your body is evaporating as much water as if it were in a desert. If your body becomes dehydrated, the likelihood of frostbite is increased because loss of water in the cells promotes freezing and acidosis, a condition that actually causes the cells to reject rehydration.

The prudent plan is to start off thoroughly hydrated. For a 45-minute to 1.5-hour ride, drink a large tumbler of water 15–30 minutes before starting. For longer rides consume 16 ounces of water or juice .5–1.5 hours before riding.

Also, be aware that anything that accelerates dehydration, notably alcohol and caffeine, should be closely monitored if vigorous riding is on the schedule. A half-cup of coffee to jump start the brain cells the morning of a long weekend ride isn't going to hurt most people and is preferable to bumbling out the door forgetting some essential item. But more than a cup is going to put the body into water debt. So increase your initial water intake to be ahead of the drying effect the coffee will have on you.

Alcohol consumption has serious consequences. Even light social inbibing can seriously upset a serious fitness regimen. If you're committed to participating in an event that demands high performance, remember that the dehydration effect of a single unit of alcohol (12 ounces of beer, 6–8 ounces of wine, or one shot of hard liquor) is pronounced even 3 days later. More than three or four units per week can negate plenty of hard work. If you must inbibe, at least drink plenty of water before going to bed (almost so much you feel bloated) and early the next day.

If you presaturated your system shortly before a ride, your body's in good position to infuse a constant resupply of fresh liquid into the stressed muscles before they become parched. If you wait until you're thirsty, your body will always be playing catch-up and will never function properly because it has to juggle emergency rehydration along with the host of other demands placed on it by the exercise (nutrition, cooling, lubrication, and exhaust venting). However, if you do feel like you're really behind on hydration, you don't want to swamp your body with too much at once. That can cause cramps and block food ingestion. You want to sip regularly and very frequently.

Simple rehydration can get complicated by the concurrent need for calories and for maintaining a steady sugar level in the blood. Carrying a second water bottle filled with a slightly sugary drink such as juice and seltzer, or juice and tonic water can provide just the pick-me-up you need on a longer ride. If your GI tract is upset by the combination of carbonation and exercise, try Gatorade diluted 50% with tap water or one of the fruity carbohydrate powders similarly diluted.

Whether supplementing water intake with homemade or commercial recipes though, remember that supplementing is what it should be. The experience of professional trainers and the current research literature indicate that:

- Plain water is still the best for most people in most circumstances.
- Electrolyte-rich and potassium-rich fluids are best taken at least 30 minutes before riding.
- Mineral- and sugar-rich concoctions can actually slow fluid uptake into your blood stream.
- Carbohydrate-rich supplement drinks need to be balanced with water.
- Even so-called single-source liquid race diets can be insufficient for rehydration, because there's not enough "free" water consumed relative to your hydration rate.
- Single-source liquid race diets have repeatedly soured people's

stomachs in extreme hot and cold temperatures, so they have problems ingesting anything, then bonk big-time.

One method that has worked for many riders is to carry both a large bottle of water and a bottle of your preferred energy drink. If you use a commercial concoction, dilute it 25% more than directed for easier ingestion. Be sure to identify the energy drink bottle somehow, maybe with cloth handlebar tape wound around it near where you grab it, so you don't mistakenly douse yourself with it.—Michael

Fat tire fuel

Dietary planning is important enough to warrant books by specialists, and we recommend reading one or more of the titles in the bibliography for a thorough grounding in the subject. But there are a number of basic concerns that should be mentioned.

There's a major difference between how your body fuels itself when dormant and what it craves when active. Sedentary subsistence feeds on fat. The active body switches to a completely different fuel system requiring mostly complex carbohydrates and water.

If you're integrating mountain biking into a lifestyle that's concerned with losing weight, maintaining a lean body, or any other version of All-American Dieting, learn to measure your percentage of body fat (most conveniently with special calipers), and understand that you want to fuel the lean body mass, not repack the entire edifice.

And despite our culture's hyperfocus on leanness, remember that cold weather requires fat reserves and that they actually play a role in health maintenance. For recreationally riding women, 15–23% body fat is fine, 12–18% for Expert or Pro/Elite female racers and recreationally riding men. Expert or Pro/Elite male racers should have between 5% and 12% body fat. (These percentages were derived from several sources giving recommendations for both minimum and maximum amounts in athletes and the general population.)

Women need to be sure they get enough iron and calcium to safeguard against anemia and osteoporosis. There is also some evidence that restricting, if not eliminating sodium, refined sugar (all sucrose products), and caffeine can reduce menstrual cramping, bloating, and sore breasts—nuisances especially for athletically active women.

Men are lucky in that they don't have to pay attention to particular elements, just be sure they get a steady supply of all major minerals and trace elements. The major minerals are calcium, phosphorous, magnesium, potassium, sodium, and chloride. The vital trace elements identified by the National Research Council are iron, chromium, manganese, cobalt, copper, flourine, zinc, selenium, molybdenum, and iodine.

It's no secret that we live in a culture that puts us at risk by clogging our cardiovascular systems with gunk and polluting our bodies with chemical carcinogens. Autopsies of cadavers from Vietnam revealed that by 20 years of age most American males are already coronary time bombs. Athletic activity such as mountain biking is generally regarded as having a beneficial effect on the body, but can put individuals with pre-existing artery plaque and genetic predispositions at risk. Reasonably conscientious mountain bikers will restrict or eliminate all saturated fat, limit cholesterol intake, and leave the salt shaker alone.

Long-time road riders often note that mountain bikes are less efficient than road bikes. The increased rolling resistance and more vertical mass just mean more calories of fuel are needed to move the same weight just as far. Such prolonged, intense athletic activity means you need to manage your food intake. Your body needs to circulate blood through the muscles and the lungs, not break down dense foods from your digestive system. On long rides, what you need to do is eat bits and pieces as you go, similar to the sipping water method.

The digestive system can get pretty selective, especially in hot weather. What your mouth even finds palatable will change under the stress of a long effort. Learn what works for you by experimenting in relatively safe, controlled-intensity situations, where you can modify variables one at a time.

Your food choice can make an even bigger difference in your cycling when you switch to a diet plan that promotes endurance. Studies have demonstrated that endurance benefits from high-complex-carbohydrate, low-fat diets. High carbohydrate in this sense means 60–70% of intake. Low fat means 15–25% of your diet. The remainder is protein. And don't forget the water—as exercise physiologist Brian Sharkey pointed out in his book, *Physiology of Fitness,* carbohydrates are stored in water in your body.

Finally, whether buying commercially packaged foods or cooking your own on-the-bike recipes, remember to include packaging disposal plans. Carry your wrappers out with you. Nothing is more disgusting than finding a trail of mylar food labels littering a track that's otherwise fared well from mountain bikers' passing.

• • Mountain Bike Aerobics

Training the Heart Rate Way

Aerobic training is the backbone of a mountain biking fitness program. Also known as cardiovascular exercise, aerobic training is the stuff that builds endurance in skeletal muscles and promotes a healthy heart and healthy lungs. It does this by elevating the functional state of the heart and lungs to what's known as your training range. To benefit from the effort, you need to exercise in your training range for at least three 40-minute sessions each week.

Mountain biking is a great means of aerobic training because it involves relatively low-impact stress on the body compared to other activities, and you can simultaneously enjoy some beautiful scenery while doing it. Also, you can easily integrate the program into your day-to-day lifestyle. If, for example, you commute to work or school on your mountain bike, there's no need to get up at 5:30 A.M. to go running or swimming or to take an aerobics class.

Throughout the training and racing sections of this book we refer to various heart rate training ranges. We do this to provide a workable system of progressive challenges that will allow mountain bikers of different fitness levels and with various performance goals to structure appropriate programs.

By riding a controlled progression of challenging efforts for specific periods of time you can significantly improve your fitness level and riding competence. Once you establish a foundation of fitness, you can manipulate the sequence and intensity of workouts to achieve specific results such as improved endurance, strength, speed, or power on the bike.

To use this plan, you need to know how long you're in each heart rate range. This is known as heart rate monitoring. We consider heart rate monitoring the most accurate means of keeping track of your exercise program and fundamental for any serious training program. Heart rate monitors are available for $100–300, depending upon the features offered. The essential items are a chest-mounted monitor of your heart muscle and a display that's easily viewed while riding the bike.

Training within specific, progressively challenging ranges of heart rate for set durations with relatively high pedal cadence, combined with appropriate recovery periods, breeds high performance motors for mountain biking. Put this motor together with technical skills, mechanical proficiency, mental and emotional poise, and an understanding of your own body's operational tendencies, and you can take your mountain bike into whatever adventures you choose with confidence.

Whatever your training goal, the trick lies in using heart rate training without becoming obsessive about the numbers or the gadgets. Once you establish what your training ranges are, warm up, get yourself cruising in the appropriate range, and then pay attention to other things, like having fun, "cleaning" a section, smelling those trees, etc.

There are a couple of concepts that should be understood about training. One is progressive overloading. By gradually increasing the demand on your body's exercise capacity you can systematically make your body capable of routinely doing a little bit more. With just enough recovery, the body trains itself to handle the new demands, and your fitness level improves.

Stress overload, on the other hand, describes when you've asked too much of your body and need to lay off from the progressive-challenge scheme in order to recuperate. If you don't back off, or if you try to train through the fatigue, you can negate the benefits of a lot of training or risk injury. How much to relax from the regimen, and for how long, depends on how extreme the stress overload, and how long it takes indicators like your morning resting heart rate to return to their regular level.

One more thing before getting into formulas—our training method uses heart rate ranges rather than specific heart rates. On any bike ride, your moment-to-moment heart rate will fluctuate. Off-road, the fluctuation increases due to many factors, especially the abrupt changes in terrain. It would be ludicrous to try to maintain a specific heart rate, but you can keep your heart rate in a range and still pay attention to the other things going on around you.

> *I use my heart rate monitor while doing everything. Well, I do take it off in the shower. Seriously, it's fun to see how your heart rate changes for very slight changes in activity, or to wear a monitor while watching a movie or reading a book to see what your emotions can do to your heart rate. Play around with it a little and the concept of heart rate training will become better integrated into how you think about training.*—Martha

Our heart rate training range formulas are based on the Heart Rate Reserve Formula used by the American College of Sports Medicine (ACSM). To effectively use these formulas, you have to know your theoretical Maximum Attainable Heart Rate (MHR) and your Resting Heart Rate (RHR).

Your MHR is a measure of your theoretical aerobic capacity. Outside of a laboratory test, you can estimate your MHR by subtracting your age from 220. RHR refers to your morning resting heart rate taken first thing in the morning before you even sit up in bed. To get a base RHR, take your resting heart rate every morning for two weeks while maintaining what's been for you a normal day-to-day routine. Then compute the average.

If you can make taking your morning resting heart rate a habitual part of waking up, so much the better. A sudden, sharp rise in your resting heart rate is a signal of stress overload and the need to alter your training accordingly. Also, your resting heart rate is likely to drop after a couple months of prolonged training as your overall fitness level improves. This will, in effect, change your training ranges, so you'll need to recompute the heart rate formulas.

Any sound exercise program first establishes base fitness and endurance so you can sustain the essential exercise activity for an expected duration of time. Then you work on special skills or abilities in an advanced program. First, we'll explain building a foundation for mountain bike riding ability. Then we'll develop the basic training program and then describe more advanced training ranges and their use.

Exceptions

Before you get busy with a pad, pencil, and calculator and go on to greater glory, let's make sure you're not an exception to the guidelines for aerobic training.

The ACSM guidelines for exercise cite a 10–12 beat per minute (bpm) variance in the general population for theoretical maximal heart rate. That means you could subtract 6 bpm from your theoretical MHR when figuring the low end of your training range, and add 6 bpm when figuring your high end, to get the widest spectrum of what your heart rate might be and still be in the "normal" range.

Whether your tendency is to be consistently high or low or on the mark is something you must learn by observing yourself or by being tested. Among the three of us, Martha's heart rate is at the low end of the variance, and Yuri's runs slightly high. Michael is an exception. His RHR of 30–32 indicates that he is outside any normal bell curve. (Nearly everyone has a resting heart rate between 45 and 75, depending upon fitness level.)

If your heart rates seem radically high or low or behave erratically, seek competent advice and consider getting tested before engaging in a rigorous program.

Also, according to the texts on the subject, adolescents should use 200 as a theoretical MHR (instead of 220 minus age) to safeguard against injury.

Cadence

Anyone getting into a mountain bike training program needs to have an understanding of pedal cadence and how it interplays with heart rate. Researchers have found that cyclists who ride their bicycles in gears that allow them to maintain fairly high pedal spin rates of 90–100 revolutions per minute against moderate resistance loads get more from their exercise than those who pedal slower with higher pedal resistance.

The reason seems to be that the skeletal muscles "fire" or pull better at these quicker rates under moderate loads than when grunting along at a slow rpm against strong pedal resistance. Also, the muscular system is better able to vent exhaust (in the form of lactic acid) under such conditions.

The most convenient way to keep accurate track of your cadence is to use a bike-mounted cycling computer with a cadence monitor. If you don't have a computer, you can use a wristwatch and count pedal revolutions, or you can count to yourself in the time-tested way, "1001, 1002, 1003 . . ." making sure one leg is going around at least one full revolution of the crank arms for every number you count.

Don't be obsessed with your cadence. Simply check it once in a while. Eventually you'll get to learn what different rates of pedal speed feel like. Also, don't try to maintain, say, 92 rpm, exactly. Begin by just making sure you stay within a range of 10 rpms, such as 80–90 rpm. As long as your cadence, or "spin" is in that range, and there's moderate pedal resistance, you're okay.

A beginner isn't likely to be able to hop on a bike and pedal at 94 rpm for an hour. So what if you get on and it's all you can do to maintain 70 rpm?

First, check your gearing. If you're new to cycling, or at least new to using it for aerobic training, start out with the chain on the middle chainring in front, and in the middle of the gear cluster in the back.

Ride on relatively flat terrain, and spend 10 minutes or so just getting comfortable. Use the rear gear shifter to move the chain one or two gears out (harder pedaling) or in (easier pedaling) as needed for any moderate slopes. After you're at ease with things, find out in which gear configuration you're able to maintain pedal speeds faster than 60 rpm.

Okay, now in a safe area—one with clear visibility and few or no cars—see if you can get the rpm number into the 80s without feeling like you're going to burst. Don't despair if you can't, and don't force yourself if it feels extremely difficult.

Find out approximately what pedal speed you can maintain for a half-hour. If it's 70–76 rpm, that's fine. As you get more fit and accustomed to cycling, you'll be able to rotate the pedals more quickly. Eventually you'll be pedaling at 75–85 rpm instead of at 70–80. Then 80–90 rpm, etc.

Once pedaling in a middle gear at about 85 rpm becomes your

standard, here's an exercise that will help nudge it up: Shift into an easy gear (such as the middle front and innermost rear cog) on a flat stretch. This will enable you to wind it up to 100–110 rpm for a minute or so. Return to your normal pedal cadence for five minutes. Do another high-spin minute. A few sessions of 5–10 repetitions of this spin cycle and high-rpm cadence will be yours.

Do note, however, that your personally preferred spin rate will be somewhat determined by your particular tendon construction, cardiovascular capability, and fitness level. For example Yuri's is 95. His wife Sally's is a tad lower. When riding their tandem on long rides, they usually end up negotiating a compromise rate in between, or going back and forth to keep each other comfortable.

The foundation

We refer to essential mountain bike exercise as training in your Endurance Heart Range, or EHR. Before you can accomplish a personal recreational goal with your mountain bike, you first have to be able to ride for extended periods. Endurance Heart Range is the range in which recreational riders get a cardiovascular exercise benefit, and in which high-performance riders lay the foundation miles for more strenuous endeavors. The formula for Endurance Heart Range is:

$$\text{EHR} = [70\text{–}75\% \ (\text{MHR minus RHR})] + \text{RHR}$$

As an example, let's take Roger, age 38, whose morning resting heart rate is 45. Roger's MHR is 220 minus 38, or 182. The lower end of his training range will be $.70 \times (182-45) + 45$, or 141 beats per minute, and the higher end of his range will be $.75 \times (182-45) + 45$, or 148 bpm. Roger's EHR is between 141 and 148 bpm.

Current research information says that the minimum program for effective aerobic conditioning is to train in your EHR for 40 consecutive minutes, three times a week. That allows for a recovery day between each workout. When you add a 10-minute warm-up and a 10-minute cool-down to each 40-minute session, you're spending a mere 3 hours per week on your fitness program. (The warm-up and cool-down are important for preventing injury. If you do them on the bike, you spin the pedals in a low or easy gear.) Endurance training establishes basic mountain biking fitness. As we said, this is the foundation from which all advanced mountain biking ability follows.

If you're using commuting or errand-running on your bike as part of your training time, you'll want to get a sense of what your exercise range feels like, and pick routes that allow you to pedal consistently, rather than continually stopping and starting.

Having mentioned keeping comfortable and "feeling like bursting" while discussing aerobic training, it's important to recognize the difference between feeling winded and being exhausted. Everybody gets winded sometimes, even the super athletes. It's a momentary condition that the body recovers from easily. If you're in particularly poor aerobic condition, you're going to feel winded quite quickly. But as your fitness level improves, you'll find yourself feeling slightly depleted or pressed, then experiencing aerobic recovery. This sense of breaking through the "winded" barrier is a major milestone in progress toward fitness.

Being exhausted can mean running out of fuel, sometimes referred to as "hitting the wall" or "bonking." But it can also mean that you're working out at a too-difficult work load for your current muscular strength. If that's the case, back off.

In your endurance training program, pay attention to time rather than miles because the human body doesn't know anything about how many miles it has pedaled at such and such a work load. It does know how long you've been at it, and that's what matters for a training effect.

Recovery range

The Rest and Recovery Range (RRR) is the heart rate range the beginning rider uses for those 10-minute warm-ups and cool-downs for the endurance rides. It's also the range that advanced riders use after extremely hard workouts. Racers frequently use this range after a particularly strenuous event, when even riding in the Endurance Heart Range would be too stressful to allow the body the complete recovery it needs, while staying off the bike would be detrimental to conditioning and future performance.

Rest and recovery rides are known in various places as "tootling" or "puttering" or some similar term. The range of heart rate should be used as a guideline for the maximum stress you put on your body after extremely hard rides, rather than as a minimum. When deciding how hard to pedal on a recovery ride, take a physical cue from your pedal resistance. It shouldn't feel too substantial.

The formula to compute the Rest and Recovery Range is:

RRR = [60–65% (MHR minus RHR)] + RHR

Basic scheduling

Rather than juggling detailed routines and seven-days-a-week rides, to begin with, just ride every other day for a month. If you begin on a Monday, the cycle will repeat every two weeks (M-W-F-Su-T-Th-Sat). After a month you can decide whether M-W-F or T-Th works better for you.

After you've decided that, you're ready to set up a four-times-a-week routine that provides the added benefit of training two days back to back. On the first of the tandemed days do a longer-than-usual workout, followed by a standard-length "light exercise" recovery day. For example, if your weekday rides are Monday, Wednesday, and Friday, make Sunday the fourth day, on which you go out for a longer training ride, say 1.5–2 hours. If you prefer Tuesday and Thursday schedules, go out on both weekend days, with the longer ride on Saturday and the recovery ride on Sunday.

As you get more fit, you'll need to intensify the training challenge on your body if you want to progress in fitness. The choices are to make the training sessions longer, intensify the resistance (using higher or bigger gears), increase the leg speed, or intensify the technical demand of the ride. All mountain bike training programs, from the basic to the most advanced, are manipulations of these factors.

Beginners should add to the duration of their time in EHR until they are riding for 70 minutes on the three standard workouts, and 1.5–3 hours on the long weekend ride. Add time to the weekday rides in 5- to 10-minute intervals, and double that for the weekend ride.

Within a month, you'll be able to ride in higher gears while maintaining the same cadence, and you may want to begin building specific cycling muscle strength or technical skills. You can either fit this training into your long ride or do it on the days between your endurance rides, just as long as you save the day after the long ride as a light-work-load, recovery day.

Once you've extended your endurance foundation to the point where you can handle three 1.5-hour rides and one 2- to 3-hour ride per week at EHR, you're ready to increase training intensity by incorporating some Race Performance Range training (RPR) into your rides. RPR is a slightly higher, in-season range used to train for the higher pace in competition or to handle the slightly elevated demands of performance rides.

The formula for Race Performance Range is:

RPR = [80–85% (MHR minus RHR)] + RHR

To incorporate this high-performance training into your program, begin by substituting 6- to 20-minute time periods in RPR for sections of your EHR rides, gradually adding more each ride, until you can ride in RPR for the entire workout. At that point, ride in EHR for the warm-up and cool-down.

Advanced training

When your fitness level is such that you're riding in RPR regularly and using EHR for warm-up, you have a lot of choices as to how to improve your fitness level or riding ability. Performance riders—those who want to be able to experience the widest range of fun they can or those who want to maintain a very high fitness level—will want to begin working in the two most intense heart rate training ranges, Capacity Heart Range (CHR) and Threshold Heart Range (THR).

Those formulas are:

CHR = [82–88% (MHR minus RHR)] + RHR
THR = [88–92% (MHR minus RHR)] + RHR

Capacity Heart Range (CHR) is the heart rate that can be maintained for 15–45 minutes of decidedly hard effort, most commonly in climbs. At the end of the longest duration you can handle riding in CHR, you are surpassing the aerobic (oxygen-using) ability of your system, which then complains with symptoms such as an extreme burning sensation in the leg muscles or in the lungs. By training with planned intervals of CHR and less strenuous heart rates for recovery, you can increase the amount of time you can spend in such upper-end efforts and improve your recovery ability.

Threshold Training Range (TTR) is the heart rate you can only sustain for two to three minutes. At this level your aerobic engine is approaching overload. This is referred to as "going anaerobic," and is thought to be the point where the body can no longer supply enough oxygen to working muscles to make fuel and so must switch to other, less efficient, methods. Whether or not your body actually begins making fuel anaerobically (literally, "without oxygen") is a subject of debate by exercise physiologists. What definitely does happen is that, at a certain level of effort, the mixture of blood gases suddenly skyrockets on the waste side and lactic acid accumulates in the muscles. Both indicate a state of intense activity that simply cannot be maintained for long.

In mountain biking this often occurs in the beginning of races, on short but very steep climbs, or in other circumstances referred to as "painful" or "exceedingly intense." One sure sign of threshold riding is that maintaining a clean line of travel or picking a line soon becomes very, very difficult.

Variety is key

Whatever your program, or whatever the stage of fitness development you're in, if you want to keep from getting bored, vary your routine every six to eight weeks. This seems to be the length of time the human body needs to fully acquire the benefits of a particular exercise regimen, but isn't so long that the body goes on automatic pilot and no longer responds to the conditioning. Pay attention to different aspects of your exercise to see if your body is "spacing out" at all. If so, shift things to emphasize a new area of improvement.

After you've been training with a heart rate monitor for several months you'll get an understanding of what your various training ranges feel like. Still, you'll want to "spot check" occasionally to verify that your perception or memory is still accurate. Some heart rate monitors come equipped with memory storage capacity, or the option to connect the monitor directly to a personal computer and "download" the memory. Both options offer sophisticated training possibilities for advanced riders.

> *I'll occasionally wear my monitor in a race, but not look at it until after the race is over—later in the day or that evening. I review the monitor's record, check the stress loads on my heart, and correlate my memory of the race with what it says. This tells me what I'm really capable of doing for an hour, or for whatever duration, and what sort of pace I can maintain without going backwards in my conditioning.*—Michael

By the way, if you notice that despite harsh terrain and intense periods of effort your heart rate just doesn't go up, it's a sure sign that you're overtraining.

• • Training

Building Your Fitness Foundation

Being a good mountain biker means more than being able to ride for a long time. Mountain biking inherently involves varying work loads (most often in the form of hills to climb, descend, and then climb again), so your enjoyment of the sport depends on your ability to quickly recover from momentarily intense efforts even as you continue. Ever gotten to a vista point and just spent the time up there gasping, unable even to enjoy the view? Such experiences pointedly illustrate that the ability to recover while continuing to function is crucial in mountain biking.

Whether you're tackling a steep grade on a personal outing or putting other competitors in your dust during a race, the ability to power through a challenging stretch is particularly rewarding when you can kick in your recovery capability and continue on without a hitch.

The good news is that all this, beginning with endurance and including on-the-bike recovery, can be established or improved with training. Endurance depends upon the muscles' aerobic capacity (the ability to oxidize or burn fuel steadily) and an efficient fuel supply system. Studies have demonstrated 160% improvement in endurance capacity over two months.

January through March is the time to build your endurance foundation. It's accomplished with long rides at a high pedaling rate in your Endurance Heart Rate (EHR), incorporating some training in your Race Performance Range (RPR) after you are well-conditioned.

Once you have this riding base built (80–100 hours of riding at your EHR and some RPR) you can build further endurance with on-the-bike climbing workouts. If local topography allows, begin by riding up hills in whichever gear maintains a high fluid spin. Once thoroughly warmed up and feeling like your engine is in its performance "hum," increase the pace to your Threshold Heart Range (THR) on relatively flat terrain for two or three minutes. Recover at a high spin in the middle chain ring until the next climb. Try to plan your route so it allows a series of spin/climbs and forced-pace flats followed by a recovery spin. Finish with a solid half-hour of 95-plus rpm spinning to get you home.

Recovery

As the season progresses and your conditioning improves, begin building recovery. Once or twice a week, do a series of climb attacks in your Race Performance Range followed immediately by the two-

Once you have a fitness base, on-the-bike climbing workouts can help build endurance.

to three-minute Threshold Range interval. Then cruise in your Endurance Range until the next attack. Bookend the workout with 30- to 40-minute high-spin rides and finish with several minutes at Rest and Recovery pace to relax the muscles and dissipate lactic acid (muscle exhaust).

Another way to develop recovery is to alternate 20 minutes in your upper Capacity Heart Range with 40 minutes in EHR throughout a long ride. Or, following a solid hour's warm-up, take on an ultra-long climb, alternating 1-minute hard efforts (that you cannot sustain for more than 65 seconds) with 5-minute puttering periods that allow your heart rate to return to your Endurance Heart Range.

> *I'll sometimes start these on the flat or rolling terrain just before the climb and do as many as 20 repeats. The first few won't feel so bad, but if you keep your intensity up even as the climbs start getting a lot harder, you have a very tough workout.*—Martha

Adding athletic depth

Once you have established strong endurance and active recovery, it's time to add strength and power workouts and to work on improving the technical skills that will add up to better times on the bike. But it may also be the time when it's most difficult to keep on with your program. Either something hurts or you just don't feel like doing anything extra. The weather may be alternating between freezing rain and genuine springtime, and the kid's bad dream at 4:30 A.M. destroyed your sleep cycle. Your body, too, reaches a crunch period in any fitness program during which the old model is still resisting being replaced by the new. Any one of a number of minor hurdles can thwart all previous earnest effort.

Usually it's only a case of the blahs. You just don't feel like riding or doing much of anything. Ironically, a good ride/workout may be just what you need.

> *When I'm feeling off, I give myself a test. If I still feel worthless at the end of my warm-up, I'll go home. Most of the time I've started to feel okay—those doldrums go away amazingly fast once you're on the bike. Then I'll do one trial interval (two*

to three minutes) just to make sure. This test allows me to rest when I really do need it, but doesn't allow me to slack off.
—Martha

Often there's a chain of hang-ups in routine, involving clothes, equipment, and transportation. Fortunately, most of these can be overcome with a little ingenuity and thinking ahead.

For example, even something as innocent as taking an impromptu "nature break" can be the glitch that does the program in for women. That's because urine, even a small amount of it, is very hard on sensitive skin and, combined with the natural chafing that happens during in-the-saddle time, it can make a ride miserable. This glitch can be avoided by always carrying toilet paper in a plastic ziplock bag. If you're driving to where you'll ride, wait to put your cycling shorts on until you get there. Once off the bike, immediately get out of them and back into your regular dry clothes. Many women—and men—find it helpful to bring a towel to wipe off the sweat from their private areas immediately after a ride.

Women who menstruate heavily may find longer rides difficult. Riding with a sanitary napkin can be extremely uncomfortable, or can cause rashes or infections. Changing tampons often (carry a plastic bag for this too) is about all you can do. If the tampon isn't enough, or if the string is irritating, go for shorter rides, stand on the pedals more, or just skip riding on the days of heaviest flow.

I always feel much better once I get on the bike and moving, although I often don't push myself hard on the first day.
—Martha

You can always do alternative training or cross-training efforts that are more comfortable—just do something or your legs will probably bloat up. If you have a very troublesome day, at least take a walk. You'll feel better for it.

Cramps can often be dealt with with over-the-counter ibuprofen (Advil, Nuprin, Medipren). Discuss it with your doctor. Or just give regular riding a shot—you may be one of those whose menstrual symptoms go away with physical exercise.

Keeping a journal

Every rider can benefit from keeping a training journal. Martha keeps a notebook in which she writes just about everything: how she feels, thoughts, training, heart rate, weather, aches and pains. Diet, too.

Every week she transcribes it to a spreadsheet, both to send to her coach and to review herself. The first line of the spreadsheet reads something like this: Date/A.M. heart rates/Workout/Duration/Ex heart rate/Weights/Comments.

The different headings translate as follows:

- *A.M. heart rates.* Measure your resting heart rate before you even sit up in bed. Then measure your heart rate 30–60 seconds later. See how much of a difference there is, and how high the rate is for both. The higher your initial heart rate and the larger the difference between the two morning heart rates, the less recovered you are from the previous day.
- *Workout.* This is what you actually do for training. Distinguish between types of rides (rd-mtn, flat/rolling/climbs).
- *Duration.* Time is most important but mileage is fun/rewarding to watch.
- *Exercise heart rate.* Include warm-up and cool-down rates if you monitor them.
- *Weights.* Done mostly in winter. Note exercises or muscle groups used and types of sets executed.
- *Comments.* Subjective feelings, diet, aches and pains, weather, trail conditions.

The spreadsheet is similar to Michael's training and racing log, in which he keeps everything Martha puts on her spreadsheets, plus race finishes, race information, and goals.

An alternative for people like Yuri who have problems with protracted diary writing is to keep an abbreviated training log—use a calendar date book or even just a calendar with big enough squares to write consistent particulars such as resting heart rate, duration, and type of workout.

For example, a daily entry might read:

- 54 (circled to indicate morning heart rate)
- 45 min. racewalk @130 (pace) w/5#ft; 4# handweights
- rollers 20 min. after

No matter what journal method you use, look back occasionally. Patterns emerge. Why something worked with your body and your lifestyle becomes evident. And what you've already accomplished supports your current efforts.

Realistic expectations

Your day-to-day responsibilities will affect your training and you have to take your other activities into account when establishing goals and expectations. How physically active or emotionally/mentally demanding is your job? Or your home situation? You'll get a better return on any training program by taking other situations in your life into account and tailoring your routine accordingly. Remember, you're mountain biking to improve your enjoyment of life, not to make yourself miserable or tired or guilt ridden.

You also need to tailor your training to your personal rhythms. For example, Martha finds that training on a seasonal basis involving blocks of several weeks works for her. Yuri has observed his body has a two-week cycle rather than a weekly one, so plans biweekly routines with a two- or three-day break in between.

A good way to learn your personal training cycle is to keep a line graph. At about the same time late each day, record how you feel on a scale of 1 to 10. (Keep this graph separate from your training journal entries; that way it's more likely to be a gut-feeling assessment of your entire day.) Watch the chart develop, and barring some major upset in your life, you should be able to see a pattern emerge. You might even notice some relationship between your training, exercise, or conditioning and the rest of your life.

Developing an accurate feeling for how training and other aspects of your life are interacting can make for more enjoyment in all areas.

Getting ready for vacation fun

If you have an extended vacation trip planned (50 miles a day for a week or more), then you've got to keep the daily miles on the schedule as well as build strength, recovery, and riding skills. Even though you can build strength and skills through shorter-mileage, quality workouts, there's just no substitute for long rides to get your body ready for the long hours on the saddle. Put in the preparation time and your trip will be a lot easier and more enjoyable—being saddle sore can put a serious damper on vacation fun.

Plan your training by counting backwards on the calendar from your vacation date. From six to three months before the big event, put in the miles in your EHR on flat to rolling terrain. Three months before, begin doing as much flat to rolling terrain riding with weighted loads as possible. Commute with pannier bags on your bike. Tow the kids to day-care in a trailer. On your unloaded rides, do strength, power, and recovery workouts.

With two months to go, you should be doing all the above and making sure you're tackling terrain as tough or tougher than you'll find on your trip. For the final month, do plenty of flat and rolling rides as well as a couple challenging terrain rides with the load you expect to be carrying on your vacation. Include three long rides each week, with at least one that's longer than your trip's average daily distance.

Maintain the long miles throughout, and when you leave on vacation you'll be in condition to enjoy the trip you dreamed of for so long.

Citizen events

Citizen challenge rides are getting tremendously popular. Even if we don't have the time or the money to race throughout a season, plenty of us seem to enjoy tackling one special event each year.

Like the dream vacation planner, mountain bikers with designs on a single-day event need to structure their training by counting back from the date of the event. How far back you count and how you structure your training depends on which of two camps you count yourself in.

— ***The Finishers Camp.*** Your goal is to simply do the event, whether that means "just surviving" or "having fun while doing it."

— ***The Placers Camp.*** You want to do well (your best), see how you place compared to some time goal, your buddies, or the whole world.

Finishers can begin preparing on shorter notice than Placers, maybe just a month or two prior to the event if they're already in fair shape. Their training goal is to be in good enough condition to handle the mileage and terrain of the event. Placers, on the other hand, want to have faced tougher stuff in training, both terrain and mileage-wise, so that the only pressure on them on event day is their own motivation.

Specific numbers on time, mileage, and intensity differ between training theorists, and number crunching can get out of hand. Below is what we consider a prudent training schedule for both Finishers and Placers for events under 75 miles. The technical demands of your training routes should roughly equal that of the targeted ride.

Performance pace (the heart rate that will be maintained for the event) differs slightly for Finishers and Placers. Finishers' Performance Pace will be at the upper end of their Endurance Heart Rate, while Placers will be at the lower end of their Race Performance Range.

Finishers' training schedule:

- *3 months before the event.* Do one ride that's 35% of event length at performance pace; weekly total = 100% of event mileage.
- *1.5 months (6 weeks).* Do one ride that's 50% of event length at performance pace; weekly total = 125% of event mileage.
- *5 weeks.* Do one ride that's 65% of event length at performance pace; weekly total = 150% of event mileage.
- *4 weeks.* Do one ride that's 85% of event length at performance pace; weekly total = 165% of event mileage.
- *3 weeks.* Do one ride that's 75% of event length at performance pace; weekly total = 185% of event mileage.
- *2 weeks before event.* Do 150% of event mileage per week in your EHR, up to 40% on pavement.

Increase weekly riding time/mileage totals 12% per week beginning 6 months before the event, if possible. During the week just before the event, concentrate on spin and low-strength and technical riding (medium demand). Ride just enough to keep loose and retain the snap in your legs, maybe 20% of the event's estimated duration per day.

Here is a training schedule for Placers:

- *4 months prior.* Do 50% of event length in one ride at performance pace.
- *3 months.* Do 80% of event length in one ride at performance pace.
- *2 months.* Do 100% of event length in one ride at performance pace.
- *1 month prior.* Do 120% of event length in one ride at 80–90% performance pace.
- *2 weeks prior.* Do 60–75% of event length in one ride at performance pace; total weekly mileage =150% of event mileage.
- *1 week prior.* Do 40–50% of event length in one ride, all at RPR.

During the weeks 3 months to 2 weeks prior to the targeted event, increase weekly ride time/mileage 15% per week so you're riding a weekly total of 200–300% time/mileage of the event.

Like Finishers, Placers should concentrate on spin and light technical rides the final week. A couple days before the event do a short, high-intensity ride to keep your system tuned up. Don't forget those rest days, at least one per week, and maybe a second easy-spin day.

Ultra-enduros

The above training plan isn't quite the ticket for an "ultra-enduro"—single-day events that are longer than 75 miles. These require building up larger blocks of training two to four months prior to the event. Include long rides that simulate conditions you'll encounter (darkness, unfamiliar terrain, temperatures, riding loads). Centuries (100-mile rides) should become a monthly training feature.

For the megarides like the L.A. 150, you should peak your regimen with a back-to-back weekend of long, deep-reserves training 2–6 weeks before the event. (The better your overall condition, the closer to the event date you can peak your training.)

Keep up solid weekly training totals, punctuated by one slightly longer, superlative-effort ride. Since surviving ultra-endeavors is a personal task, listening to your body is much more important than any training formula and cannot be overemphasized.

Finishers' training schedule:

- *3 months prior.* Do 50% of event length in one ride at performance pace; weekly total = 100% event mileage.
- *1.5 weeks prior.* Do 60% of event length in one ride at performance pace; weekly total = 110% event mileage.
- *4 weeks prior.* Do 60% of event length in one ride at performance pace; weekly total = 120% of event ride.
- *3 weeks prior.* Do 45% of event length in one ride at performance pace; weekly total = 135% of event ride.
- *2 weeks prior.* Do 35% of event length in one ride at performance pace; weekly total = 150% of event ride.

Placers' training schedule:

- *4 months prior.* Do 50% of event length in one ride at performance pace.
- *3 months.* Do 80% of event length in one ride at performance pace.
- *2 months.* Do 100% of event length in one ride at performance pace.
- *4 weeks prior.* One ride at 80% of event length; weekly total = 130% of event ride.
- *3 weeks prior.* One ride at 70% of event length; weekly total = 150% of event ride.
- *2 weeks prior.* One ride at 55% of event length; weekly total = 170% of event ride.

150-plus-miles mega training

Hopefully, you'll know about an event like this and your intention to ride it two to four months beforehand. If you've been racing or regularly knocking off high-performance club rides and citizen's events, you just switch over to longer and longer rides.

Since there's no feasible way to duplicate percentages of your estimated riding time in an event like the 210-mile Iditabike in Alaska or the 24-hour Montezuma's Revenge in Colorado, training becomes a steady build-up of total weekly training and increasingly longer sessions on the bike. For an expedition event in which you are required to carry gear, train with loaded panniers the final six weeks.

In this chart, all percentages are the percentage of estimated event riding time.

Time Prior	Weekly Total	Longest Day
3 months	100%	15%
2 months	110%	20%
6 weeks	120%	20%–25% (15% next day)
4 weeks	130%	25%–30% (15%–20% next day)
3 weeks	140%	20%–25% (20% next day)
2 weeks	150%	15%–20% (15% next day)

All percentages = percentage of estimated event riding time.

Assuming a solid training base, mental conditioning becomes two-thirds of doing well in an Ultra. Begin training early on in strange conditions. Make yourself go out on long rides that push your reserves and force you to get back on your own (no car ride home or bailing out allowed). Change your daily habits to reinforce a sense of self-reliance. Develop a sense of humor about things that go awry (such as headers) and the unexpected. Learn to persevere by pacing your emotions as well as your body, and get plenty of rest—a minimum of eight hours a day.

• • Annual Planning

Scheduling for Racers and Rec-heads

Okay, maybe you're not out there to be the first at the finish line. But strength training, developing a "jump" (momentary power), trick handling skills, and recovery ability are important nonetheless if your pastime happens to be mountain biking.

No, you don't have to refine such skills to have any hope of enjoying a mountain biking vacation. But being able to climb in stride and recover well, to quickly put some distance between your bike and a weaving motorized dinosaur, or to handle an 11% rock-strewn grade with boulders behind every corner without being terror stricken, are abilities that pay you back with increased enjoyment on your bike. Structuring exercise routines and planning the season are as important for the "personal best" or vacation-planning mountain biker as they are for racerheads.

On the other hand, if your brand of entertainment is seeing just how you measure up in speed compared to other fee-paying, licensed, fat tire funaholics, the information in this chapter is for you, too.

Endurance plays a large role in any rider's training regimen. That large volume of time spent continuously pedaling at 88–98 rpm in EHR is Joe or Josephine Seven-Speed's season-long standard. But where your program develops from there depends on what your goals are for the forthcoming year (if you believe in "goals" as a valid part of recreation) and whether or not there is a targeted Big Event on your mountain biking calendar.

So, what kind of recreationalist are you?

Do you let yourself off the fitness hook between Thanksgiving and Super Bowl Sunday? Or do you simply lighten the schedule a little during the months short on daylight?

If you slough off any appreciable amount (it only takes two weeks for muscle mass to begin disappearing), you're going to need a two- to three-month re-ignition period on the bike. This will be a time to rebuild stamina, aerobic capacity, and muscle tone, and reprogram habits like sleep, diet, or social routines to those that reinforce the realization of your mountain bike hopes. Then count on a one-month transition phase during which your body and/or mind may vacillate between enthusiasm for the new fitness lifestyle and the less demanding existence in the La-Z-Boy.

> *I use my heart rate monitor a lot in the spring to see how I'm doing in my early season training. For two solid months I use it for three or four out of every five hard riding days. You can get tired of looking at it, though, so have a relaxed frame of reference about progress, maintaining training ranges etc., even as you stay with your program. You don't want to get sick of the heart monitor, because it's very useful.*—Michael

Racers

For a serious racer January 1 means jump on the bike if you actually got away from it for any length of time. It's time to build your training foundation. When setting up a schedule you build by time rather than distance. Record 80 hours of high spin pedaling (95–100) at your EHR during January and February (about 10 hours a week) for your foundation.

It doesn't matter what kind of bike or indoor trainer you ride during January and early February. It's the time and heart rate and cadence that count. Just be sure your riding position is similar to your normal summer riding posture. By the end of February you want to be doing some outdoor training, and spending some time off-road.

In March you want to begin technical refresher sessions, and start riding in your Capacity Training Range (CHR) 20–40 minutes twice a week. Use common sense—start with short sessions and see how you recover. Make sure you warm up and cool down with 20–30 minute spins in your Endurance Heart Range.

Plan your training around your life: If you work full time, don't expect to be able to train the hours and intensity of a fully sponsored racer. Everyone needs rest, relaxation, social intercourse, and entertainment. Set realistic personal goals annually, monthly, and weekly.

During April make a transition from an EHR-pace standard to your Race Performance Range (RPR), substituting 15% per week so that by mid-May EHR is used for warm-ups, cool-downs, and specific recovery periods in workouts. Structure technical skills rides as technical intervals at EHR, alternating with RPR periods of 15–20 minutes.

Begin doing power intervals once a week in which you get your heart rate up to your THR for two or three minutes. Spin in an easy gear for 10–15 minutes between intervals until your heart rate is around 130 bpm. Do five or six intervals, then ride home tapering from EHR to Rest and Recovery heart rate.

Continue the capacity training twice a week, and don't forget the day off, most commonly Monday after Sunday's hard effort. Every five or six weeks, depending on your body's cycles, take three to five days for rest and recovery. Ride if you want, but don't play hard at all. (Sometimes not touching the heart rate monitor helps you stay sane.) Don't let things on these days get beyond EHR.

After mid-May your training depends on your local geography, when the race season starts for you, and what your target events are. Face each challenge as it comes—don't let fear take over, but don't go way beyond capability. (Then you'll just make a BIG MISTAKE and really have food for thought.) Remember that to improve you have to push yourself and test yourself, but you must manage the rate of challenge.

Women have to be careful that one of a zillion socialized cop-outs doesn't take root, such as the "I'm a woman, I'm naturally more cautious than men because my body's used for childbirthing, et cetera, et cetera" excuse not to try. If you're honestly not ready, fine, but the point is you need to emphasize Capacity Heart Range training and Threshold training as much as the guys do (who have their own excuses to overcome).

That's because all mountain bike races generally start with a bang.

People striving to be at the front ride above anaerobic threshold for a while, and then a break usually forms. Everybody settles in and rides at anaerobic/lactate threshold or close to it. Then there's often another selection process during which you go anaerobic again.

The cycle repeats itself. How often depends on whether the race is a loop or point-to-point course and how long it is. You don't recover much because you're trying to hold your position, and you're trying to stay alive—the technical requirements tend to keep your heart rate up even higher than in a road race. If the race goes through sandy stuff it changes from a test of anaerobic capacity to a power session.

To be able to handle that sort of race, women are battling all the physical challenges that men do, plus the lifelong saturation bombing with the propaganda that they're physically inferior to men, even though muscle biopsy studies have indicated that women physiologically may actually be superior to men for endurance sports like mountain biking. It all comes down to the fact that in athletic competition, performance ability is largely mental. Since a female in our society has already been socialized to the idea she is sub-male by the time she is four years old (often despite the best efforts of egalitarian parents and teachers), we'll probably never know the answer to the "Who's physiologically better?" question, because we'll never have athletes raised without that cultural influence. In lieu of that opportunity, women need to be sensitive to whether an urge to back off is a genuine signal to take it easy or another performance-inhibiting sexist cop-out rearing its ugly head.

If you're trying to stop yourself from becoming too one-dimensional in your mountain biking and want to continue taking long recreational rides with friends, be aware that long weekend rides can be great for training but they also extract a toll. A five-hour mountain bike ride can mean two or three days of recovery during which the most you want to do is easy, restful spinning. In this respect, aggressive recreational mountain bike riding is much like marathon running—there's a high tear-down factor on the human body.

Using a road bike for up to 40% of your riding will mitigate this injury risk whether you use it for recovery riding after an event or for pre-event training. But using a road bike requires long climbs to get and keep the heart rate up to the intensities required for mountain bike racing. Pounding it out on road flats and rolling terrain can develop power and speed but requires strong mental discipline. If you ride a lot on the road, be sure to keep the remaining off-road work technically demanding.

Weekly and monthly planning

If races are weekly Sunday events, your training weeks should look something like this:

- Monday is a rest ride.
- Tuesday is an CHR ride, maybe including some speed work.
- Wednesday is a RPR ride of 80–100% of the forthcoming event's duration.
- Thursday is for THR training.
- Friday is a rest ride with technical work.
- Saturday you pre-ride the course at a pace hovering between EHR and RPR. Include a few hard bursts for three to five minutes, either sprints or short hill attacks to prepare for Sunday's effort.

Wednesday and Thursday workouts can be interchanged. Just see what order your body responds to best.

If there's more than a week between targeted events, use an unimportant race on the in-between Sunday as a training ride. Similarly, try to use travel time, family time, and time spent meeting everyday responsibilities as relaxed recovery instead of cramming to get them out of the way for training.

Peaking

"Peaking" and "tapering" are frequently used terms in talking about structuring training intensity. Peaking is the result of a training system in which you use a progressive, varied program with both long and short recovery periods so that you're rebounding to your highest performance potential the day of a targeted event. By manipulating training volume and intensity in a wave structure (including recovery), you avoid overtraining and injury that can result from a linear build-up of both volume and intensity (not to mention getting bogged down in a repetitive schedule that may actually inhibit event performance).

Tapering involves reducing training intensity for a period prior to an event so you're fresh and rested the day of the contest, ready to use the strengths you gained in your training. On the days before an event, you cut back the intensity/duration of workouts just enough to let your body recover from training.

Both peaking and tapering are easily applied to one popular program used by many recreational competitors, the Hit of the Month scheme of racing. That is, one event per month gets targeted for your best shot. If these targets can be structured close to a month apart, the peaking/tapering plan should be something like this:

- Half a week following the last target race is recovery riding—low mileage at moderate intensity.
- Then two weeks of normal intensity/duration training, one of high mileage at moderate intensity, followed by one of the highest mileage but the lowest intensity.
- Half a week (3 rides) higher than race intensity/duration. This should be the lowest mileage of the month at the highest intensity.
- One week tapering to target event, using moderate mileage at low intensity and building to moderate intensity.

A low-intensity week means only one moderately hard ride, all others being fairly easy efforts. A high-intensity week means two or three hard rides, each incorporating intervals with brief recovery. Surround such intensity with recovery periods. The most intense ride should be sandwiched between either a rest ride or low-intensity ride the day before and two rest/technical-skill-riding days afterwards.

Always use your tapering period rides for technical-skills sharpening along with mental relaxation, and be very disciplined about your diet and rest. Two nights before the big event is the night to get a full, solid night of sleep. The day before an event, either pre-ride the course at EHR, making mental notes and practicing technical sections, or do a technical skills workout.

A common predicament for recreational competitors is the discovery that several outstanding events clutter a particular section of the calendar, in effect creating a miniature race season within the overall season.

If that's what your calendar looks like, you must build up during the two or three months prior to the miniseason and launch yourself onto a performance plateau that you can hold for the duration of the miniseason.

Structure waves of high-intensity/shorter-duration training days and rest days so you are on an intensifying wave as the targeted days approach. This is where knowledge of yourself and your body's cycles, gleaned from your training journal, becomes important. This is also where the self-discipline learned in early-season rides through lousy weather and aching muscles will kick in.

Young riders

Juniors have to learn to hold back on their ambitions in the interest of self-preservation. Juniors should hold power work and anaerobic capacity training to 70% of adult training work durations.

One particular concern is whether an adolescent is going through his or her "spurt" period of rapid growth. During the spurt, power work should be carefully coached and executed to protect joint structures. For the same reason, riding position and bike sizing should be closely monitored.

On the other hand, this a great period of life for consistent EHR with some RPR training and technical skills work. These will provide an incredible foundation from which future athletic training can launch in a couple years.

Finishing kick

No matter what your age, always try to finish long training sessions with a strong final power segment. That's because the final place to wind it up and go at it in a race is in the last five miles. If you get to that five-miles-out spot with too much left, or you're still not happy with where you are in a race, that's the time to take some water, get dialed-in and pick up speed.

Besides training for that circumstance, the feeling of having done the final tough segment well can keep your spirit up even if the warm-down spin is a 20-minute slog through rain and sleet.

Also, try designating a start/finish point for your training session that is a 15–20-minute ride from home. Use that 15–20 minutes for warm-up and cool-down, not working training time. This ploy is especially helpful when participating in group rides, which typically start and end with all-out efforts. Get that warm-up and cool-down time in and take care of your body.

Rec-heads

When the weather breaks, the club rides get ambitious, or the organized events on your hit list come up, achievement-oriented, personal-best riders are into their performance season. Keep one day a week just for endurance riding (high rpms, mileage, no attacks on the terrain). Regulate your program according to your schedule: for example, if you do one big (it could big mileage or demanding strength) ride per week, allow a spin day and a complete day off to recover. That leaves four days, of which one is a pre-big-ride, easy-ride day (work on skills not strength).

The three remaining days can be split between recovery, power, and whatever. How you organize those three days depends on your plans and your other responsibilities.

Annual plan

Here is a suggested annual plan for performance-oriented recreational riders who want to organize their training to build for the prime months.

- *December-March.* Endurance, stamina rides, flat to rolling terrain, three or four rides per week at high rpms in your EHR, a more-than-the-daily-norm stretching program, and maybe a weight work program.
- *March-April or April-May*, depending upon where you live. Four to five rides per week, Saturday's a little longer and harder (EHR-RPR), followed by a long spin on Sunday in EHR. At least one of the other rides each week a strength or power workout. Reduce weights or cross-training to twice a week.
- *Performance season* (May/June through October/November, depending upon location). Work on improvements according to desires. Precede the peak ride of each week with a more moderately paced technical-skills-sharpening ride. Follow it with a spin-recovery day in your EHR.

• • Gut Strength

Manufacturing Muscular Magnificence and Fluid Style

Mountain biking is an endurance and power sport more than a speed sport. Endurance is the ability to carry on continuously and is the foundation for all other athletic capacities. Power is force compounded by velocity—or the ability to deliver force to the pedals to propel your mountain bike over a segment of terrain at a certain speed.

Power for a climb, a technical stretch of single track, or the waning miles of a long ride can only be developed if you reinforce endurance and recovery training with gut strength. Now, "gut strength" can be a term for abdominal muscular magnificence and is essential for successful intense riding, but in mountain biking it refers to being able to ride well in the face of gnarly circumstances. In its most advanced or developed state of execution, it means riding with technical fluidity, speed, and power all the way through a particularly demanding race or ride. This kind of powerful play on a mountain bike, or practicing to be able to do it, is referred to in some places as "gut-bucketing."

But before someone can reasonably expect to be able to attempt "gut-bucketing" with much success they need to build torso strength and power spinning.

Torso strength

Although most of the muscle in mountain biking, or any cycling, is in the legs, everything that propels something has to work against some other structure to exert force in a specific direction. In cycling, your legs rotate the crank arms by exerting force leveraged against your stable upper body (torso).

Your abdomen is crucial in holding that platform for pedal force together. Simultaneously, it also provides support for the upper body, which is working much harder to steer accurately than on a road bike and is getting tired from bumps and shocks from the terrain.

Total abdominal conditoning includes working both the upper and lower abdominals, and the muscles that wrap the sides of your lower torso. Good exercises include partial sit-ups or "crunches," various leg lifts, over-the-knee-reach partial sit-ups, and alternating V-ups. If your abdominal muscle tone is negligible, begin by lying on the floor and simply raising your shoulders and head off the floor and holding for 5, 10, then 15 seconds. Be careful to raise the upper

Upper body strength is essential on demanding terrain and also helps provide a counter force to the legs.

body as a unit, not leading with the head and curling the neck unintentionally. When doing any partial sit-ups or crunches, don't go too far off the ground, thereby working your thigh muscles instead of the abdomen.

> *I lift up so the shoulder blades are just off the floor. Then I make small hinged movements, traveling about half an inch up and down. Killer exercise when you go slow.*—Martha

Leg raises can be done in many forms, the important thing being to stabilize the rest of the body so that you're working the lower abdominals. The vertical bench is an apparatus designed for that purpose. You can also use a set of gymnastic parallel bars, holding yourself with straight arms and raising your legs taut together until parallel to the floor, and then down again. Do either of these as slowly as you can while keeping your upper body still.

Alternating V-ups, in which you alternately touch each elbow on the outside of the opposite knee, extending the other leg straight 6–10″ off the floor, are excellent for the oblique or side muscles.

Power spinning

In mountain bike training, like everything else, what goes around comes around. After devoting hours to steady rides for building endurance, and who knows how much time and effort into strength and technical skills, you return to the principle of spinning.

Being able to maintain a high spin is a hidden component in truly effective power. Lactic acid is the exhaust from the combustion that happens in the muscle fiber. If it isn't removed from the system it just clogs things up. A higher spin rate promotes flushing the lactic exhaust from the muscle. Those who can maintain a higher spin, say above 75 rpm on extended climbs, are going to make it to the final lap of a race with a lot less lactic acid, and therefore a smoother-firing muscular engine.

So it behooves anyone dedicated enough to instigate power sessions in their rides to transfer the high-rpm training from the off-season endurance period to their power sessions. Doing so can make a pretty good mountain biker into an irresistible force able to scale the immovable object (usually the side of a ridge or hill) with nary a break in tempo.

The key is to build on your existing strength with quick-paced, higher-resistance workouts. Take on a series of one- to two-minute climbs or devise a loop bringing you back to the same climb with just enough time to recover your heart rate to around 130 beats per minute.

Take the first climb in a gear that starts taking your breath away but is no serious struggle to complete the entire climb in. The second time around, just before you can see the top of the climb, shift to the next highest gear (rear cog) and attack. Repeat the same procedure for the third climb. For the fourth time up, attack for the whole climb in what by now is a vicious gear, doing whatever it takes to keep the pedal spin as high as possible. Spin for five minutes and then repeat the cycle. Work up to three or even four sets of four hill attacks. Finish with 30–45 minutes of rolling spinning at high rpm (95 plus).

Practicing

Gut-bucketing is practiced for by planning training rides whose third one-quarter or next-to-last 20% is a varied rolling terrain in the upper third of your technical proficiency. Ride the first 50–60% of the ride at a pace in which you can talk a little with fellow riders, should they be there. Make certain you are well hydrated. When you hit the designated "guts" stretch, crank the effort up to your Capacity Heart Range.

The challenge is to keep the momentum up and the work level constant while cruising the terrain and making all riding position and shifting changes smoothly. Not only do you train anaerobic capacity, but you train technique while your tongue hangs out.

Ride the final stretch in whatever gear maintains a fluid 90–100-rpm pedal speed. When doing such intense training, warm-up, cool-down, stretching, hydration, and quality carbohydrate replacement become increasingly important.

A variation on the theme is to ride 45 minutes at EHR, then begin alternating 20-minute sessions at CHR with 45-minute EHR periods for two, three, or four cycles.

Both are useful training for fortitude under unexpected circumstances and retaining poise and technique in particularly harsh races, i.e., not letting them see you're hurting.

> *At the first Iditabike I learned never to underestimate another rider's ability or background when it comes to sprinting for the finish after 200 miles on the snow, even if he appears tired and less capable than me. And I vowed that in the future, ultra-endurance events will not come down to a finish sprint.*
> —Michael

At such times, keeping your head together benefits from having your head supported by strong neck muscles. Here's a simple set of isometrics that will help prevent your neck muscles from fatiguing while the rest of you still has plenty left.

1. Jut your chin out and then down to your chest. Cup your hands behind your head and work to lift the head backward against the hand resistance. Hold 5–15 seconds. Repeat three times.
2. Move the head backward as far as it will go comfortably. Hold it there 5 seconds. Work it against hand resistance on the forehead 5–15 seconds. Repeat three times.
3. Move the head directly sideways, without lowering the ear toward the shoulder. Hold 5 seconds. Work to return your head against hand resistance on the side of head. Repeat two times. Repeat other side.
4. Turn your head to one side, keeping your eyes looking forward. Hold in furthest position 5 seconds. Let eyes swing back to look to the rear and rotate the head some more. Work to rotate the head back to normal against resistance from the palm of your hand. Repeat two times on each side.

Important: Always start and finish with the head in the same forward and upright position.

Another power exercise can be done on the flat final 20% of a rolling or hilly two-plus-hour ride. Get your speed up and then shift into the big gear and give it all you can for 10–20 pumps with each leg. Sit down and spin for one to two minutes. Then stand up and do it again. Try five sets. These are best done on logging roads or similar wide trails where terrain and steering aren't a primary concern.

They're also especially beneficial if you can find a stretch of freshly graded roadbed—loose, chunky stuff.

You can also cadence train for power by simply riding at a moderate effort of 90–100 rpm for 20 minutes or so, and then shifting up to a larger gear that requires hard concentration to maintain 90–100 rpm. You should feel the exercise in your thighs and calves. (Shift down before your cadence falls below 90 rpm or if you feel continued stress in, or just above, your knees.) Downshift after 15–30 minutes. Repeat the entire exercise.

Time trialing

Then there's time trial training, or racing against the clock, for power. Select a one- to three-mile rolling stretch, and time yourself on it for two to four near-maximum effort attempts the same day. Ride a distance at a moderate pace so that you almost recover between timed hard efforts. By comparing your times and striving to maintain similar ones for each ride, you can learn to judge your subjective effort level and be more consistent.

Another way to use time trialing is to time yourself over a three- to eight-mile course once every two weeks. These are best done on gradual uphill routes. By challenging yourself to improve your time on the same slightly uphill course regularly, you're forced to deal with the weakness in your technique—the bits and pieces that fall apart when you're already a little exhausted and still demanding power from your body. Like all other power workouts, be sure you've warmed up for 15–30 minutes before the effort, and follow it with a 30–45-minute spin.

• • Upper Body

Conditioning and Weight Training for the Rest of You

In mountain biking your upper body, besides withstanding the repetitive shocks from uneven riding surfaces, also works to maintain steering, clear away obstacles, and provide the maximum leverage for power on the drivetrain. So developing a strong upper body will greatly improve your performance on the bike.

You can improve general upper-body conditioning by consciously doing a variety of tasks that work your upper body, but systematic weight training allows for a precisely managed program that results in balanced strength. Balanced strength is important. Any time a muscle is working, another muscle is stabilizing the action. The relative strength of the stabilizing muscle is just as important as that of the actively working muscle for both high athletic performance and long-term fitness. Weight training will also improve your overall conditioning and strength.

Fortunately weight training is a fairly uncomplicated way to undertake selective muscle remodeling and can be used in the off-season to bring your network of active and stabilizing muscles into harmony. But you do need to be disciplined in following a basic set of principles to ensure safe development of strength and to avoid bulk.

Correct form is essential. If you're not doing precisely what you should be in any weight exercise, you are, inevitably, not working the muscles you want to the way you want to. The results can then be something quite different from what you expect. And should you progress to heavy weights, incorrect form can result in injury.

Should you use machines or free weights? The choice is this. Free weights demand extra care with form and safety. With machines like Universal or Nautilus you need to be keen on intensity and execution to get the complete benefit of the exercise.

In weight training, you develop particular strengths by isolating specific muscle groups. This depends upon "setting" the rest of the body so it supports the moving work without wiggling, counter-balancing, or otherwise doing more than the most minimal movement. Complete, careful execution of each exercise through its full range of motion is necessary to work the entire section of muscle and will help prevent injury or unnecessary tightness in the muscle.

Weight training works by challenging muscles to work to their fullest ability, but the challenges, or overloads, must be carefully controlled. The pace, rhythm, or tempo (however you want to think about it) of even the toughest strength sets needs to be methodical in execution, not attacked with a jerky, bouncing style.

And you should keep these cycling-specific guidelines in mind. Calf exercises should always tend toward high reps. (The Donkey Calf Raise seems to isolate and work the muscles best, but is an advanced exercise which requires a partner.) Be careful to work both legs equally, possibly doing one leg at a time. Also, keep the toes straight ahead, or slightly pointed in.

Leg curls should handle 50–66% of the weight you can do in the leg extension exercise (along with higher reps, eventually). If you can handle two or three times as much weight in leg extensions as curls, concentrate on leg presses for thigh strength, or do very slow, controlled lowering of extensions to bring calf strength up to par.

Safety in knee-joint exercises, such as half squats and power cleans, requires a complete warm-up of the legs prior to the exercises. Keep the center of your kneecap over your second largest toe throughout the exercise and don't bounce in or out of any bent-knee position. Control the movement.

Squats remain the object of debate amongst trainers. The strong spinal stress involved, which can inflict long-term injury from relatively slight form mistakes or crossing a personal weight threshold, keeps them off many people's list. An alternative is to do lunges, either with a barbell on the shoulders or a pair of dumbbells. Squats are excellent for the quads, hamstrings, and gluteus muscles.

Mountain bikers who do do squats should do half-squats. They should be executed with the feet straight ahead, not turned out, and a little closer than shoulder width apart. This will slightly emphasize outer thigh muscles and reduce the build-up of mass on the inner leg.

Besides observing the above principles, you can help prevent injury by always warming up and stretching before a weight workout. Also, during periods of intensely stressful riding or racing, or during a personally stressful period in your life, lighten up the weight routine by either lowering the weights used or the numbers of reps or sets executed. In other words, don't try doing too much.

If you have any doubts about an exercise, have a gym instructor demonstrate to help you get the form correct. You can also consult a good book on technique. Two that we recommend are *The Complete Weight Training Book*, by Bill Reynolds, World Publications, 1976; and *The Encyclopedia of Modern Bodybuilding*, by Arnold Schwarzenegger, Fireside Books, 1985. The Reynolds book is a concise presentation of the basics and has stood the test of years. Schwarzenegger's book is oriented toward bodybuilding, so you'll have to adapt its lessons to your purposes, but it's exemplary in its illustration of correct execution and technique, and discusses a host of training guidelines relative to all sports.

Preadolescents should not work out with weights. Their bones are too soft. The architecture they will have to live with for the next 60 years (joints, tendon structure, etc.) is still forming. Overall conditioning, and a positive inclination toward it, is best established through a variety of demanding activities such as soccer, cross-country running, lacrosse, basketball, and swimming. Teens still in their growth or spurt years should work out only with weights with which they can do high repetition sets: 15–30 reps for upper body exercises; 25–40 reps for lower body exercises.

Presumably you're weight training to supplement your mountain biking. Therefore, you're trying to develop strength without building excess weight or bulk, which can hinder you on the bike. (If you do develop a personal interest in building raw strength in a particular area, that's fine, just as long as you're reconciled to the added weight you'll be toting up hills.)

Some riders worry about losing their pedal speed, or spin, as a result of weight workouts. As long as you make a point of spinning on the bike, whether on rollers, an indoor trainer set on low resistance, or on the road at high rpm (95 plus) at least two or three times per week throughout the winter weight program, you'll gain in strength and keep those muscle fibers trained for good pedaling technique.

Getting started

When beginning a weight training program, first establish what weight you can handle in each exercise for 2 sets of 10–15 repetitions with good form. (That is, do one exercise for 10–15 repetitions, rest a moment, and do it again.) Then take three to four weeks to break in your body to the new training program by only doing two sets of each exercise. Concentrate on learning correct form. Get a feel for each exercise in your mind's eye, so the memory of how correct execution feels will be in the background, like a safety function, when you go on to heavier weights.

After the break-in month, to build strength without excess bulk, do 3 sets of 12–20 reps for upper body exercises, and 1 set of 20–50 reps with lower body exercises to build toward your goal weights. (Goal weights are expressed as percentages of your body weight—in parentheses in the suggested workouts.)

For upper body exercises add reps in a 12–15–18–20 pattern. For example, when you can do 3 sets of 15 reps for two or three workouts in a row, then move on to 3 sets of 18 reps. When you can do 3 sets of 20, add 5 or 10 pounds of weight and begin again at 3 sets of 12 reps.

For lower body exercises, use either a 20–25–30–35–40 reps pattern or a 30–35–40–45–50 reps pattern, depending upon the difficulty of the exercise. Lower body muscle groups can generally take larger resistance jumps, so add 10–25 pounds when starting the cycle again.

Keep track of your progress in a notebook or log. Not only is it rewarding to look back on what you've accomplished, it also makes planning next winter's weight training easier if you can review your previous progress rates. Here is a suggested notebook format (terms are explained below):

Exercise	Goal	Standard	Tue	Thur	Sat
Bent Rows	(85)	3/15 (65)	3/15 (65)	3/15 (65)	3/18 (65)

Goal is the maximum percentage of your body weight we suggest you lift for the sets and reps, expressed in pounds. (In the example, it's 85 lbs.)

Standard is what you are able to handle at the end of the previous week. The fraction is the number of sets over repetitions. The example is 3 sets of 15 reps. In parentheses is the poundage executed, in this case, 65 pounds.

Tuesday, Thursday, and Saturday's executed workouts (or Monday, Wednesday, Friday) are entered in the same format as the standard entry.

Depending on how you structure your weight routine you can emphasize endurance, strength, or power. Generally speaking, endurance benefits from massive amounts of reps (repetitions per set), usually with lower weight. Strength is directly related to muscle mass, although that muscle mass doesn't need to get bulky. Organizing intense resistance work against heavier weights at low reps is fundamental to strength-building. Power builds on strength with moderately long sets (15–30 reps) with heavier weights at a quick pace.

Breathing

A good time to practice proper breathing is during your weight workouts. Full, rhythmic, dynamic yet stable breathing is essential to supply enough oxygen to muscles during exercise. By rhythmic we mean it must be in sync with the activity of the whole body, dynamic means it must be able to adapt to momentary changes in demands, and stable means the rate of breathing and the extent to which you completely utilize your lungs should not be overly changed by mood swings (that's why mental poise is so important in sports).

You're probably familiar with the notion of diaphragmatic breathing—filling your lower as well as upper lung with each breath, expanding your diaphragm to insure use of both areas. But your lungs can also expand to the back and sides. You can train your body to do this by having a partner gently place his or her hands on these areas while you practice total breathing and letting you know when he or she feel your lungs expanding.

During fast-paced weight sets, practice consciously breathing fully for every two reps. On slower, higher-resistance strength reps, practice a complete, forceful exhale on the press portion. This not only aids breathing, but can provide the extra oomph needed to complete the exercise.

Schedules

October is an excellent month in which to begin a weight training program. Starting then allows you time to break in, get comfortable with weights, and develop some strength over the winter without risking your in-season activity or overstressing your body.

If you want to use weight training for total body conditioning, plan on three workouts a week. You can do one total body weight routine three times a week, or you can alternate upper-body and lower-body days.

If you're using the weight room strictly for upper body conditioning, work out two or three times a week, after your usual bike workout, if possible. During the riding season try sandwiching your weight workout between a short bike ride and the 20-minute spin home. It helps if you lift weights at a gym where you can keep some sneakers, a bike lock, and gym clothes, saving you from carrying them each time on the bike. Be sure not to let too much time pass between the time you get off the bike and the time you begin doing the weight circuits.

Many racers only spend time in the weight room during the winter, but total body conditioning should be maintained through the summer as well. If you quit weight training entirely, within a few months you'll lose almost all but the cycling-specific strength you gained through the winter. Then in mid-season, when you need the conditioning to fight fatigue, it won't be there.

To simply maintain your strength once you reach your weight goals, do two sets of each pair of exercises, with no or minimal rest between sets. Work up to 20–25 reps per set at 40% of your maximal lift in each exercise.

If your overall strength and conditioning is already satisfactory, but you want to build more lower body strength, use the maintenance scheme for the upper body while you concentrate on strength and power development in the lower body.

Daily abdominal workouts should be a fact of life for intensive mountain bikers. As little as 15-minute workouts on the days when you're not doing heavy weight training or intense on-the-bike workouts can bring real improvement. Be sure to work both upper and lower abdominals and the obliques—the muscles that wrap from the side of the body. (If you cross-country ski in the winter you can get the same benefit from double-poling sessions.)

Specific routines

Here are some suggested weight routines for developing specific areas of strength. For a description of each exercise, ask your gym instructor or refer to one of the books mentioned above.

Do the exercises in couplets: 1.a. and 1.b. for 2 or 3 sets, then 2.a. and 2.b., etc. (That is, do one set of 1.a., one set of 1.b., and then back to 1.a.) Try to minimize the break within each couplet and take no more than a two-minute break between couplets.

Upper Body Routine

Exercise	Long-term Max. Weight Goal (% of body weight)
1. a. Good mornings	50%
b. Clean & press	40%
2. a. Bent rows	66%
b. Bent arm pullovers	40%
3. a. Bench press	100%
b. Side laterals	15% each arm
4. a. Alternating military presses	33%
b. Reverse curls	33%
5. a. Shoulder shrugs	66%
b. Upright rows	50%
6. a. Front laterals	33%
b. Incline bench, supine flies	15% each arm
7. a. Incline V-ups	n/a
b. Back hyperextensions	n/a
8. a. Wrist curls	33% each arm
b. Reverse wrist curls	20% each arm

High-performance mountain biking takes endurance, strength, and power, and a special combination of incredible endurance and strength we call deep reserves—particularly in the thighs, calves, abdomen, and back. To meet those demands we added the "emphasis" column for this routine and the one that follows. The letters indicate the number and kind of reps you need to do to develop deep reserves through that exercise.

- *W.* These exercises are warm-ups for the workout ahead—don't get carried away with high weights.
- *R.* Sets of 15–30 reps.
- *R/S.* Sets of 15–25, developing strength through form, slow reps, or percentage of maximal lift, "short" reps.
- *RR.* Sets of 20–40 reps.
- *RRR.* Sets of 30–50+ reps.

Lower Body Routine

Exercise	Long-term Max. Weight Goal	Emphasis
1. a. Good mornings	50%	W
b. Step-ups	50–66%	W
2. a. Leg extensions	33%	R
b. Leg press	200%	RRR; R/S
3. a. Half squat/lunges	100%	R/S
b. Calf press	100%	RRR
4. a. Power cleans	50%	R/S
b. Leg curl	20%	RRR; R/S
5. a. Vertical bench leg raises	n/a	RR
b. Donkey calf raise	100%	RR

Total Body Routine

Exercise	Long-term Max. Weight Goal	Emphasis
1. a. Good mornings	50%	W
b. Step-ups	50–66%	W
2. a. Bent rows	60%	
b. Bent arm pullover	40%	R
3. a. Leg extension	33%	R
b. Leg press	200%	RRR
4. a. Half squat/lunges	100%	R/S
b. Calf press	100%	RRR

Total Body Routine (*continued*)

Exercise	Long-term Max. Weight Goal	Emphasis
5. a. Alternating military press	33%	R
b. Reverse curl	33%	R/S
6. a. Bench press	100%	
b. Side laterals	15% each arm	R
7. a. Shoulder shrugs	66%	
b. Upright rows	50%	R
8. a. Power cleans	50%	R/S
b. Leg curls	20%	RRR
9. a. Front laterals	15% each arm	R
b. Incline bench prone flies	15% each arm	
10. a. Incline V-ups	n/a	RR
b. Hyperextensions	0–15#	R
11. a. Wrist curls	33% each arm	R
b. Reverse wrist curls	20% each arm	R
12. a. Vertical bench leg raises	n/a	RR
b. Neck raises	20%	RR

If you want to keep things simple and to the point for biking, combine an upper body maintenance routine of two circuits with 5 sets of 8–15 reps of lower body exercises to build strength in your transmission. The five sets can be done a couple ways: (a) begin with 5 sets of 8 reps, then progress to 10, 12, 15; or (b) take what you can do 3 sets of 10 reps and just do 2 more sets, as many reps as possible.

Here's how you can open a deep reserve account. Find out what your maximal weight is for 3 sets of 10 reps in, for example, the leg press. Do the three sets. Immediately after the third set, reset the weight resistance for 60% of the weight just executed. Go for 40 reps and see how it feels. Then adjust the weight up or down accordingly. It can help if a friend is there to immediately lower the weights for you, minimizing the time lag to the long set and acting as a spotter.

Some folks have taken this fourth set to 60, 80, even 100 reps. If you get into it, remember it's important to work up in reps and not to rip through them. Squeeze the muscles mentally as well as physically with a controlled tempo. Do this on the leg press, where you have back support; do not do this scheme with squats.

The extraordinary hamstring strength you want can be prodded by doing some custom sets of leg curls that work different portions of the muscle group. First do two standard sets. Lower the weight resistance 20%. Then do a couple sets of 7–10 reps, bringing the ankles up only halfway. Follow with two sets of 7–10 reps in which you repeat only the upper half of the leg curl movement.

After building basic conditioning and endurance for at least two months (not including break-in) you can manipulate the sets and reps for strength development in four-week segments, or keep with the outlined program until you reach your percentage weight goals.

If weight training is nothing but an aid to improve your ability in high-performance riding or racing you'll want to emphasize different development as the season approaches. Focus on strength from mid-January to mid-February, and deep reserve and power development from mid-February into March. By April you should be tailoring the workouts towards endurance or deep reserve strength or doing strength-maintenance circuit training while increasing the emphasis of on-the-bike workouts.

Strength plus

When you decide to concentrate on specific strength development, take a day to find out what your maximal one-rep lift is in the exercises for the muscle groups you want to concentrate on. (Any of the R/S or RRR exercises are automatic candidates.) Make sure to do a complete warm-up, then do one single circuit of your usual exercises. Then return to the exercises in which you want to discover your maximal single rep. At each one, increase the weights as you do five, then three, then one rep.

On strength-development days, do either two single-set rounds of your whole routine, or a tempo execution of the routine doing two sets per exercise. (Choose whichever lets you keep moving with minimal down time.) Then return to the exercise or exercises you want to work for strength. Complete the following routine in each exercise before moving on to another.

Sets/reps	Weight, % of max
1/5	66%
1/3	75%
1/2	87.5%
5/1	95%

Depending upon the exercise, and the options available with the equipment you use, once you handle the 5 sets at 95%, add 5–25 lbs. and start the sequence again.

If you're using free weights for this, use spotters you can trust—being trapped under lots of weights is no joy, and if you're having exceeding difficulty completing a rep (like it looks as if you can't do it) have the spotters relieve you of just enough weight pressure for you to complete that exercise's range of motion before they put the bar back in the rack.

Another sure way to build strength is to do sets adagio, at a very slow pace, after executing a standard speed set, or to control large amounts of weights on a single drop. After doing standard sets, work through to a single rep of 95% of maximum, as in the program outlined above. Then, working with conscientious spotters, add weight to make it 110% of your maximal lift. Get their assistance to help get the weight off to the peak of the movement, then, with the spotters prepared to assist if necessary, lower the weight very, very slowly. The spotters return the weight to the rack after you finish lowering the load.

Do strength-focused workouts for a month before beginning power or deep-reserve workouts. During weeks one and three make one of your three workouts strength-development focused. Weeks two and four, make two of the three weekly workouts strength-development focused. After that, you can begin mixing things up. You can either alternate power and standard workout days, deep-reserve and standard workout days, or all three. Just make at least one workout for every three per week a standard workout.

Power packing

Mountain biking power can be built in any of the RRR value exercises by first pre-exhausting the muscles with a pair of endurance sets. Then do three sets at 60% of your maximal lift for 15–20 reps. Work to do the reps with a determined, sharp tempo, but don't get reckless or bouncy in pursuit of quick completion. Rest just long enough between sets for your heart rate to settle down to about 120 bpm.

If it doesn't feel like your muscles have had enough, take a walk to the water cooler (which should take 1–2 minutes). When you come back adjust the weight resistance to half of what you can do for 3 sets of 10 reps as we discussed earlier, and go for one super-endurance set of 40 or more (until failure).

Another concise double-whammy workout is to do the deep-strength sets, immediately followed by the heavy-tempo reps of the power workout. This mix comes in handy in the spring when racers and performance riders want to minimize weight time and maximize time on the bike.

Circuit training

When warmer weather returns, the workout emphasis shifts from strength and power to endurance and power. Time in the weight room is best spent in circuit training. This requires organizing the weight room exercises so that you don't pause between single sets of each exercise. Besides being a bit quicker than standard weight routines, circuit training also benefits your aerobic conditioning.

If you want to change over from weight training to circuit training, begin in early April by substituting circuit training for one weight workout per week. Do this for three weeks, then increase the circuit training to half your workouts. By Memorial Day, you should be spending more of your training time on the bike, with two weekly workouts consisting of slightly up-tempo circuit training.

You can either do two to three sweeps of one total-body circuit, or break the circuit into upper- and lower-body exercises and do two to three sweeps of each. Either way, take a break of no more than two minutes between each circuit.

Here are two possible circuits.

- *Circuit One.* Bent Row . . . Leg Extension . . . Leg Press . . . Bent Pullover . . . Half Squat . . . Alternating Military Press . . . Calf Press . . . Reverse Curl . . . Bench Press.
- *Circuit Two.* Power Clean . . . Side Laterals . . . Shoulder Shrugs . . . Leg Curls . . . Prone Flies . . . Wrist Curls . . . Upright Rows . . . Front Laterals . . . Reverse Wrist Curls.

You can also go through both circuits consecutively, pausing for a minute or two only after the final exercise (reverse wrist curls). By continually moving from one exercise to the next, it's surprising how little time it can take and how well you can keep your heart rate elevated. Circuit training is particularly effective when sandwiched between rides.

Fixing problems

Besides improving overall strength, weight training can also be used to correct specific riding problems. Let's take one common complaint—fingers and hands going numb from braking. Assuming correct brake adjustment, your only hope for improvement lies in strengthening your hands, fingers, and forearms. There are a number of devices for doing this—the familiar coiled hand-grip squeezer, in-line tension grip exercisers, and super-tennis-ball grip exercisers. Take your choice and use it while watching TV, sitting in the car (passenger side or at a long traffic light), and other such moments. Begin with 50 repetitions, building up to 500 reps in increments of 10.

If your hands and fingers don't wear out, your wrists or forearms probably do. Wrist curls, reverse wrist curls, and reverse curls with dumbbells work best for these. As a starting point, do a set with whatever weights you can manage in good form for 20–30 reps.

Standard mountain bike handlebar gripping, especially when the upper body is bent over, exposes the elbow to strain injury. This risk can be minimized with lots of reverse wrist curls and reverse curls.

• • Stretching and Massage

Forging Flexibility and Strength

"True strength is the combination of power and flexibility." That maxim has held up through years of research, fads, and exercise-theory revision. The sticky wicket seems to be how to develop the two together.

Stretching has been shown to increase range of motion in muscles and relieve pain symptoms due to connective tissue damage. It can also reduce muscle spasms and assist lactic acid dissipation. Our experience and the educational material available both indicate that stretching should be an integral part of every exercise routine.

Stretching eases muscles from a relatively semi-static state to a more elastic condition, making them better prepared to undertake the repeated vigorous contractions of exercise. Stretching also assists blood flow, which fuels and cleanses the muscles.

All these things happen more easily if the body is kept in a pliable state on an ongoing basis, which means a daily stretching and flexibility program. We're talking about 10 or 15 minutes each morning and evening, with quickies as allowed during the day. (We've found it helpful to do something first thing in the morning before stretching to get the blood flowing into the muscles. Martha and Yuri often walk their dogs. Mike does calisthenics.)

Pre-exercise stretching is trickier than post-effort stretching. Mentally you may not be motivated to do much, or you may be so eager to get out on the bike that you have little patience for stretching. Physically you're probably cold, too. So the last thing you want to do is ballistic stretching, the bouncy, "wham-bam" approach too many of us were first taught. Instead, do 10 to 30 seconds of a steady static stretch that ever-so-gradually increases the opening of a joint or the range of motion of a muscle group.

But cold muscles don't stretch well. A good solution to this problem is to do some light stretching, then a short warm-up on the bike, followed by another flexibility session. Start with some stretches in which you work the major muscle groups involved in cycling. Then ride a few miles (15-plus minutes of moderately high spinning, very low resistance). The on-the-bike warm-up gets blood into the muscles and oxygen into your brain. Then do a thorough stretching session. Concentrate on the muscles that work the bike, but don't forget the antagonistic groups—the muscles that pull in response to cycling's power contractions—or the muscles that do the static work of holding your upper body in position for hard riding.

If you're meeting others for a ride, get to the meeting point a little early and stretch while waiting. Usually folks will join in and everyone will benefit. Make it a regular part of group rides. Likewise, after rides, stretch while chatting rather than just standing around raving about what a great time you had.

Your mountain bike makes an excellent portable ballet barre for standing stretches, but be careful if you wear shoes with cleats or you might scrape the paint off the top tube. The ubiquitous long-sleeved cotton T-shirt makes a great foot sling for quadricep stretches.

On really long rides, a quick stop and stretch a half-hour to an hour after starting can be especially helpful for the innermost muscles. These take the longest to warm up yet are in the crux of the action.

> *I do some stretching whenever I've climbed a hill and I'm waiting for the rest of the group, or during a feed break. Just make it casual and it won't be hard to make it habitual.*
>
> —Martha

One of the tricks to productive stretching is to remember to change your attention from how much is done to how it feels. Awareness of your usual range of motion, or how far you can stretch, is fine as a reference. But understanding the intense internal feeling of cautiously increasing the elasticity demand on the muscle without making it go too far, and keeping muscles properely aligned are far more important.

Regarding alignment, there's no need to get neurotic about it, but be alert to body position. Whenever any part of your body is not positioned just as you want it during a stretch, muscles are being worked or stretched differently than you may want them to be. On the positive side, this means you can change stretches a bit to get the exact effect you want, and you can avoid positions that may be injurious to a nearby joint while still stretching muscle tissue that needs it.

Pay attention too, to your personal quirks and habits. Everyone has subconscious patterns of movement and posture. Some of us have different-sized right and left parts, or injury-caused idiosyncrasies. These quirks affect how you function on the bike, so pay particular attention to these parts when warming up or cooling down.

Post-exercise stretching should include the whole body with particular attention to the thighs, gluteus muscles, hamstrings, ankles, shoulders, neck, and back. (Concentrate on stretching the back muscles vertically, not twisting or torquing the spine.)

After a hard ride or race, muscles may be in a vulnerable, almost traumatized, state. Make sure you cool down sufficiently. (You'll know because your heart rate will be lower, your body temperature may feel cooler, and a layer of sweat may discharge over your entire body.) Continuing the cool-down process from light spinning on the bike to walking sometimes helps. Dress warmly, maybe in sweats, to prevent the muscles from getting too cold, then stretch.

If you have the time, a two-part, after-ride stretch routine maximizes the feel-good return of a great ride. Stretch the major cycling muscles, take a hot shower (use it as a massage to relax the outer muscles), then do a thorough stretch session.

Here are some stretches relevant to the muscles used in mountain biking. They can be done as a daily routine, after a ride, or at a rest stop.

Head Circles: (not shown) Do five times in each direction.

Foot Point and Pulls: Seated on the floor or ground, with the legs side by side in front of you, sit up straight, using your arms to support the back if need be, and alternately point and flex your feet. Begin the action from the top of your thigh, with the muscle-tightening traveling like a ripple down your leg. The knee should bend slightly before you flex your foot and straighten as you point it.

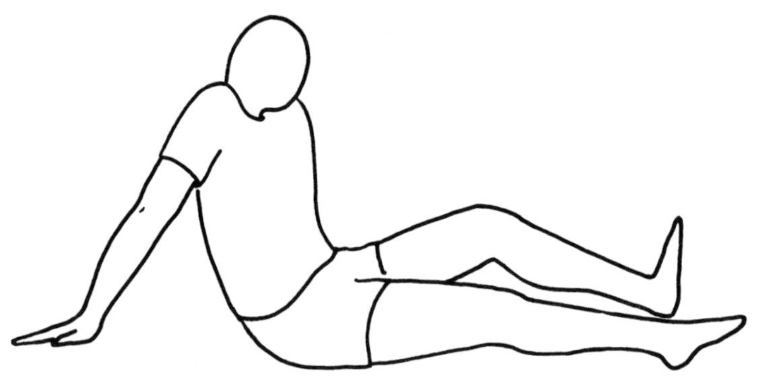

Cross Toe Touches: Open the legs to a comfortably large V shape, then rotate your upper body, trying to touch the opposite big toe with each hand (for example, right hand to left foot), turning only as much as you can while keeping the hips square and on the ground.

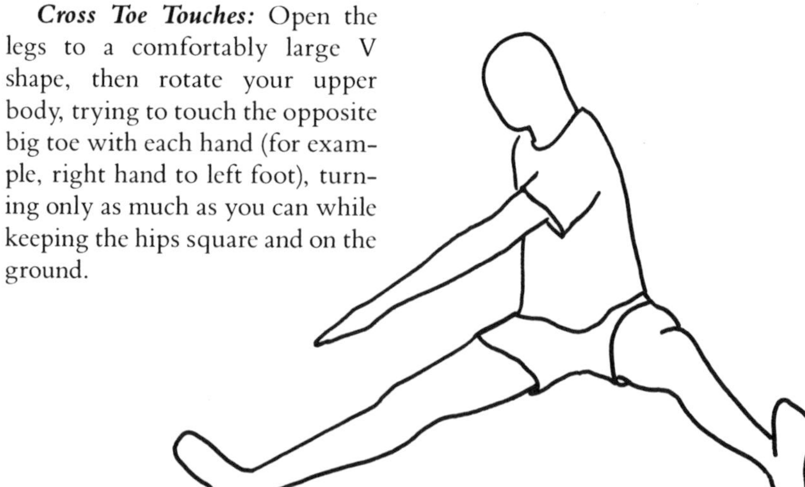

Knee Fall: Put the bottoms of your feet together, then lie on your back. Relax with each breath, and slowly let the weight of your knees carry them closer to the ground.

Back-of-the-neck and Shoulder Stretch: Lying on your back, put your feet on the floor and bring your knees together with a comfortable bend in them. Place your hands behind your head, and lift

your head, tucking your chin into your chest. Concentrate on extending the muscles that join the neck and shoulders out sideways through your elbows.

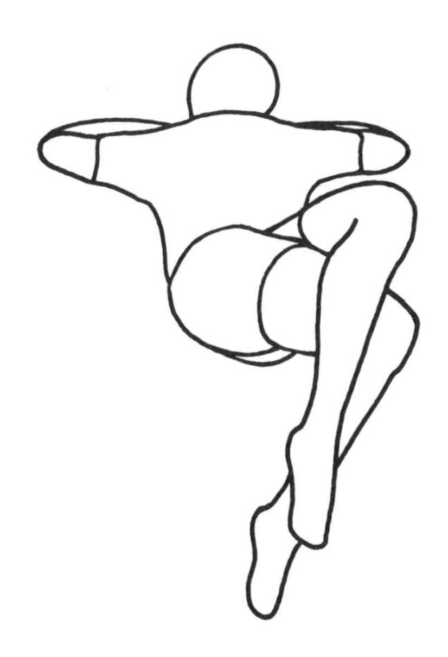

Knee Fold-over: Still lying on your back with your knees bent and feet flat on the floor, cross the right leg over the left, hooking the right leg's knee on the outside of the left knee. Gently let the weight of the right leg stretch the outside of the left leg as it's weighted down to the side. This will probably lift your left hip off the floor. You'll feel it in your outer left thigh and hip. Repeat other side.

Small Back Press: Sit up and put the bottoms of your feet together so that your legs make a diamond that gently stretches your inner thighs. Lift through the spine out the top of your head to straighten the back and press forward slightly with the entire upper body.

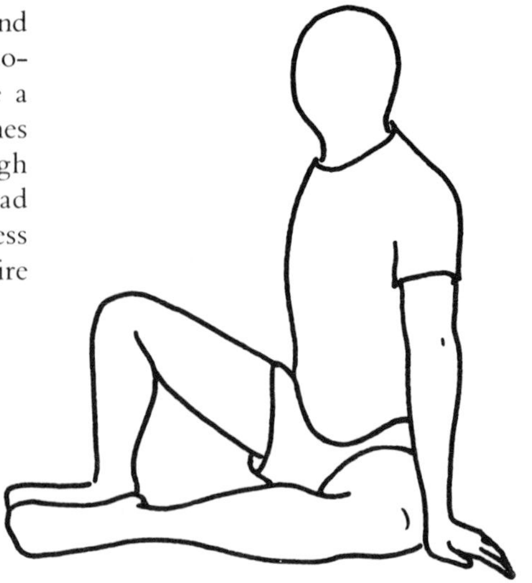

Foot Rotations: (not shown) Straighten the legs and place your right foot on top of your left thigh. Rotate it slowly in each direction five times with your hands, gently manipulating its flexing action at the same time. Switch legs and repeat.

Thigh Stretch: With your weight on the left hip, swing both legs to the right and bend the knees so that you're almost sitting on your right heel, while the left heel rests in front of your right knee. Lean back with the upper body, keeping it in line with the right thigh until you feel the stretch on top of the right thigh. After 15 seconds, press up with the hips to increase the stretch for a few seconds. Lower the hips, swing the legs front, and repeat on the other side.

Hamstring Stretch: Lie on your back. Roll a long-sleeved T-shirt into a rope while holding it by the sleeve ends, loop it under the arch of a foot, and straighten the leg while holding the foot just off the floor. Use the shirt to gently lift the leg, pulling it up and toward your head. Raise the leg only as much as you can while keeping

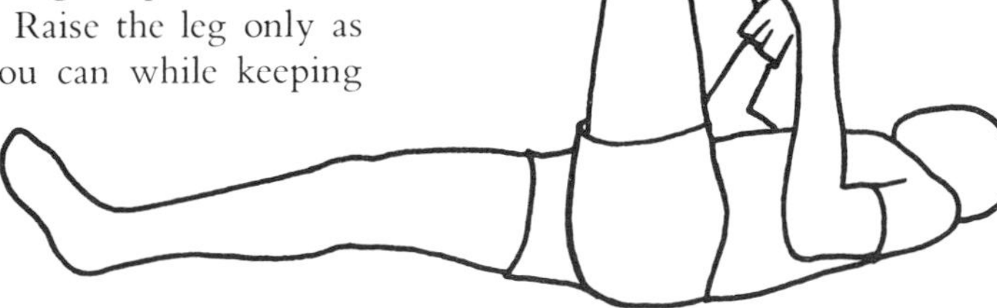

your back on the floor and your hips square. Repeat on other side.

Squatting Gluteal Stretch: Rise to a squat on your feet, taking care that the feet are wide enough for your bottom to hang between them. Keep the feet and knees aligned with the middle of the knee cap over the second toe.

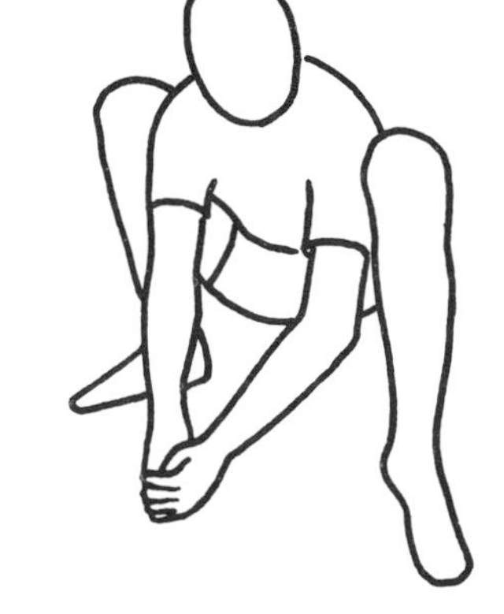

Lunge Stretch: Put your hands on the ground on either side of your knees. Bend one knee and extend the other leg back. You should feel the stretch in the groin and upper thigh of the rear leg. Repeat on other side.

Ankle Stretch: Standing with your feet slightly less than shoulder-width apart, bend your knees slightly, and lower your upper body just enough to feel the hips pivot forward slightly and the small of the back flatten. Gently move your upper body to each side, then forward and back by only moving the ankles. Once you get comfortable with this stretch, try circling the upper body, keeping it level by moving only at the ankles.

Standing Thigh Stretch: Standing straight, lift the right leg behind you with a bent knee. Hold the ankle with your left hand. Raise the ankle up with your hand and extend the leg rearward until you feel the stretch on the rear leg's thigh. Use the right hand to hold onto something for balance, or counterbalance by extending it forward and up. Repeat on other side.

Barre Lunge: Using your bike's top tube, a fence, log, or piece of furniture of about the same height, rest one foot on it while standing on the other foot, two to three feet away. Bend the rear knee and lower the hips. Repeat on other side.

Shoulder Rolls: (not shown) Hold your arms out to both sides. Emphatically roll both shoulders forward 5–10 times.

Hand Hooks: Put your left hand behind your back. Reach your right hand over the right shoulder. Hook your fingers together and after an initial static stretch, have the lower hand pull the upper arm down a little, and then vice versa. Repeat on other side.

Wall Walks: (for your wrists and forearms) Stand facing a wall nearly arm's-length away. Place your palms on the wall with fingers up. Walk the hands down the wall as far as comfortable stretching allows. Reverse the fingers to point down, then walk the hands up the wall.

Calf Stretch: Rest your forearms on a wall. Place one foot back a couple feet. Bend the front knee and lower the hips toward the wall to stretch the back calf, working to keep the rear heel on the ground. Repeat on other side.

Shoulder Blade Hang: Place both hands on a wall (or the saddle and stem of your bike). Step back until you can bend over at the hips to hang the weight of your upper body from your arms. (Keep your feet parallel to and next to each other.)

Wrist Stretches: Place the palms of your hands together in front of your sternum, elbows up and out so the forearms are parallel to the ground. Lower one hand so the fingertips are in the palm of the other. Pressing gently with the palm of the upper hand, drop and raise the hands with the forearms. Then move them forward and back. Reverse hand positions and repeat.

Rearward Arm Raise: Intertwine your fingers behind your back and straighten your arms. Raise the arms enough to feel the stretch in your upper arms and shoulders.

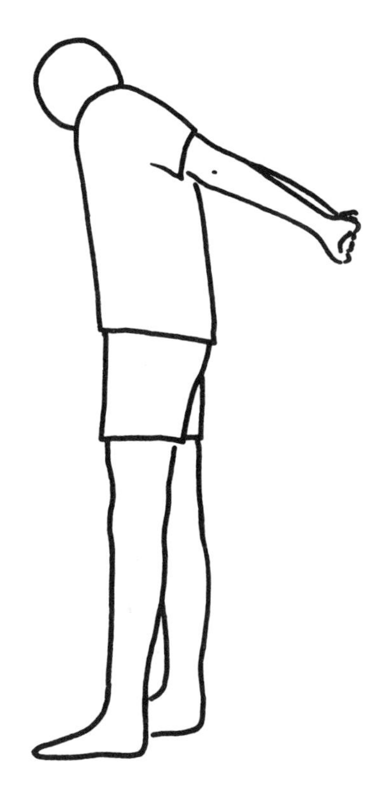

Massage

There are cycling coaches and trainers who consider massage so essential to daily recovery from training that they think you're wasting a third of your effort if you ignore it.

Self-massage is actually quite easy, and can be effective whether worked in after your shower and stretching session or at the end of your active day. Here's how you do it:

Start with a vigorous massage of the bottoms of your feet, a couple minutes per foot. Lie down on your back with your legs propped up on the wall, or on the couch, or anywhere that will elevate them at a 45- to 60-degree angle. Give them a little jiggle, then let the blood flow out of the lower extremities for 10 minutes or so. (This is an excellent time to review your training, do some visualization exercises, or read the comics.) Jiggle your legs again (sort of a vibrating/shaking action); then ease your legs down and sit with your back supported.

Reduce friction by using a natural oil, massage ointment, or body lotion (depending on how slick you like your skin to be afterward). Work each leg from the foot up. Begin by stroking towards the heart. Then use light to moderate circular pressure with the thumb and knuckles on particular muscles.

You have narrow and wide muscles, and muscles that taper in width. Calibrate the size of the bearing surface of your hand to the size of the muscle being worked on. Be careful not to rub so hard as to cause bruising. You want solid pressure but not sharp pain. You may have to use both hands, one on top of the other, to get enough pressure on your quadriceps.

Return to a stroking movement, and finish up with another light jiggling or shaking of each leg.

Next, do each arm from hand to shoulder, again using oil or liniment and stroking toward the heart. Follow with rotating pressure with the thumb, and maybe a little kneading, then stroking again.

After your massage, clean the skin with a washcloth. A little rubbing alcohol will remove oil-based substances.

Complete body massage is a full treat for a mountain biker. So if you have a spouse or friend who is willing to regularly perform the service, you may want to shave your legs. The friction from even moderate amounts of leg hair on an amateur masseur's hands is outrageous, sometimes painful. Give your masseur a break. The relationship might survive and the service continue.

Try to have some form of massage every day that you train 1.5 hours or more. Serious racers or devoted performance riders should try to get a total body massage on a weekly or biweekly basis. Don't stop in winter either. That's the time you and a professional can work deep on problem areas, work that shouldn't really be done in mid-season.

• • Alternative Activities

Mixing It Up Before You Crack Up

Excessive amounts of mountain biking to the exclusion of any other recreational activity can backfire with emotional burnout, fatigue, and even injury. And too much mountain biking, to the exclusion of all other athletic activity, can leave you frustrated when the weather and your schedule conspire to make riding impossible.

Missed training days and blasé efforts can result in poor race results, but even that would be getting off cheap. Single-sport overtraining injuries can range from ligament damage to muscle cannibalism.

Damage control calls for alternative recreational exercise (also known as cross-training) to relieve boredom and to give your muscles a slightly different experience, while still providing supplemental conditioning. The time to start cross-training is before you feel lethargic for days at a time, or your legs feel like they've turned to stone, or you have problems sleeping, or irregular heart beats (all symptoms of over-training).

The alternate activity should support the aerobic conditioning you're used to at your mountain biking intensity level. Don't fret too much over what's "closest" to cycling. One of the paybacks on alternative activity is that no matter how close the activity is to mountain biking kinesthetically, there will be just enough difference in muscle stress to relieve some overuse risks.

Probably the two most popular complementary sports for cycling are cross-country skiing and speedskating, which come into their seasons at a convenient time of the year for cyclists. Nordic skiing gives us the outdoors we love only with the terrain covered in snow. The exercise is similar to cycling, too—you grunt up the hills, then get the downhills for a reward (or another challenge).

Most mountain bike racers use ski-skating instead of diagonal striding because of its closer match to cycling. With diagonal striding you can shuffle along and barely get into your training range, whereas with ski-skating there's no way to cheat yourself out of a good workout. Cross-country skiing is also a lot warmer than cycling in below-freezing temperatures.

Speedskating also offers a good aerobic workout and develops a strong back and abdomen, typical weak points in bike riders. The advent of in-line roller skates, roller skis, and indoor ski trainers means these sports are now year-round options. (Use poles with them and your upper body will get a workout, too.)

Racewalking is another good alternative, particularly if you do a bastardized version of the traditional technique that incorporates hand-held weights. Standard racewalking strengthens muscles around the knee joint and the abdomen. But be aware that racewalking also demands a good deal more technical (form) conscientiousness than say, running. If you're averse to technique-intensive activities, you might pass on this one. The hand weights condition shoulder and arm muscles, and increase the aerobic demand just enough to raise the heart rate of a regular mountain biker into his or her training range. Begin with low weights (one to two pounds per hand), and increase gradually. Only use amounts of weight that allow a vigorous arm swing for the entire exercise period.

Hill and stair running will help your aerobic conditioning and prepare you for when you need to run your bike up that darn hill in a race. Trail running will sharpen your balance and alertness. It will also give you an entirely different perspective on the trails you're used to riding.

On the bike

Racers can't totally give up their bikes, even in the winter, but they can benefit from saving the bike for enjoyable riding—including long exploratory rides to keep endurance up—and doing their serious November to January workouts off the bike. Keep rides in the Endurance Heart Range and don't worry about speed or power. These relaxed winter rides are great for getting reacquainted with cycling friends who don't race-train during the season, and for enjoying the scenery more fully.

If you just can't keep away from contests with a bike, you may want to try cyclocross racing in the fall and winter. 'Cross racing is a combination of on- and off-road riding and cross-country running. The traditional 'cross bike is a road bike with a high bottom bracket, cantilever brakes, and sometimes a single chainwheel up front with double guards. Many mountain bikes can be retrofitted with lighter 700 C 'cross wheels and tires.

Courses are usually one to two miles in length, although they can run up to eight miles. They usually involve steep run-ups, mud zones, roads, hills, fields, and single-track trails strewn with fallen-tree-type barriers. Being able to run and hop across all kinds of terrain with a bike on your shoulder and to accurately judge when to ride and when to run are handy skills in this sport. 'Cross develops bike handling, and dismount/remount skills. A skilled 'cross competitor is almost balletic through these transitions. Better courses and races help you develop a sense of tempo—when to go hard and when going all-out is wasted effort.

If you get interested in cyclocross, build a cross-country running base during late summer/early autumn, gradually adding sprints and stair running. If enough riders in your area get interested in 'cross, you might be surprised how open your parks and recreation department is to developing courses or even holding races. It's an

Cyclocross is a terrific fall and winter companion sport that improves overall conditioning and bike handling skills.

exciting, entertaining sport with lots of spectator appeal, and it doesn't demand miles and miles of trail.

Many ex-roadies rightfully dread the loss of high-spin habits (90-plus rpm) that can come from mountain biking. Make a point to maintain some regular road riding year-round specifically for the high-rpm habit. Up to 40% of your in-season riding can be road work, with large amounts of it in the late winter to ingrain good pedaling habits.

Track racers who need a change of pace but don't want to get off a bike have taken to off-road because they find the strength and handling demands of mountain biking complementary to the skill and athletic requirements of velodrome competition. Their ventures haven't gone unnoticed by other backwoods riders, and track programs in Seattle, WA, Colorado Springs, CO, and Portland, OR, are beginning to attract cosmopolitan mountain bikers for the same reasons the trackies went to the woods.

Indoor training

Nothing says an alternative workout has to be an outdoor workout.

Fencing is a terrific thigh-and-stamina builder. Its unique demand for hand-eye coordination helps precision steering on the bike.

A stair-running machine can be beneficial if you use full leg extension and don't rest all your weight on the arm rests. One- to three-minute intervals not holding on at all are also a challenge.

Lap swimming works for many people as an alternative activity because the environment is totally different from mountain biking. While the kinesthetics are not exactly complementary to cycling, swimming is a great aerobic sport, and there's a nice effect on the back and spine from the constant drag of the body being pulled by the arm muscles through water.

If you've got riding technique, aerobics, and strength all dialed-in, but maybe you're just too tight or suffer from rigid, awkward back posture, maybe you should consider taking your Lycra-clad bod into a dance studio. Modern jazz dance will help loosen your body and develop coordination that can make you more relaxed on your bike.

Those who want to concentrate strictly on stretching the muscle groups in the legs (especially the quads and hamstrings) and developing clean, independent leg action, should give ballet barre sessions a try. Barre sessions are 30- to 45-minute periods that precede ballet classes in many studios. As the name implies, you don't do floor routines. You are strictly working on stretching.

Four-wall handball can be just the ticket to help you get through the winter and early spring doldrums. Admittedly, walking through a down-sized door to hit a ball around a cement room might seem like the last place a mountain biker might want to be. But when played intensely, handball is great aerobic exercise, develops hand-eye control, quick reflexes, and left/right balance, and it helps keep your upper body flexible.

Those who want to ensure shoulder/arm conditioning and flexibility might consider year-round training with a boxer's speed bag. It, too, helps hand-eye coordination and reflexes but can also be just the thing to loosen up arms that stay pretty much in the same position all the time on the bike.

Our preferences

What do we do?

Martha hikes and trail-runs with her dogs, rides and races on the road, goes cross-country ski-skating, and lifts weights.

Michael lifts weights three times a week, jogs a little, skis (both downhill and cross-country), and uses a bike to ride to and from skiing or the weight room.

> *I've seen PVC tubing bolted to the sides of rear racks to hold skis vertically. I've strapped cross-country skis to the rack and top tube, and bungee-corded the poles and boots on top of the rear rack.*
>
> *I try to mix it up as much as possible in the off-season, to keep me fresh and enthused toward cycling. I'll play tennis, basketball, and swim laps once a week. I'll also ride rollers up to an hour twice a week to sustain leg speed. Generally, I try to do some exercise for four to eight hours a day, five to six days a week.*—Michael

Yuri rides a road bike year-round, racewalks with hand weights (often doing circuit training sessions of rollers/racewalking/windtrainer/more rollers in the winter), lifts weights, hikes, intermittently rides track bikes, does a couple months of lap swimming or some cross-country skiing.

• • Trailside Trauma

Being Ready When Things Get Too Gnarly

We don't like to think about it, but a lot of things can happen to you out on a mountain bike ride—things that may be merely annoying or something quite serious. The easiest and most practical way to deal with such prospects is to follow these three rules:

- Always pack a small first-aid kit.
- Learn enough about first aid to be able to assess the seriousness of an injury and stabilize the situation.
- When heading out alone, always tell someone where you'll be riding and when you plan to be back.

The first-aid kit is fairly straightforward. It should include:

- sunscreen
- aspirin or ibuprofen
- butterfly bandages
- gauze pads
- small roll of cloth first-aid tape
- water-treatment pills or filter
- moleskin
- antiseptic
- snakebite kit
- thermometer in protective case

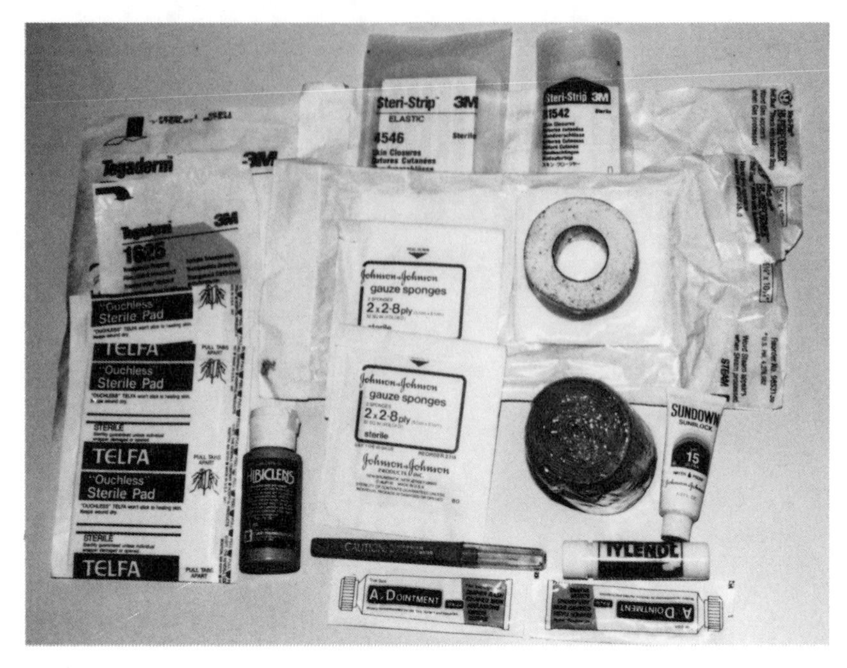

When riding far from medical services, you should carry a complete first-aid kit. This one includes gauze pads, sponges, bandages, antiseptic cleaner, skin sutures, tape, elastic wrap, sun block, ibuprofen, thermometer, and anti-bacterial ointment.

Wrap the kit in a zip-lock bag to keep it dry.

Knowing how and when to use the above items will get you through most situations. But if you have worse luck, not knowing how to assess the extent of an injury could have serious consequences.

Most of what you need to know is covered in the standard Red Cross first-aid course, an eight-hour course that covers injury surveying, heat exhaustion, frostbite, hypothermia, shock, and adult CPR. This course is often required for teachers and shop personnel who must meet OSHA requirements.

The Red Cross also teaches a certified, advanced first-aid course that takes 50 hours to complete. The advanced course goes into all the topics in the standard course but in more depth, and it presents treatment procedures in more detail.

If you've already had some first-aid instruction, but just want to refresh your memory (or you'd like some cue sheets to bring along on rides), the Red Cross sells the standard course manual for $7.50 per copy, and sells a 6″ × 7″ "pocket guide" to first aid for $3.50.

Your local community college or university physical education department may also be a source for first-aid instruction. Many such institutions offer wilderness first-aid courses tailored for situations likely to be encountered in the outdoors.

Of course nothing works like preventive medicine, and for mountain biking that means wearing a helmet (all the time), staying well hydrated, having dry clothes on hand to keep you warm, and not riding beyond your capabilities. Sometimes, preventive medicine also means having the right eye protection.

> *By the second day of the inaugural Iditabike I think was almost in a state of hypnosis, but I was also glare blind. I couldn't focus more than a few feet in front of my bike because I didn't have dark enough lenses for my glasses. Until nightfall, every chance I got, I rode on Dave Zink's wheel. Fortunately it was a pretty straight shot that day down the rivers. If there had been a need for extreme maneuvers, I would have been at a loss.*
>
> —Michael

Besides minor scrapes and bruises, the most common injuries in mountain biking are damaged wrists, broken collarbones, and concussions. But you don't have to have a traumatic incident to get into trouble out on a bike. Hypoglycemia, heat stroke or exhaustion, frostbite, and hypothermia have all struck unwitting wanderers of the outback.

Hypoglycemia, or insulin shock, is the rapid loss of sugar levels in the blood stream. Fainting is likely if hypoglycemia occurs during intense exercise like mountain biking. A gnawing hunger, a case of the jitters, cold sweat, dizziness, or reduced vision may forewarn the fainting spell. Then again, there may be no warning.

The important thing is to maintain a supply of blood sugars by pre-ride diet and to carry easy-to-digest fruits and juices on the bike (and to eat them). The prompt ingestion of such easy-to-absorb sweets is imperative once the condition develops.

Heat stroke is marked by an extremely high body temperature (105–106 degrees) and a malfunction of the body's cooling system. (You stop sweating.) The skin often becomes red, hot, and dry. This is a life-threatening condition. Sponge the body with cool water until the temperature drops to below 102 degrees. Do not give the person stimulants, including products containing caffeine.

Heat exhaustion involves fatigue, weakness, and sometimes collapse from dehydration. The body's temperature can be nearly normal, and the skin can seem cool and/or pale because of capillary constriction. Fainting, nausea, dizziness, or cramps may be present.

The victim should lie down, elevate his or her feet several inches, loosen his or her clothing, and drink water. If the victim is vomiting, give very small amounts of fluid at frequent intervals.

Hypothermia is a much greater risk than most people realize. The seemingly ideal cool temperature range for riding, say 40 to 55 degrees, is the range in which people most often contract hypothermia.

Hypothermia is tricky to discern because the early symptoms are the same as just being hammered—a slight loss of coordination, speech difficulty, and shivering. It can also be a problem to self-diagnose because impaired thinking is another one of its hallmarks. If you begin to wonder if you have hypothermia, don't brush that thought off as paranoia. Make sure of your situation (*everything*, including where you are, where you're going, how long it will take you to get there, the status of your food, clothing, and water supplies, even what your name is).

You may not want to do it, but if your innermost layer of clothing is wet or damp, you'll be much warmer if you remove it and put a dry garment next to your skin. (For women, this means removing damp bras, too.)

If a riding companion becomes too cold to want to keep on or to eat or drink, he or she is near the edge. This person must be kept warm, rehydrated, fed carbohydrates, and kept moving. To lie down and curl up is the kiss of death.

If the person has stopped shivering but is still cold, he or she is on the edge. Getting the person covered with maximum insulation and immediately evacuated to medical attention is imperative.

Frostbite occurs when ice crystals form in the skin and the area just below the skin. Dehydration, wet clothing, and constricted circulation from overbundling often contribute to the development of frostbite. In the early stages the condition is sometimes painful, but more often the area just feels cold and numb. This can make early frostbite tricky for the mountain biker to perceive since some cyclists' hands and feet often go numb even in warm weather.

The frostbite victim is often unaware of his or her condition until someone points it out. (This is what happened during the first Iditabike. A rider only found out he had frostbite when he was asked to remove his boots for inspection at a checkpoint.)

A light case will have hard skin that's white or grayish, but underneath the hard surface, the area will still be soft to pressure. More serious cases develop blisters, and the frostbitten area will seem thoroughly cold, hard, and insensitive.

Since damage can be worse if a frostbitten part is thawed and then refrozen, only rewarm a frostbitten part if you know it can be kept warm. Rapid rewarming with 102–105-degree water is best. (If you don't have a thermometer, test the temperature as you would baby formula on your inner wrist—it should be just slightly hot.) Elevating the frostbitten part, but not bandaging it, and drinking warm liquids helps.

Concussions. A Snell- or ANSI-certified helmet will protect most heads in most cases, but should you hit hard, take the time to promptly think about what happened and assess whether you were knocked out (especially if you are alone). Being knocked out for longer than a few seconds is cause for concern. Severe headache, fluctuating pulse despite being still, and foggy consciousness are symptoms of head injury.

Train yourself to conduct a quick systems check after every fall. Begin with the ABCs of first aid: is the Airway passage clear, is Breathing okay, is Circulation functioning properly—check for bleeding, swelling, and pain.

Even after a minor tumble, ask yourself where the pain is first. Then systematically go over the whole body. Doing the body check in a controlled, thorough pace seems to allow the brain to quit rattling and get back into operation.

Swelling can be reduced with an ace bandage wrap, although nothing is better than ice. But since you're unlikely to be dragging an ice chest along, swelling around localized injuries can be treated by cold treatment when you're back in town. If you're away from home, buying a bag of frozen corn has advantages over a standard bag of ice cubes. The small kernels conform to the shape of your body better, they're inside a sealed plastic bag, and you have something for your dollar besides dirty water when you're done.

For bang-ups that seem more serious—when the degree of pain may indicate a fracture or serious sprain—first stop any bleeding.

Elevating the wound and mild compression will help keep a wound from reopening and will reduce swelling.

Wash the wound with soap and water if you have it on hand. Squirts from your water bottle work fine if you're not near a stream. Small cuts will stop bleeding on their own. Large wounds require pressure to clot. Rinse the wound with antiseptic and allow the antiseptic to air dry. After drying, cover it with sterile gauze. If the cut keeps bulging open, see if a butterfly suture helps pinch it together.

Then check again for pain—pain upon movement or pain upon pressure. A broken collarbone or injured wrist won't want to take the pressure of riding, especially downhill riding. But if you rode alone out into the boonies, it's likely you're going to have to get yourself back. A bike can be a nice thing to lean on, but if even pushing your bike is too difficult or painful, consider stashing it and returning for it later, especially if you have a long way to bushwhack.

If the injured area can't take any pressure or do any movement without protesting loudly, it'll need a padded splint, and prompt medical attention. Likewise, if tenderness, redness, or swelling haven't subsided in 24 hours you should have the injury checked out by professionals.

Once you know you're physically stable, make sure you're warm and dry—your body can chill quite rapidly after it stops exercising suddenly. If you think you can ride, then take it slow. Riding will allow any less obvious injuries to reveal themselves, and an easy pace will keep blood flow down. (With more catastrophic accidents there's always the chance of internal bleeding.)

Finally, don't think you know first aid because you read this chapter. We're merely passing along practical advice confirmed with medical personnel. Take the first-aid courses and encourage as many of your riding companions as possible to do so as well so that group rides are likely to have two people along who've been trained in first aid.

• • The Racing Scene

Exploring the Courses, Classes, and Categories

Mountain bike racing takes place in a wide range of formats in which contestants test themselves in skill, strength, and on-the-trail self-reliance.

Most races are conducted under the auspices of NORBA, the National Off-Road Bicycle Association. This governing body sanctions more than 300 races each year, licenses more than 5,000 competitors, and ties in with international cycling competition through its parent organization, the U.S. Cycling Federation (USCF).

From 1987 to 1989 several so-called "World Championships" were staged in both the U.S. and Europe, the result being that no one could lay legitimate claim to world titles. In 1990, however, the UCI (Union Cycliste Internationale, the world governing body) began sanctioning an annual World Championships in which professional and elite amateur racers compete on national teams for world titles in downhill and cross-country events.

The ambience at a mountain bike race is often compared to that of nordic skiing competition. Typically, the not-so-serious far outnumber the fanatics. Most mountain bike racers are there just to have a good time with their bikes.

Mountain bike racing remains an individual sport because, unlike in road racing, drafting does little good and usually extracts a toll from the following rider by making him or her choke on dust, smart from pebbles and sticks propelled by the lead rider's rear wheel, or get smothered in flying mud.

Most recreational competitors are there simply to beat their times in last year's edition of the race, to cross the finish line ahead of friends who are also competing, or just to see if they can complete the event.

There's often a festival atmosphere, highlighted by an awards ceremony after the event. Sometimes there's a cook-out or barbeque. Competitors who have to travel great distances to events sometimes camp out the night before or after, trading race stories, discussing equipment, or simply socializing with other mountain bikers.

As larger amounts of money have come into mountain bike racing, a Pro/Elite class of racers has emerged. These are serious competitors, many of whom are attempting to make careers out of racing mountain bikes. But there remains a friendliness, an unpretentious honesty, and an egalitarian social order at races. Sometimes it seems like even the Pro/Elite race is just an excuse to get the tribe together to socialize. Competitors from different teams are often seen after national events goofing around together on sand dunes, star gazing on ridge tops, or eating Mexican dinners together.

Racing is a pretty relaxed, fun gig to be involved with. But before you foster an affinity for it, you should realize that a commitment to a season of racing involves some cash, whatever your level of seriousness. Entry fees and travel costs must be added to the inevitable wear and tear on equipment and to the increased food bill to fuel the activity.

Race formats

In just over a decade, mountain biking has developed a wide variety of competitive formats from short, slow contests of handling skill to injury-defying downhilling and three-day expeditionary contests. Here's a brief description of the options.

Cross-country point-to-point races. These can be either mass-start or individual-start competitions held on forest roads, wooded or field trails, or unpaved dirt or gravel roads. Race distances range from 15-mile beginner courses to 100-, 150-, and 200-mile "ultra-enduros."

Cross-country circuit races. These are mass-start competitions held on terrain similar to point-to-point courses except the course begins and ends in the same spot. Courses are usually fairly short (4–12 miles), and competitors cover the loop a number of times, the number of repetitions and distances varying according to Class and Category. The one ultra-enduro circuit race we know of is called Montezuma's Revenge. It's a 24-hour timed event in which racers compete to see who can cover the most distance on seven different loops emanating from St John's, CO.

Hillclimb or uphill. The officially sanctioned version of a hill-climb is a timed event in which the finish line is at a substantially higher elevation than the start. The race can be either an individual time trial or a mass-start event. Another popular version is the "widow-maker," an individual-start event on a hill that is so steep that the contest is to see who can pedal the furthest up the slope before putting a foot down.

Downhill. These are individual time trials with the start at the top of a challenging descent (although some have been known to climb a bit first). They represent the ultimate challenge of a rider's bike-handling skills and ability to read the terrain at speed. Such skills are most apparent when the racer attempts to execute course turns, jumps, and drop-offs.

> *I competed in one mass-start downhill in France's Alps where about 50 competitors began simultaneously. It was a frightening start.*—Michael

Classics. Cross-country point-to-point racing and downhills were the earliest forms of mountain bike racing. The "Classics" combine both on courses that racers do one time, en masse. The courses usually cover 30–60 miles and include at least one, but more commonly two, major climbs (1,500–5,000 feet of elevation change) and subsequent long descents.

As mountain biking grew, formats from other sports were adapted to fat tire fun, and now an assortment of hybrid varieties are growing in popularity.

Dual slalom. This is an event similar to the winter version in downhill skiing in which competitors race side by side (or "head-to-head") down parallel courses. The courses are set using poles, pylons, or flag gates.

Stage racing. Similar to the events of the same name in road racing, competitors are required to complete a series of events. Times or points are combined to form a cumulative time or score. A popular practice is to combine several types of events over a few days to determine the best all-around, "most gnarly," or most versatile rider. Sometimes bonus points or time reductions are awarded for winning significant stages. In France some stage races include "specials" where you might ride an uphill in the morning, then transfer by bike as a group to the start location 10 or so miles away for a circuit race, then transfer again to another start, maybe a time trial.

Observed trials. These are contests of balance, as well as terrain and obstacle management. Competitors must progress through an obstacle course. Colored ribbons mark the right and left boundaries between which competitors must remain. At each significant obstacle a judge is stationed to observe and record how well the competitor executes the section. Each time a rider touches a hand or foot to something for support he incurs a "dab," which adds points to his score. The rider that completes the course with the lowest score wins.

Obstacles can include naturally occurring or constructed barriers. Logs, cable spools, tree stumps, creeks and streams, gullies and drop-offs, rocks, ramps, bridges, and muddy terrain have all been used. "Cleaning" sections (to execute without a dab) may require bunny-hopping, stair-climbing, stair-descending, rolling jumps, stationary pivot turns, or other deft handling skills.

There are specialized events in which competitors ride bikes made just for Observed Trials. At some events though, competitors must ride the same unmodified bike used for the cross-country events.

Scott trials. These events consist of a chain of trials sections separated by significant cross-country trail sections. (Scott trials are usually ridden on a standard mountain bike.) They're conducted as individual time trials in which each rider attempts to combine the quickest ride time between trials sections with the fewest number of dabs. The trials sections in these events usually include obstacles commonly encountered in recreational mountain biking, and although they may be difficult, they're not extremely severe or contrived.

About the different races

The popularity or predominance of the various formats changes from year to year as the sport accommodates pressures from land-access politics, promotional and commercial concerns, spectator interest, and participant preference.

Although Classics are the type of races many of us got hooked on and are often referred to as "real mountain bike racing," they're difficult to scope out before you jump in. That's because in the typical Classic the racers depart in a cloud of dust or splatter of mud, only to emerge from the woods and hills one by one a few hours later.

The courses are usually marked well enough that you don't get lost if you pay attention to the markers. Usually you find your own pace. Then you're alone out there for most of the time. It's you against (or with) the terrain—an ultimate individual challenge.

To preview such racing you usually have to either ride out on the course in advance to get to an observation point, or take shortcuts to various observation points with your mountain bike or a four-wheel-drive motor vehicle. Of course, a primary rule if you try this is to coordinate with the race director and stay off the course whenever riders may be near. An excellent way to check the scene out is to volunteer as a water-station worker. (Most Classics have one or two water stations out there somewhere.) You can also listen to the stories of finishers at the end of the event.

Circuit courses of 4- to 12-mile laps have grown in frequency over the past few years because they provide easier spectator access and the logistics of organizing are simpler than a cross-country event. Spectators can usually ride or walk to numerous points where they cheer for friends and favorites. For the racer this experience is quite different from the solitude of a Classic cross-country event. You always know when you're approaching a high-crash zone or muddy stretch because that's where spectators gather! Besides not being nearly as lonely as a classic, knowing who's in front or behind you, by how much, and whether you're gaining or falling off from your pace has helped make circuit racing popular with participants.

Although NORBA classifies any race over 75 miles in length as an ultra-endurance event, the most common distance for an ultra-enduro is 100 miles. There's a 150-miler in southern California, the aforementioned 24-hour mass time trial in Colorado, and the ultimate challenge to one's stamina and sanity, the 210-mile Iditabike in Alaska.

To many people's surprise, quite a few off-road cyclists have contracted "ultra" fever. Maybe it's because we're all getting older and endurance is the one riding factor that can be improved despite the effects of aging, or maybe it's just because humans are attracted to doing things on a grand scale. Whatever fulfillment they offer, ultra-enduros are for experienced riders and outdoors adventurers who have trained enough (meaning a lot), are relaxed and self-reliant in the outback, and who want a very peculiar experience of life as we know it.

Equipment

Every competitor in a NORBA sanctioned race is required to wear a helmet that's passed either the ANSI Z90.4 or Snell Memorial Foundation standards test, and is so identified. Racers are usually also required to wear a shirt, shorts, and fully-enclosed shoes.

The bicycle must have brakes that will stop the bike within 20 feet from a speed of 20 miles per hour. All tubing ends must be plugged and finished smoothly. (Most often this is a handlebar check.)

As a relatively young sport, mountain bike racing has a fairly concise set of rules. The "Competition Introduction" from the NORBA handbook succinctly explains the premises and philosophy of mountain bike competition.

"The sport of off-road bicycle racing evolved from recreational off-road bicycling. Recreational off-road cyclists must be prepared to reach their goal self-contained and return on a functional bicycle. To enhance the continuing evolution of the off-road bicycle, NORBA competition events place an increased emphasis on equipment reliability, and individual ability. It is in the spirit of self-contained, self-reliant, back-country cycling that NORBA competition events are conducted."

Whether a sanctioned NORBA event or a spontaneous pick-up game, mountain bike races true to the tradition of the sport maintain a core of standards, such as:

- All racers must finish the event on the same bike they started with.
- All repairs are conducted by the racer. No outside help.
- Any repairs must be made using only parts carried by partici-

Staying on top of an intense athletic game like mountain biking is intensely satisfying at any age.

pants, without cannibalizing other bikes. You may borrow parts or tools but only from other racers.

- Foul riding, unsportsmanlike behavior (including profane or abusive language, littering, and short-cutting or cutting switchbacks on trails) warrant automatic penalties or disqualification.

Classes and Categories

In the nomenclature of off-road racing, age groups are divided into Classes, and skill/ability level is divided in Categories. If you get a NORBA license, both Class and Category are identified on it.

NORBA procedures are to put you in a Class according to your age on December 31 of the year you register for a license. The license will be good for 12 months from the date of issue, and the age Class listed on the license is the one race directors are instructed to allow you to compete in. The Classes are:

- *Junior*: 15–18 years of age
- *Senior*: 19–34
- *Veteran*: 35–44
- *Master*: 45–plus

Regardless of age, you can register to race in whatever Category you think you can handle. The Categories are:

- *Beginner*: generally first-time competitors and novice riders
- *Sport*: intermediately skilled racers
- *Expert*: racers with advanced athletic and biking skills
- *Pro/Elite*: highest-level competitors

There are no regulations regarding sand-bagging in your first race, so you might consider riding in the Beginner Category once or twice to find out what it's like. If you're fit and feel you can handle a bike fairly well, maybe try the Sport Category race. The thing is that once you race in a certain Category (say Sport or Expert), NORBA does not allow reclassification to a lower Category without a formal written request.

On the other hand, once you complete five Beginner races, you must become a Sport entrant. A Sport rider must move up to Expert once he or she has three top-three finishes or six top-six finishes in one calendar year.

Pro/Elite categorization only follows submission of a written resume to NORBA.

Race directors are supposed to divide race starts first by Class. It's then their prerogative whether or not to divide age Classes into Categories. The director may also divide the Senior Class into subcategories.

Women are not supposed to be combined with men in the same competitions unless there are fewer than four women present when all Categories are combined.

When fewer than four racers preregister for a Class or Category of events, they may be required to race with the next respective Class or Category.

The pros

The NORBA Pro/Elite racers can compete in a National Points Series in which points accumulate toward the National Championship. The final race of the Points Series is also the National Championship for Juniors, Vets, and Masters. The Points Series is also instrumental in selecting the U.S. National Team for participation in the World Championships. The National Team consists of up to five members per gender class.

In 1991 a World Cup competition was inaugurated, consisting of a series of events in Europe and North America. The winner in each gender class is determined by cumulative points garnered in World Cup events.

• • Beginner Racing

Getting Fired Up about Competition

If you're a first-time off-road racer, go out just to have fun. Races are places to meet new people who share your love for mountain bike riding and to learn about new places to ride. Have a great time, get a good adrenalin rush, and spend the rest of the weekend trading race stories with companions.

Martha's first couple of races were like that for her.

> *My first race—The Gant Challenge—was an eight-mile course in a Minneapolis city park. I won a helmet and almost won a bike, and thought 'Wow, this is pretty cool.'*
>
> *My second race was an experience I'll never forget and what really got me hooked on racing. It was the Chequamegan Fat Tire Festival, when it was pretty small. It's a 40-mile point-to-point race through a national forest, part of it on the Birkebinder Ski Trail in Wisconsin.*
>
> *I almost had to cancel because on the Thursday before the race I got food poisoning. I'd been camping out for a week, ate some bad food after a long ride, and spent the night going in and out of the tent. I drove to Cable (the race town) on Friday. Got a couple pieces of toast down, then got a hotel room and slept until nighttime. I ate a light dinner, got more*

sleep, then was on the bike at 10 A.M. *Saturday to see if I could do it.*

It was the first time since high school that I'd pushed myself that hard physically. (I was thankful for the Gatorade at the checkpoints!) I not only finished but came in second. I had that exhausted, exhilarated feeling you only get when you've set yourself a big challenge and succeeded. And, just as important, I met four people who are still my friends.

The entire experience is what kept me coming back for more: meeting race buddies, eating pre-race meals together, camping out together, eventually organizing weekends of biking and camping when there weren't any races. And these weren't 'pros' or 'elites' or anything like that, just people who liked to ride bikes, eat well, and be in the woods.—Martha

Almost anyone drawn to racing wants to be sure to finish, if not finish well (whether that "well" means a personal standard or relative to others). The absolute raw rookie can do a couple things to help ensure positive results.

- Ride off-road before the race. It's amazing how many people show-up at NORBA races and have never been off-pavement before. You'll be asking a lot of your sense of humor to handle your first dirt ride in a race situation.
- In the days or weeks before the race, take rides of a distance similar to that of the race.
- If the time and opportunity exist and it's a short-course race, pre-ride the course at a leisurely, observational pace before racing it. This will save you from nasty surprises such as encountering an unexpected three-foot drop-off or an obstacle just as you come bombing around a corner.
- Don't put yourself to the front of the starting-line pack at your first event.

Besides having fun, your most important priority is finishing the race, so pace yourself as well as you can. Learning pacing is a personal thing. (We all had our problems learning it.) If you have a knot in your stomach, don't go any harder. On the other hand, if you're 5 miles into a 10-mile race and you feel like it's been no big deal and that you can go hard and still finish without bonking, then go for it. After all, it is a race!

Space yourself from other riders in the race so you're no danger to them and they're no danger to you. Remember, everyone else in the race is a novice, too. And start with a race over fairly gentle, nonintimidating terrain. For example, don't pick a mountain criterium for your first race.

Some women have found it useful to train with female rather than male companions. When a solo woman begins training for mountain bike racing, the initial foray is too often a ride with a bunch of guys, which may leave the woman vowing never to ride off-road again. ("It's too hard, there were too many falls, had to walk half the time, we got lost, and the bugs were horrible.") Even when guys are considerate in their pacing, there's not as much intimidation about relative ability with other women.

> *If you watch a male friend clean a technical or downhill section, you might say to yourself 'Yeah, but he's a man. He's been doing this forever.' But if your female friend does it just as nonchalantly, you'll have to face the fact that women can and do do these things, do them well, and have fun doing them!*—Martha

Whether male or female, even if you've road raced for years, you have to realize that dirt races are a whole new game. A getting-by-as-best-you-can effort is fine as long as you can maintain a relaxed attitude about things that go askew. If, no matter what happens, you remember that basically you're riding your bike through the woods/mountains/outdoors with a bunch of people who like doing the same thing, you'll probably continue to have a good time.

If you enter a Beginner's race to get your feet wet and finish too well rested to feel good about your effort, then go harder at it the next time, maybe staying just off the leader's pace.

If you're two-thirds or three-quarters through a race using that method and still feel like there's plenty left, then go for it. If you do, keep in mind that you'll feel a lot better about yourself if you finish without bonking. It's difficult to ride "on empty" and the experience may make you wish you hadn't entered. Prepare mentally for the time when this happens, because if you continue to race, there is bound to be a time when you discover your limits.

If you go for it a couple times and finish an outrageous amount of time before your competitors, move up to the Sport Category for your next race.

● ● Sport Racing

Dialing-in and Staying with It

Okay, you're hooked. You're traveling to races more often, you don't see your nonriding friends much during race season, and maybe you've won a couple trophies (or almost did). Your rides have become "training rides" and you've started reading magazine articles and asking other riders questions on how to improve your technique.

You're still in it for the fun, but you're a little hungry for results. To get those paybacks in Sport Category competitions you need to be training a minimum of two to three times during the week, every week, for 1.5–2 hours per session. Add to that one long weekend ride (3–4 hours) or a race. If your weekend training is a race, then your midweek training ride (Wednesday or Thursday) should be a longish (3 hours) endurance ride.

Also, one of your weekday training rides each week should be a skills and technique session. Look for steep, technical trails, or a Threshold Heart Range hillclimb followed by a technical ride home.

There's no reason why a long midweek endurance ride or a couple of the nontechnical rides can't be road riding as long as you keep the work load (heart rate) up to match the power demands of off-road riding. If you're one to mix road and mountain bike training, match the setup of your two bikes so your position is the same on each, and pay attention to the differences between road and mountain hill climbing (position, gearing, pacing).

Skills acquisition plays a key role in improving results in the Sport Category, and the importance of handling ability never really goes away, so ride a lot of different terrain.

> *The Trans Vesubienne in southern France involved a 60-kilometer course that descended 8,000 feet and regained 5,000 feet before finishing. The winning time was somewhere around six hours! We started above treeline, rode along cliffs and down stair sections that seemed to go on forever. A lot of the trails were tight switchbacks with boulders. You either dismounted or did a trials maneuver to get around each corner. I still need to practice those things.*—Michael

Which points out the need to get comfortable with dismounting and quickly remounting your bike when you can't execute the ace maneuver, or after a fall or hiking section.

Begin to pay attention to what happens to your body and your psychological state under different circumstances. Just as you think you've found a new, fun love in your life, things may seem to be off a little or not quite clicking. You may need an attitude adjustment. Deciding to become "athletic" can be a major change. The psychological challenges anyone faces in making a commitment to athletic competition include:

- pushing through fears
- finding compatible training partners and coaches
- transforming from simple fitness motivations to the desire to become stronger and more skilled in order to have even more fun or accomplish a tougher challenge

All these challenges are magnified by the spectator-sport cult in our society. The spectator-sport ideology convinces the average person that intense athletic accomplishment is beyond his or her abilities, the prerogative of an elite minority or the passion of the obsessive or egotistical. This thinking begins with the intramural, junior-varsity, and varsity selection in youth and is maintained in the emphasis given spectator sports in newspapers, television, and radio where participant sports are minor afterthoughts. It serves to deny people the self-reliance and confidence that results from participation, and it underlines a notion of a spectator status in the world, paving the way for a condition of powerlessness and victimization. (This line of propaganda is even more magnified in its strictures on women.)

For too many of us, hesitation to participate often is compounded by negative body image. It often has less to do with how we actually look than how we feel about ourselves.

> *My thighs have always been too big, my shoulders too wide, my feet too big, my legs too short, and on, and on, and on. Competitive cycling has removed a lot of the excess from my frame, given a raison d'être for my large quads, and made me much more comfortable with this less than so-called ideal body.*
>
> *Each time I finish a race or long ride during which I've asked my body for power or speed and gotten it, I rejoice and feel pride for that body I see in the mirror. And it seems that the self-confidence I've gained from getting stronger through racing is reflected in other attitudes. I now look at most models and women I used to think were beautiful and find myself thinking 'but she has no shape to her legs; she has no muscle tone.'*—Martha

Intermediate racing, and all categories thereafter, demand that you learn to stay on the bike while going into oxygen debt, or "going anaerobic." Each individual has slightly different reactions to such physiological stress, but symptoms include the following:

- narrowing vision, tunnel vision, or dimness of vision
- a burning sensation in the lungs or leg muscles
- a "head rush," almost like you're hyperventilating
- a funny taste in the mouth

In the midst of such sensory bombardment while trying to control and accelerate your bike, you need to breath deeply, throw out bad or negative thoughts, and concentrate on pacing until you're back into an aerobic state. To avoid seizing up, the lactic acid, or exhaust material, that will have built up in your system must be dissipated. This is best done with a high pedal speed and rehydration.

Pre-race notes

Managing the race will be easier if you can pre-ride the course to nail down some of the details. Check the terrain to determine what kind of tires are appropriate and which tire pressures might offer the optimal compromise between traction and rolling resistance, and shock absorption.

> *I generally stay within 30–40 psi, with approximately 2 pounds less in the rear tire than the front for climbing traction. On a strictly downhill course I might push the psi above 40 pounds.*—Michael

Michael weighs about 150 pounds. Adjust your tire pressures approximately 5 pounds for every 25 pounds that you're above or below that weight.

Inspect any tricky technical sections and ride through them a few times, if possible. Make mental notes about food and water requirements for longer courses.

You won't always be able to pre-ride courses, so practice handling strange territory. Play follow-the-leader on training rides, during which the designated leader takes you on trails you haven't ridden before.

Besides practicing chasing down a rider, get used to reacting to riders in close quarters and to riding through strange sections with someone on your wheel. On dusty trails, whether flat or downhill, you'll find it best to stay right on someone's wheel (within five feet) because the dust is much less of a nuisance. But you have to get good at reacting quickly. Start by practicing drafting on county roads, not on a trail.

Racing

It's no fun riding behind a herd of cattle, and the situation isn't much better in the increasingly crowded Sport Category races.

Get near the front as soon as possible. Races are never won from the back. Of course getting near the front may put you into oxygen debt, so you've got to get good at maintaining your line under such circumstances because you don't want to be in other people's way either.

You'll need to be sensitive as to whether you've gone into momentary oxygen debt, blown up, or bonked. If you've bonked it will be self-evident—you'll have completely spent your energy and nothing will seem to work. If you suspect you've blown up from an effort rather than gone into momentary oxygen debt, slow down and drink both water and carbo-mix fluids. Ride at a total-control pace until all your systems seem "go" again.

Whatever happens, though, remember the adage, "It ain't over until it's over."

In 1988 I went to Europe to race for Fisher Mountain Bikes in the European World Championships. There were 400 starters for the two-lap, 24-kilometer course. There was a one-hour-long climb on each lap. I wasn't seeded near the front as were Ned Overend, John Tomac, and other favorites. Needless to say, I was frustrated when I discovered this moments before the start. I thought my chances were ruined; the trail narrowed to a single track just a quarter-mile from the start. Experience had taught me that starts and starting position can mean a lot. But I decided to show that I wasn't just another 'wanna-be.'

Chasing down another rider is a skill that should be practised.

When the gun went off I started sprinting and tried to pass as many racers as I could before the trail narrowed. I surprised myself by moving up to about 20th overall, about 30 seconds back. I could see Overend and the other leaders. Having spent precious energy that would be needed right away, I settled into a pace that left me two minutes down on Overend as I crested the summit of the first lap's climb. But I was in fourth place, just seconds behind Tomac! On the second lap I was able to catch Ned Overend halfway up the climb, and I finished nearly four minutes in front.

So never succumb to defeat before you even begin, and use your energy in a positive sense (racing), not negatively (grousing about it).—Michael

Martha learned the lesson from both sides.

My first and most humiliating defeat was at Chequamegan in 1986. It was a competitive race for me. One woman was ahead, but faded midway. The only woman I'd seen at any other race was with me. I pulled ahead, then passed the leader. I began just cruising. My back was hurting, so I really slowed down during the final miles. But I was feeling confident, and last I looked, I didn't see anyone.

Then, a minute from the finish, a figure sprinted by me. I didn't react quickly enough and ended up in second place. She won an expensive bike and sponsorship the following year. I was in pain physically and emotionally.

At the second Iditabike Race, Sara Ballantyne was 1.5 hours ahead of me at the halfway point. But I remembered Chequamegan and decided the only thing to do was race 'til I dropped—after all, the race was only half over.

Fifteen miles later I was suddenly ahead of Sara due to her getting disoriented and off the trail. My carrot gone, I lowered my pace again. Not from overconfidence this time, but, I think, a combination of exhaustion, confusion, and concern—'Where was she?'

When Sara caught up to me again, I shook myself out of that state, telling myself 'If she wants to get by me she's gonna have to hurt even more than me.' And I put six minutes between us.

So never give up.—Martha

●● Expert-Ease

Refining Super Stuff

A question keeps running through your mind: "Do I just keep doing this racing/training stuff for fun in my spare time, or do I see how far I can go?"

Or maybe you've begun to find your various worlds clashing. Your boss wonders where you are most of the time, because your attention isn't always on the job in front of you. Are you daydreaming about being the champ? Figuring out how to get the day's ride in?

Do some of your nonriding friends wonder what's going on since you never hang out with them any more? Do even your riding buddies think you're weird because you don't do intervals "their way" or because your weekend's race is more important than the Friday night party?

Are you looking at everything else in life according to how it supports your race habit? And do you feel okay about it because you've improved a lot and are working hard at it, reading books on training, querying better riders on what they do, how they train, what they eat, etc., etc.?

These are common predicaments for the Expert Category racer. Maintaining or improving your abilities once you're in the penultimate Category is a peculiar recreational proposition at best. This is when you find out what you're willing to do in the name of fun, because here is where the little things do add up. Alcohol restriction, everyday and race-day diet, even sleep-rest-activity-cycle management can be instrumental in standings.

For all Expert or elite racers, training makes a transition from gross improvement to incremental upgrades, and the line between enough stress and overload is a fine one. Too much time riding off-road at race or near-race intensities can tear you up.

Use your effort and time to realize specific goals. Accentuate training that you know your body responds to, but train your weaknesses too. That is, make sure you're working to improve abilities that need strengthening, not simply focusing on what you may be more at ease working on.

Rest more. Use recovery as part of training. Depending on your physiology, structure shorter, more intense sessions or blocks of training sessions followed by recovery periods. Find a group of riders a pinch better than you to train with occasionally.

To compete successfully in Expert races, you'll have to make a total physical commitment. And women, on top of all else, you have to think about the possibility of amenorrhea (the cessation of menstruation). At first this may seem like a desirable side-effect of intense riding and training, but it can lead to early osteoporosis. This is because as a woman becomes amenorrheic her estrogen level drops and restricts her ability to retain the calcium needed to maintain bone mass.

Most Pro/Elite off-road female racers who replied to an informal survey reported few problems with amenorrhea. Some have skipped one or two periods during the height of their racing season, but menses resumed when the stress was reduced. Temporary amenorrhea doesn't seem to be a major concern, but if you have prolonged problems of this type you should consult your physician.

Just because you're racing and training intensely, if you're not bleeding it's not automatically because you're not ovulating. Birth control may still be important. The risks and advantages in using hormonal therapy for amenorrhea, birth control pills, or non-hormonal birth control change with intense exercise. If you're concerned about symptoms or health implications of your lifestyle, consult a physician. Take the time to find a physician familiar with the circumstances of an intensely physical lifestyle, and who is supportive or at least open-minded about your desire to be athletic.

Discuss all the options, and be sure to be candid about your sexual activity and exercise.

Target your training

You should be getting to more races, but you also need to target specific events and develop travel priorities to realize your goals. By "targeting" races we mean identifying races in which you want to do especially well. Use other races as training for those personally important events.

In training races, do what it takes to stay with or follow the better riders, but don't put pressure on yourself to win. Use these events to learn, maybe risk blowing up just to see how hard you can go before you do. (If you try this, have arrangements made in advance to accommodate your post-ride condition, such as someone to drive you home.) Don't take Saturday off the day before a relatively shorter training race.

You can learn a great deal about your body and how it reacts to racing by wearing your heart rate monitor during training races.

> *I like to wear my heart monitor in the local Tuesday night races where there's nothing at stake. After the race I review the monitor's memory of my heart rate and compare it to my memory of what different sections felt like and how I did.*
> —Michael

If you discover you're the best rider at a training race, ride a tactically smart race within your limits until the appropriate time comes to make your move. Then make the move stick. Use the attack to build your confidence for your targeted event.

Whether training with slightly better racers or keeping up with someone during a training race, you need to be able to react instinctively to changing situations. Racers who play chess and are familiar with chess clocks can develop pattern recognition, split-second decision-making, and reaction capability by playing Blitz. This is a chess game in which players use a chess clock with two clock faces. Each clock is set for the number of minutes each player has to make all his moves. (Usually it's three minutes.) After making a move, the hand that moved the chess piece must be the hand that touches a button or switch that stops your countdown timer and starts your opponent's clock. When you run over your time, a flag drops, signifying checkmate.

Visualization exercises before a race and quickly seeing the correct line of travel during a race are two of the most important mental abilities for an expert racer to develop. Chess, which is all about visualization (seeing the line of play on the board), is perhaps the best mental exercise widely available that helps develop visualization and line recognition ability. Blitz, which incorporates intense time pressure, develops mental stamina for the stress of important or big-time events and split-second line recognition.

The key is to get into the game enough so that your competitive inclinations make it important for you to win. It's incredible how the pressure can build in your mind as you try to figure out what to do, quickly, while battling the clock as well as your opponent.

A chess set (and clock) travels easily. Having it along gives you one more option when you want to take it easy physically but still do something productive.

Travel tips

Traveling is one thing that can take a lot out of a racer. If nothing else, it deprives you of training time. Plan your travel so you're fresh for the target events. If you think you really need to ride the day you travel, it's usually better to get up early and put the cycling miles in before you drive or fly. That way, if anything delays your travel you've already gotten the riding in. If you can travel the day before a race, get there with enough daylight left to inspect the course with a moderately paced technical refresher.

> *When I'm driving to an event with a friend, quite often I'll head out early on the bike and have them pick me up along the way. One of my favorite options along these lines is a round of leap-frog in which one rides while the other goes ahead in the motor vehicle to a predetermined point. The driver then takes off on his bike, leaving the vehicle for the original rider to drive to the end of the second rider's training segment.*
>
> *If two or more are traveling through open country, we take turns driving while one of us rides. If the roads and location are appropriate, and you're practiced at it, these can also be times to motorpace.*—Michael

Staying on course

Don't get mesmerized by who's in front of you in a race. It's too easy to get off the course by following someone. You have to know how to race in strange territory and follow markers on your own, even though you may frequently discover that on the longer duration Expert courses, directions aren't always as well marked as they should be. Nevertheless, staying on-course is your responsibility. You have to stay alert and make sure you hear details at pre-race meetings, especially on how turns, downhills, and dangerous sections are marked.

The problem, of course, is that navigation is compounded by your exercise work load and race stress. When flying down the trail at 30 mph, you can miss a pair of ribbons all too easily. It's surprising how often this happens. That's why we're going to tell you about a martial arts exercise that increases peripheral vision. It's also good for seeing someone coming up on you when you can't hear them yelling "track" (or when they're not saying it).

After a stretching session, stand about 10 feet from a large wall in a relatively quiet place where you'll be uninterrupted. Wear sweats and sneakers or other loose, comfortable clothing (no cleated shoes). Stand with your feet parallel, just less than shoulder width (about pedal distance) apart.

Take a few deep breaths to relax. Exhale and lower your upper body slightly by bending your knees just enough to feel your back flatten out and your pelvis rotate down and forward a nudge, flattening the small of your back.

At the same time let your arms float up, elbows bent, similar to the position you use holding the bars. Keep your back and neck vertical, head level, shoulders down and relaxed, and fingers extended, but use a minimal amount of muscular energy to hold the position.

Maintaining this position and breathing fully but easily, relax your visual focus to use your passive vision. ("Active vision" is what we most often use, whereby we subconsciously or consciously focus on an object and then focus the remainder of our field of vision relative to that object.) The task is to look at the entire field of vision equally, without giving priority to any one thing. Gradually you'll become aware of an extended range of view.

Your mind's eye should circulate in the background, quietly

checking that each body joint is relaxed, open, and not using any more than essential effort to maintain the pose. (This same function should happen subconsciously, in the background, while you're racing.) Your mental voice should be still, not discussing today's ride, yesterday's ride, or what's for dinner, etc.

Begin with a three- to five-minute session. Sometimes people report feeling that their muscles are quivering, but when they check, nothing is moving externally. Should the quivering sensation get pronounced, finish the exercise. Walk around for a couple minutes afterward.

The exercise can be increased to 10 or 15 minutes per session. People have reported 30- to 60-degrees of improved peripheral vision subsequent to steady use of the exercise.

Pre-race routine

Set aside the two or three hours prior to your event for your standard pre-race routine. Eat your meal at least two hours before the start. Drink a bottle of water an hour ahead of the start. If you go for easy-to-digest racer bars, eat one with 40 minutes to go.

Ride rollers or spin in the vicinity of the race start for 15 minutes. Then do 10 or 15 minutes of stretches, wearing a training jacket if it's cool or a spare jersey in warm weather. Then ride some more in some bigger gears. Stand on the bike; then sit down again and spin for a few minutes. Break a sweat on your skin. Stretch on the bike, and then do some rapid pedal-speed sessions in various riding positions.

> *I usually go out for 45 to 90 minutes, starting very easy, stopping to do the stretches, and then continuing. Then 10 to 20 minutes of fairly hard riding. Then easy again for another 10 to 20.*—Martha

Change to your race jersey, double-check your bike, tool kit etc., relieve your bladder. (It's awful to race on a full bladder.) Stay covered enough to stay warmed up. If your system can handle it, drink a little more water.

Be finished with your routine 10 to 15 minutes before the start. You'll be well warmed up, so don't let it bother you if the start is delayed.

Do your pre-race procedure either by yourself or with friends with whom you can simultaneously relax and concentrate on your preparation. Stay away from the start/finish area until 10 minutes before the actual start.

At many events a women's Category and the next lower men's Category are on a course at the same time. Women, use the men as rabbits, with you as the greyhound. It makes for more exciting racing in both Categories.

At altitude

Most major national and international events are held at moderate or extremely high altitudes. If you plan to compete in a highly competitive event held in thin air, locate yourself at a similar altitude for 7 to 10 days, minimum, before the race. This is so that your blood cell count, which helps determine oxygen uptake ability, can adapt to the lower oxygen density of high altitude atmosphere.

In 1987 at the Bishop 7500 (named after the 7,500-foot climb in the first 26 miles) I found myself a little slow starting out. Midway up the climb I found myself a minute or so back, but as the climb got higher I got going, and at the summit I was two minutes up on an oxygen-starved John Tomac. I'd been living at 8,000-plus feet, whereas Tomac and many of the others were training at elevations below 5,000 feet. I was able to beat Joe Murray's King of the Mountain time by less than a minute, and lengthened my lead during the 20-mile descent to more than 4 minutes.

The flip side to that tale is that in 1989, following three months of racing and training in Europe at low elevations, I returned to the States for a few races. Two days after arriving at altitude I entered a local weekly mountain bike series. I had never been beaten in a local mountain bike race in Vail, CO, but things were about to change.

Two close friends and I took a quick lead. I decided to push the pace, and then as the climb continued, my now not-so-close friends decided to attack. This left me chasing and in oxygen debt. Although I was able to regain all but seven seconds by the finish, I was reminded of the effect racing at altitude can have on the unacclimated.—Michael

● ● Extreme Environments

Riding beyond the Horizon

A mountain bike makes getting into almost any version of extreme outdoor predicaments easier than ever before. So when going into any relatively remote and unusual situation, be it an ultra-distance race or an expedition (any tour in an area where you'll be out of touch with support services), you need to prepare your body and bike, carry a basic survival kit, and know a few survival skills.

A basic survival kit isn't hard to put together. It should include:

- a small folding knife
- waterproof matches or lighter
- a magnesium fire block
- iodine tablets
- a wire saw
- a strobe light or flare, and a hand signal mirror
- aspirin, antiseptic, and butterfly bandages
- a compass and map
- a candle
- coffee or tea, bouillon, and foil
- two high-calorie food bars
- a "space blanket" survival blanket
- a steel cup or small aluminum pan

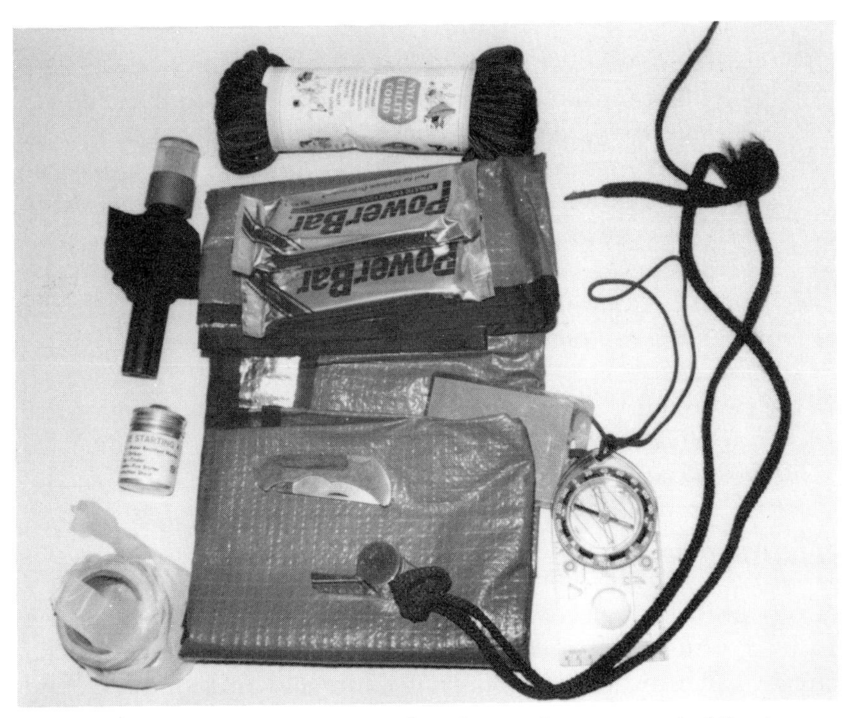

For extended trips and in bad weather the prudent mountain biker's survival kit might include a strobe light, nylon cord, two PowerBars, space blanket, fire starter with matches, fluorescent trail tape, pocket knife, whistle, compass, and mirror.

Despite the length of the list, such a kit barely takes any significant space out of a pannier bag or rack-top stuff sack.

> *Michael and others have been incredulous regarding the amount of stuff I sometimes carry on a ride—even though it's usually just my tool kit and the survival kit. 'No wonder you're so slow,' they say. But for five years when I lived on the northwest Oregon coast I would regularly go on three- to six-hour solo rides in the vast lumber company lands in the coast range. One winter day the maze of logging roads and mountain ridges and river valleys became just that. It was getting near dusk, my wool was damp with perspiration, and I had none of the above items (except an apparently outdated forestry map). The temperature was around 40 degrees and dropping.*
>
> *I took one last plunge into a watershed, figuring it either*

was the Lewis and Clark River down there, or I was in for a long night staving off hypothermia. Five minutes later I found the main spur along the river and began an 18-mile time trial home to beat total darkness. I was lucky that day, but the experience drove home the point that it only takes one mishap to create a personal tragedy.

Now, besides carrying all that stuff on long rides, I also make sure to leave a note at home stating explicitly where I'm going and my estimated arrival time back.—Yuri

Many community colleges offer courses that teach you how to use such a survival kit to make a bed or survival shelter, signal for assistance, or administer first aid.

Treating water

A very probable concern for the adventurous mountain biker is how to treat water. The days of drinking refreshing, cool mountain stream water are over. All untreated water should be considered contaminated. Giardia, salmonella, amoebic dysentery, and hepatitis are a few of the dangers you're likely to encounter in drinking raw water.

When beyond the range of potable water from home, you have three choices for treating your resupply: boiling, filtering, and chemical treatment.

When you're pressured for time, or just want to keep moving, mixing in the iodine treatment and continuing to ride is very handy. Otherwise, boiling is the most effective and least costly method to treat water. Here's how we arrived at that conclusion.

Boiling has strong advantages. It's effective and costs little. You need only to bring the water to a rolling boil, unless you're at high altitude, when longer boiling times are required. The disadvantages are the time it takes, and, in warm weather, the fact that you end up with hot water.

Filtering varies in effectiveness according to the system used. Anything other than a relatively expensive Katadyn porcelain filter should be used with caution. One-quart treatments are fairly quick, but volume water treatment with a Katadyn is laborious.

Chemical treatment can be effective. Chlorine treatment has been replaced by iodine products because of their ease of use, lower cost, and longer shelf life. Of the iodine methods available, tincture of iodine, in a 2% or 7% solution seems the most viable. It can handle large volumes, is easy to use, and has a reasonable shelf life.

To use tincture of iodine, get a bulk bottle (2% or 7%) from a pharmacy, along with a nose-drop bottle and dropper. Using the eyedropper, add iodine to each liter of water (2 drops of 7%, or 7 drops of 2% solution). Wait a half-hour before drinking. If the water is exceptionally cold or dirty, either add additional iodine or wait longer before using the water. (Be sure to clean the water bottle cap and lip to make sure they're not contaminated.)

Iodine has one disadvantage—its taste. This can be overcome with a few drops of lemon juice or some powdered fruit-drink mix.

Climate factors

Both hot and cold climates increase your water needs. Most people realize that in hot weather you're going to need to consume more water because your engine's running hotter than usual. Riding a bike can be deceptive because of the cooling effect of airflow, but the need for hydration is real. But many people don't realize the extraordinary water demands of cold-weather climates, where your engine is effectively running harder simply to maintain body warmth.

In both situations, you have to be prepared to handle larger volumes of water. Prepare your bladder by slowly increasing your daily water consumption during the months before your expedition. By the time you're out there, your bladder shouldn't have to relieve itself too frequently.

Temperature extremes also affect your aerobic ability, so be prepared for lowered aerobic performance. The performance ceiling on hot-weather athleticism is a lot lower than for cold weather. Your ability to function aerobically comes to an abrupt end at anything more than 100 degrees Fahrenheit. Then you easily risk heat exhaustion or stroke. At the cold end you can function athletically to very frigid temperatures—around minus 30.

Acclimating

It takes at least a week to adapt to temperatures significantly hotter (15 degrees or more) than those you're used to. If you're going to be riding in a hotter climate, cut back activity to 50% of norm the first day or two you're there, then increase the work load (duration or intensity) 5–10% per day.

Be sure to wear loose, well-ventilated clothing that also protects you from the sun. The shaded air between your skin and the hot exterior actually amounts to an insulating microclimate.

Exercise physiologist Brian Sharkey, author of *Physiology of Fitness* and consultant to the U.S. Forest Service for firefighter training, suggests that taking 250 milligrams of Vitamin C a day helps you acclimate to a hot climate.

Whereas hot weather drains your energy, very cold weather impairs your energy production. According to Defense Department studies, at 0 degrees Fahrenheit, your aerobic capacity decreases 33% from what it is at 60 degrees.

Layering of clothing becomes critical. Weather may change. Your insulating requirements will quickly jump when you take a break from intense activity like mountain biking. Staying dry, mostly by dealing with perspiration, is a constant concern. Overdress and you'll overheat, not only accelerating dehydration, but soaking your clothes with moisture that will chill you as soon as you pause. A synthetic super-wick foundation layer followed by wool and then by a breathable shell garment has proven the best system.

You have to be especially careful of your extremities. The human body seems willing to sacrifice fingers and toes for the survival of the animal. Double the insulation over your boots and quadruple the insulation over your toe box. Insulated hand and forearm covers that fasten around the handlebar grips and controls have proven worthwhile. Men should consider wearing a wind brief.

As for your bike, standard grease turns to paste in very cold temperatures. Thinning grease with Triflow and repacking bearings for below-zero riding can help. Coating your chain with a slick surface agent can retard icing, and rubbing alcohol carried in a small squeeze bottle makes a good emergency de-icer. Lowering tire air pressure to below 30 pounds can improve traction but causes tire migration on the rim. As this can end up shearing the valve stem, you may want to glue your tires and rims.

If ice is a concern, you can stud your tires with 3/8-inch × 8 or 1/2-inch × 8 Phillips pan-head sheet-metal screws. Use tires that have large tread blocks (Standard Fat Tracks, Racer X-1, Hi-Lite Hots, and Motivators are good candidates) and drive the screws from the inside. Line the tire with a tire liner, such as Mr. Tuffy.

Because there's less weight on the front tire, and it turns and leans more, the most important placement is a line of screws on either tire edge, where they'll assist in cornering and straight-line riding. Slightly better traction can be had by running a single or narrow pair of lines on the middle of the tread as well. For more consistent grip, the center line of screws should be on alternate rows of knobs from the outer lines (forming form a chevron pattern).

If all you need is a little more traction and control, you can sometimes get away with a single line of screws down the middle of the rear tire. Your weight compresses the rear tire a bit more than the front, ensuring more center-strip contact.

As always when making any significant alteration with your bike, practice riding and stopping on the studded tires in a safe spot—the bike's braking and handling characteristics will be altered dramatically.

At altitude

When at altitude (above 5,000 feet), take more time to warm up, spend more time cooling down, and remember to drink more: higher altitudes tend to be drier.

If you plan to go to high altitude, try to do intervals below 8,000 feet and endurance work above 9,000 feet to stimulate red blood cell production and acclimate your cardiovascular system to the thin air. Also, doing anaerobic work at lower altitudes increases lactate tolerance and builds fiber strength.

If you get hooked on riding in thin air, you might be interested in Mountain Baggers, a registry for mountain bikers who've reached the top of exceptionally high land forms. To qualify you need to have made 75% of the ascent on your bike, and completed the final 100 meters riding your bike. For information, contact Mountain Baggers of the World, P.O. Box 554, Stillwater, British Columbia V0E 1N0, Canada.

Night riding

If you're enthusiastic about these rather out-there mountain bike pursuits, there's a good possibility you'd like night riding.

Lightweight, long-lasting rechargeable illumination now makes it possible for mountain bikers to ride year-round. Night riding is great for improving your reflexes, and it teaches you new body-

English techniques (like bending sideways instead of just forward to duck below a tree branch). Riding in groups is highly recommended. When planning night rides, count on averaging a quarter to a third slower speed than on daylight rides.

Equipment should include first-aid and emergency survival kits, a handlebar bell for communicating location (it's much nicer than yelling intermittently), clear eyeshields (branches surprise everyone at some time), and heavier long-sleeved protection and shin protection than you'd use for the same weather in daylight (same reason as the eyewear).

Lighting systems are available either for helmet mounting or handlebar mounting. See the chapter on tools for more on lighting.

Expeditions

Getting extremely far from home on a mountain bike is one of the greatest adventures a rider can have. The mechanical advantages and load-carrying capacity of a mountain bike allow you to carry genuine home-cooking provisions and real food while on extended camping and backcountry touring trips.

The basic equipment requirements are strong, multipoint-mounting racks and pannier bags made for off-road touring. The best racks are made of tubular chrome-moly steel, although TIG welded aluminum will work. Some people prefer higher-riding front racks for ground obstacle clearance, while others like the lower

One of the rewards of a mountain bike expedition is the satisfaction of being a self-sufficient traveler.

center of gravity of low riders and the protection lower bags give the front spokes. Think about your needs and what you're likely to encounter on your trips. Whichever you choose, you'll still be traveling at immensely greater ease than riders did just three generations ago.

Compartmentalize your packing by putting the different types of clothes and belongings in stuff sacks that then load into your panniers. (This will help keep things clean and dry as well as make getting them in and out easier.) Place the denser objects at the bottom and on the inner side of the panniers.

It also helps to keep your food pantry in one bag, stoves and equipment in another, clothing and toiletries in others. Distribute the weight approximately 40% front, 60% rear.

Of course you want to go someplace inspiring, but check to verify that the terrain is within your ability. Compare your planned expedition routes with your regular rides by comparing topographical maps of the same scale. Also, check for probable weather patterns, available resources, and camping sites at likely daily stopping points. Set slightly lower-than-challenging daily mileage averages and you're apt to have more fun. You can always go off for some extra riding after setting up camp, but you'll spoil things with disappointment, or worse, if your estimated campsites are out of reach each day.

> *Weight watching can get back at you. On one trip Sally and I discovered we could make our sleeping quarters either bug-proof or rainproof, but not both. We got by, but only after a couple of exasperating nights.*—Yuri

Practice getting along with a smaller amount of gear and you'll find gram counting won't be necessary. You really don't need to replace everything in your closet with the latest and lightest hi-tech wonder. You can keep things simple, as well as light, by just reducing duplication, making better use of each item. And that way your back-country expedition remains a journey into the natural world instead of a retreat to commune with your equipment.

In this regard, read all the old adventure books you can get your hands on. The low-tech possibilities and personal resourcefulness that previous generations got high on are inspiring in our age of gadgetry.

• • Map Reading and Orienteering

Getting Around without Street Signs

A U.S. Geological Survey topographic map, along with a county or state forestry service or National Forest Service map can tell you just about all you need to know about going anywhere on your mountain bike. But first you have to understand a little about the standards of mapping.

USGS "topos" illustrate the terrain features—elevation changes being the most crucial—but they also color-key ground cover and watersheds. They'll also note landmarks, such as radio towers, service buildings, mines, and ruins. Once you get a grip on the language, a topo map will spare you from too many adventuresome surprises.

Unfortunately, many sectors of the nation haven't been updated recently, and for that reason it behooves a mountain biker to ask around and find out which public land agency publishes the most current map. It may be the state forestry service, the Bureau of Land Management, or the county. These agency maps will often give you more accurate road and trail information than some USGS quadrants (maps).

The National Forest Service publishes maps of each of their units that can be had for about $1 from any ranger station. The maps cover large areas, color-code land according to whose jurisdiction it is (USFS, BLM, State, Indian), and often show more current roads and trails than the USGS. Forest Service roads by the way, are numbered, which makes route-finding easier if you can locate the markers.

There are also private maps published by regional companies that sometimes work as well as any government agency map, and some active mountain bike shops put together their own maps. Some newly published maps are printed on weather-resistant stock and fold to bike-jersey-pocket size.

Reading contour lines takes some getting used to. Because you're often apt to be checking your map when you're dazed from hard riding, begin now by drilling into your memory that the closer the contour lines are, the steeper the slope is. Next, practice thinking about how a road or trail line would appear on a topo map. Use your imagination to envision a relatively level road that slowly descends into a valley. On a topo map the road will run in the same direction as the contours then cut across them at acute angles. The more steeply the road climbs or descends, the more perpendicular it is to the contour lines.

Route planning

Planning your ride benefits greatly from a home library of USGS maps and recent road maps. The USGS topos come in different scales, the most common two scales being 15- and 7.5-minute maps. (A minute is one 60th of a degree of latitude or longitude.) This is how they compare:

- 7.5 minutes = scale of 1:24000 (1″ = 2,000 feet); covers approximately 6.5 × 8.5 miles
- 15 minutes = scale of 1:62500 (1″ = 4,000 feet); covers approximately 13.5 × 17.5 miles

The two sizes of USGS maps are helpful whether used on their own or integrated into a comprehensive home library of trail information. The 7.5-minute maps are significantly more detailed, but are a difficult size to work with on the bike, so they're for home reference.

Maps are available at U.S. Forest Service headquarters, local ranger stations, and regional USGS Public Inquiry Offices. Some cities have bookstores or travel stores that specialize in maps, but they will probably charge a dollar more per map than government agencies.

Martha likes to copy detail notes and cues from the 7.5 map directly onto the 15-minute map and take that into the field. Yuri makes photocopies of the state forestry map, copies notes onto that, and takes the forest service photocopy and the 15-minute map in a zip-lock plastic food bag, with a cardboard stiffener in between them. Michael highlights routes on whichever USGS quadrant he has and stuffs that in his pocket.

All of us have built up a collection of both 7.5- and 15-minute topos for the area roughly 30–40 miles from our homes. Martha has a full map wall in one room, which holds nine 7.5-minute maps, margins trimmed and tacked together to form one huge area map for easy planning of the week's rides. New routes get highlighted as they are explored. It's become a game with her to see how many can be marked.

Annotate any corrections to an area as soon as you return from a ride. It'll help you remember what an area is really like, and after a while, build a reference so that when you take a new route someday, you'll be able to reasonably guesstimate what it's like, based on your experience and what's on the maps.

Planning with maps can be a pleasant diversion on cold, rainy, or slushy winter days when you're itching to get out on the bike. Spend some time planning a completely new route; then get on your wind trainer or rollers using your expectations of the new ride for imagery. For that matter, you can go over favorite routes on the maps and then ride the stationary trainer to your memory of them.

Orienteering

"Orienteering" is the term for using topo maps and a compass to find your way around in the field. In a maze of logging roads or trails or monotonously similar rugged terrain, orienteering can be your only hope for finding your way quickly.

The basic method is to look at the topo map while holding it so that it aligns with the land, using any nearby landmarks to help you rotate the map to its correct position. If physical landmarks aren't obvious enough for you to do this, then use a compass to align the map. Put the compass on the map and rotate the map until its north-south magnetic lines parallel the north-south lines scribed on the compass. Now you're set to go, using terrain features as guides.

If you're still disoriented, you need to "take a bearing" or "shoot an azimuth," to use navigational jargon, using the orienteering arrow on your compass. Here's how:

- Line up the side edge of the compass base on the map so it connects where you are with where you want to go, with the arrow on the plastic base pointing toward your destination.
- Turn the round housing so that the inscribed lines inside the round part of the compass parallel the map's north-south lines, the inscribed arrow pointing to north on the map.
- Next, hold the compass level at waist height with the destination arrow pointing straight forward. (Make sure you don't move the compass housing.)
- Pivot on your feet until the red end of the compass needle lines up with the orienteering arrow of the compass.

You should now be facing the direction you want to go, with the destination arrow on the compass base pointing the same way you're facing.

If you ever want to recheck, hold the compass as you just have and rotate your body until the red magnetic needle point lines up with the orienteering arrow.

The front edge of the compass base makes a handy tool for estimating distance. If it doesn't already have a scale inscribed on it, place some white cloth tape or masking tape along the front edge of the clear base and transcribe the map scale to the tape before leaving home. Then when checking your bearings, you can use the scale to estimate distances. When you're riding across unmarked territory, "declination" becomes important. Declination refers to the deviation between true north and magnetic north, and it varies according to where you are. All USGS maps give declination information in the map border.

Nothing makes using a map and compass more user-friendly than making a sport of it, and orienteering has been established as an outdoor competitive sport for runners and cross-country skiers for years. It's a natural for mountain bike club challenge rides, too.

There's an orienteering time trial event at the Chequamegan Fat Tire Festival held each fall in Cable, WI. You're given a map at the start line; then you're sent off with 8–12 target checkpoints to find. It's a great contest between "rabbits" and "tortoises," as faster riders tend to miss turns on the fly, while slower but more skilled orienteering mountain bikers make systematic progress without a hitch.

To set up a course, pick a series of "control points" or targets. The targets make a course loop, and everyone participating has to make it through all the points and back to the finish.

You can verify that competitors actually reached all the checkpoints by hanging different styles of paper punches at each location with which participants punch an index card. Or have a volunteer dispense buttons, dried beans, or other colored bits into a 35-mm film canister that each entrant carries on his or her bike. The winner is the first person to complete the course and return with all the punches or tokens from the targets.

The targets don't have to be in a loop. In fact, it's more of a challenge if each target has several approaches of differing technical difficulty.

Orienteering instructional aids are available from American Orienteering Service, P.O. Box 547, LaPorte, IN 46350.

The administrative organization for the sport of orienteering in the U.S. is the U.S. Orienteering Federation, P.O. Box 1444, Forest Park, GA 30051.

• • Family Fun

Making Fat Tracks with Rug Rats

"Ah, you're finally going to have to settle down." Such are often the sentiments of relatives when a couple starts having kids. But whatever "settling down" might mean, it doesn't have to mean forsaking mountain biking.

Yuri and Sally just added the Family Hike 'n Bike to their repertoire of recreational outings. For these, their first daughter, Roxanne, got to sit in an infant carrier—beginning with a cloth, frontal-positioning type, and later the pack-frame type with a hip belt.

For Hike 'n Bikes, Yuri and Sally take the shortest of their mountain bikes, which has a long enough seat post to accommodate Yuri's leg length. Picnic lunches, bottles, diaper changes, and sometimes the dog come along as well. Then the two adults take turns—one riding the bike and the other carrying the infant. Never ride a bike with your child on your back in a carrier.

Having noticed that Hike 'n Bikes are excellent opportunities to practice slow-speed technical riding, Yuri and Sally began taking them on more rugged trails. Soon enough the bike rider was the one being left behind in many stretches, as he or she worked and reworked difficult sections.

The advantages to Family Hike 'n Bikes are that the family gets an outdoors outing together, both adults get to ride the bike that day, and the child gets to see both parents mountain biking and so gets a better understanding of what a parent is doing when he or she leaves home to ride without the family.

It's also a terrific method for encountering hikers on joint-usage trails in a context that builds positive relations. Speed isn't an objective, so there's little risk of negative surprise encounters. And the hiking parent often gets to tell hikers that "my spouse is coming along on a mountain bike." Yuri says he hasn't yet had a negative encounter with hikers on a Hike 'n Bike.

The Hike 'n Bikes have continued, even with two little girls now in the family (the elder child walks), as has another family-way training method: Trailer Training. Hauling your children around in a bike trailer is a terrific strength-training device due to increased air resistance and the weight of trailer and child. You'll usually have to drop down a gear or two to maintain the same cadence on the same roads you travel solo. Once you're used to it and warmed up, you can do some quality intervals by maintaining the same gearing and cadence you normally would without the extra load. (We're talking paved roads or relatively smooth dirt roads here—most child trailers don't have clearance for rough dirt roads, and none of them can take single tracks without tipping.)

Depending upon where you live, the training or exercise options with a tight family schedule can be relieved with a trailer. If you have a good napper like Yuri and Sally's Roxanne was, the long weekend aerobic training ride (two to three hours) can be undertaken during the child's afternoon nap.

And whereas some parents take emergency car drives to help put kids to sleep, Yuri's taken plenty of bike rides with the trailer and gotten some cycling out of it as well. With two children, turning afternoon naps into long training rides isn't as easy, but it can happen.

Shorter Trailer Training rides sometimes mean the difference between riding or not riding at all. They can be done prior to or following a wind-trainer session or a short unhitched ride for longer training benefit.

It helps to pick routes that feature something for the kids. Passing water fountains that seem gigantic to the trailer passengers is always a hit, as are rides past pastures with cows or horses, or even a brief destination stop with something for them—a playground area where you stretch while watching them, or a cafe with appropriate treats for each age group.

The options for family fat tire fun seem as endless as a parent's flexibility—the bike certainly accommodates anything, including family camping, mountain bike style. As mentioned, conventional child trailers can negotiate smooth dirt roads, and in many parks and National Forests, that's what you find leading to campgrounds.

Older kids love few things more than being able to ride their own bike on a camping trip. Of course the parent carries the gear, but you also have a lot more gear options than the children do. Child-scale multi-gear mountain bikes are now standard in many bicycle company product lines, but a 20-inch BMX bike is also easily modified to a 5- or 6-speed trail bike.

And if you can go on camping expeditions together, you can take day rides together. For both, rides have to be selected according to the child's strength, endurance, and riding abilities. Children tend to go in spurts, too, instead of maintaining a steady pace, and they'll need front and rear adult escorts riding "point" and "sweeping" the trail, both for riders and litter.

Finally, parents can get their exercise in on weekdays by using their mountain bike for commuting, even if commuting involves dropping the kids off at daycare. The latter means having a trailer with a weatherproof top. To handle riding on pavement, you can simply pump your tires up to road pressure, but a better option is to get a second pair of wheels with street "slick" tires. (That way you can easily switch to knobby tires for weekend rides.) The street slicks hold more air pressure and roll along quicker than knobbies, and stop quicker than the off-road designs do.

If you're always changing back and forth between knobbies and slicks, your tire sidewalls will wear more quickly from constantly being taken on and off the rims. But if you have the spare wheels, you can even have a rear cog cluster for commuting and another for off-road. The only trick is to make sure you have the same rims on both sets of wheels so your brakes work equally well with both.

Having Mom and Pop split up the daycare and preschool busing also adds workout options. If your child's facility has a secure place to lock the trailer, then you can divide drop-off and pick-up duties according to whose work schedule best accommodates which run. Splitting the towing gives each parent a share of strength-building, loaded-trailer pumping. At the same time you get to keep the money-guzzling motor vehicle at home, and make the house look like someone's home all day.

Whoever doesn't have the trailer can leave for work a little early or ride a little longer afterward to turn an everyday commute into a scheduled workout. Maybe do hillclimb repeats to work off some job-related frustration, or sprint home and see if you get there quick enough to have dinner ready by the time the covered-wagon contingent arrives.

In other words, far from being another fun activity that gets restricted by having children, mountain biking and family life can be combined into a recreational lifestyle that involves everyone, isn't horribly expensive, and doesn't waste the planet your kids will inherit.

• • Mountain Bike Polo

To Some It's Just Horsing Around

"Have fun! If you're not having fun, you're dangerous!"

How can you not be interested in a game with that No. 1 rule and that's played on mountain bikes?

Traditional horse polo, the oldest recorded team sport in western civilization, "The Game of Kings," is only slightly less expensive than training for the America's Cup, and about as staid. But by substituting mountain bikes and fat tire biking's off-the-wall ethos, mad-hatter mountain bikers have come up with one of the more comically entertaining enterprises invented by American baby boomers.

Bicycle polo has been tried before—early in this century, primarily in the United Kingdom. But it never really caught on. Whether mountain bike polo does we'll have to see, but Americans have historically been intrigued by any sport that involves a hitting implement and a ball, and this seems no exception.

The game is played by two teams of four riders on a playing field approximately 160 feet long. It's divided into 10-minute periods known as "chukkars." The objective is to score goals by hitting the ball through a 10-foot-wide goal at either end.

At the start of each chukkar one player from each team rides from the goal line (where the rest of the team waits) toward the center of the field to "joust" the ball. The players from both teams then pour onto the field and soon the prevalent sound is that of laughter, accented by clicking of mallet and ball.

Contemporary mountain bike polo started in 1981 when Lou Gonzalez and Trice Hufnagel were in Crested Butte, CO, for the Fourth of July. Lou and Trice were playing croquet with their hosts after mountain biking. The lightning bolt of inspiration struck, and that September they debuted Mountain Bike Polo at the Fat Tire Bike Week Festival in Crested Butte. The first stand-alone mountain bike polo tournament happened in Boulder, CO, in July of 1988, and local league play has been sprouting up all over ever since.

Devotees of polo point out that you don't have to be in great shape to play, because much of the play is at low speed, involving maneuvering for the ball. At the same time, adherents claim, the game helps you develop an ease in riding close to others, an explosive sprint, a safe falling technique, high- and low-speed turning skills, and the ability to feather your front brake.

The rules, which seem designed mostly to protect the players, are easy to learn. For example, play on the ball can only happen from riders moving up and down the field, and a rider playing the ball has a seven-yard right of way in front of him or her. That, and the use of

Mountain bike polo brings the fun of bike handling to urban and suburban settings in a low-impact, safe context.

a hollow wiffle-type ball eliminates much of the injury potential. And by mandating that each team must have a bi-gender squad on the field at all times, the World Bicycle Polo Federation adds a dash of contemporary egalitarianism to the sport.

There's also plenty of excitement when opponents approach the ball in a joust, when a player attempts a dribbling advance, and when teammates make synchronized soccerlike passes down the field.

Although any mountain bike can be used, many polo players recommend that people use their No. 2 bike or a less-expensive set of wheels. Smaller-diameter tires are the rule, for quick accelerating and minimal field impact. (The Know Fun Club, official suppliers and coordinators of the sport, say they can supply references from institutional groundskeepers testifying to low or nonexistent field damage from the game.)

Players have also developed opinions regarding whether to use standard mountain bike gearing and brakes or fixed-gear track-style fat tire bikes. Fixed-gear advocates like the maneuverability and control, while others prefer the braking ability of a standard bike. The preference in fixed-gear models is for a 47-inch fixed gear, either a 40 × 22, or 28 × 15 combination.

Either way, all you need is a bike, a helmet, and an inclination toward fun, but eyewear and kneepads (to protect against stem/knee hits) are also recommended. But before you get enchanted with this latest twist of fat tire fun, be forewarned: participants' bikes have been known to sprout streamers, Sesame Street Honker Horns, spokey-dokeys, and bizarre paint jobs.

To find out if mountain bike polo exists in your town, call the local mountain bike shops, which often buy a league set of mallets for a local club to use in matches. If that doesn't turn up anything, and the local mountain bike club provides no leads, contact the Know Fun Club, P.O. Box 1039, Bailey, CO 80421, 303–892–8801.

They're also the home of the World Bicycle Polo Federation, the sanctioning organization for tournaments and the publishers of *Chukkar Times*, the sport's official newsletter.

• • Wildlife

Snuggling Up to Nature on a Mountain Bike

The thin crust of three or four inches of snow that had fallen a couple days ago gave off a continuous crackle and crunch as my Fattrax tires writhed forward on the six-mile ascent of Davis Point. A constant westerly breeze blew perpendicular to my line of travel up the relatively straight logging road, but the low, straw-yellow winter light kept me warm.

Three deer had spooked at my approach a half-mile below, but now the enormous form of a majestic North American bull elk appeared before me, completely unconcerned. Tail to me, the elk grazed on the left edge of the roadbed, ignorant of my awe-struck observation 20 yards downhill. The wind apparently kept my scent from reaching him and the sound of my tires had failed to cause alarm. I straddled the bike, watching the largest elk I'd ever seen, and I began to chill as my body temperature dropped.

So I clicked my brake levers to get his attention. He seemed puzzled by the mountain bike centaur. I managed a double count of his incredible rack (seven and six) before he figured out what I was. Of course I didn't have a camera.—Yuri

Whether your passion is to record critters and fauna on film, fill a fishing creel, bag a bighorn, or simply see more species with the naked eye, your mountain bike can be a vehicle to greatly expanded encounters with wildlife.

This is especially true out west, where automobile road closure commonly controls access to an interesting biological range or choice mountain lake. With a mechanical advantage greater than you'd find on a horse (but not requiring feed and water), a mountain bike eases the initial entry to rugged territory. With the addition of a trailer you have a rig fully capable of hauling all your gear, or, in the case of hunting, taking home the steak. And since there's so much less contact between your body and the ground, a biker leaves less scent along a trail.

The hunter's bike

Standard mountain bike accessories are easily modified for hunting. Bows, quivers, and arrows can be carried slung across the back, sideways across a rear rack, or mounted on handlebars. Rubber-coated bolt-on racks available for motorized all-terrain vehicles work well enough, but with a couple evenings' time a bow hunter can craft a custom rack system out of aluminum rod and inner-tube rubber. The rod is easily bent to clamp around the handlebar and stem, away and back from the seat post, or on a rear rack. Some riders prefer to carry things sideways, while others like designs that

The quietness, low impact, and high mechanical advantage of a mountain bike make it ideal for accessing isolated animal ranges.

hold objects like bows and arrows vertically along the side of rear rack struts. It's just a matter of what you're comfortable with.

Gun hunters don't have as many options. A fine rifle and scope can be carried safely if securely lashed to a loaded trailer. The slower pace and the padding afforded by clothes, tent, and sleeping bag will protect your prize hunting rig. But when actually hunting on a bike, carrying your rifle off your shoulder or across the back seem the only reasonable options. It's also the only place that allows the quick access you'll want.

A back rack can be fashioned from half-inch white plastic plumbing tubing that's light, quiet, and keeps the knob of the action out of your shoulder blades. A front-hanging shoulder sling is preferred by some for granny-gear stalking times. Long-barreled-pistol hunters can strap their holster to the bike's top tube just behind the head tube. (This is also an excellent place to holster emergency magnums in grizzly country.) The challenge and reward of mountain bike hunting then becomes one of riding as close up as you dare before taking your shot.

Much of a mountain bike's advantage becomes evident after a successful hunt. Too often it's an early evening kill, and instead of being able to relax and savor the accomplishment, you have to work hard to beat the sunset, most likely on an empty stomach. A mountain bike can make transporting average large game such as deer a much more manageable chore and reduce elk hauling from four trips to two. Aluminum poles can be lashed across handlebars, between two bikes, or paired to make a travois behind your mechanical steed. For those wishing to go first class, Glacier Cyclery in Whitefish, MT, is experienced in helping mountain bike hunters outfit their rigs.

Carrying gear

Fisherman and birders have the easiest time carrying gear. Sectional rods are easily carried on a rear rack, and panniers are easily modified to carry creels or gear bags. A fishing vest is often just the right amount of clothing on pleasantly cool days, although we'd hate to take a header with a chest pad full of flies.

The optics that are the essential tools of birders can be padded and carried on handlebars, rear rack, or cinched to the rider's torso.

Packing equipment for outdoor photography is a bit more complicated. A rider's body is the best place to carry such sensitive mechanisms because it's most protected from shocks. The easiest thing to carry is one of the small, point-and-shoot 35-mm cameras. A urethane-foam sleeve provides extra protection and hardly adds any bulk or weight. The package easily fits into rear jersey pocket or fanny pack.

Those with ambitions involving single-lens-reflex cameras and extra lenses can carry a camera, two lenses, and a flash in a variety of bags. There are a couple camera-dedicated fanny packs available. Their only disadvantage seems to be the weighted feeling that grips at your waist at the end of a long ride and the perspiration that builds up between the pack and your body.

A number of companies market a roughly Y-shaped camera bag that will hold a body and long telephoto or a body and two shorter lenses. Usually there's a film pouch on the inside of the top flap, and a small outer pocket for filters, lens cleaner, or a small flash. These will work fine if, in addition to its shoulder strap, you rig a waist-wrapping or belt-loop strap to hold the bag in a comfortable spot. Otherwise the bag shifts while riding, dropping to an awkward spot that interferes with pedaling uphill.

Of the non-camera-dedicated packs, the Overland Lassen fanny pack works best. Really more of a lumbar-region pack than a fanny pack, the weight of your gear is held closer in and more precisely cinched by a myriad of straps. Its Achilles heel is the extra-wide belt—you may want to replace it with a narrower one to avoid accidental unbuckling while you ride.

With any of these arrangements, urethane sleeves or bubble packing held with rubber bands helps to protect your gear, but just wrapping them in your spare long-sleeved T-shirt will help a lot.

The other nemeses of photo gear are dirt and moisture. Both are defeated with zip-lock bags around each individual unit, although these hamper quick-draw shooting. Conscientious cleaning of everything after each ride is a must.

The strongest of tripods can be managed on a four-bolt rear rack. Even a simple blind or collapsing reflectors can be mounted to the rack as well.

But you don't need to haul 20 pounds of accouterments for sharp photos. Gel-filled saddles make excellent telephoto lens rests, as does the mountain bike frame with a shirt or jersey acting as a pillow between the lens and bike.

• • Dogs and Bikes

Canine Company Can Be Fun

As most cyclists know, dogs have held one of the all-time longest grudges against man for inventing the bicycle. This occurred after canines had been *Homo sapiens'* best friend for centuries, accompanying him in work, at play, and even at war. Suddenly, man got obsessed with tinker technology and abandoned the loyalty and companionship of another living animal for a machine. Who wouldn't feel slighted?

But finally, more than a hundred years later, a lot of mountain bikers are mending relations with their favorite mutt. Many are simply introducing their dog to the joys of cycle-paced running. Dog sledders are running up to six dogs on leads in front of their mountain bikes for summer training, and others are fashioning a new hybrid sport similar to the cross-country ski-and-dog activity known as Skijoring.

Many begin such activities when they realize that because they're off the streets now, they don't automatically need to leave the pooch whining at home. If you honestly enjoy outings with your dog, give this a shot, but remember to follow a few exercise and trail-use guidelines.

If Fido hasn't been running a lot lately, you'll have to ease him in to cycle-running. Dogs bonk just like people and can overheat a lot sooner in warm weather. (And there's nothing more fun than attempting to carry home a 50-pound best friend whose legs have gone out.)

Think about your dog's genetic strengths and weaknesses—every breed has its limitations. Martha's Staffordshire Terrier is so much stouter than her pitbull-terrier mix, he just can't handle the longer-legged half-breed's quicker pace. Tailor your rides to the breed and conditioning of your dog, or buy a dog whose genetic ability matches your riding aspirations.

Think about where you're going to go with your dog. Rock or gravel can be great fun to ride on, but merciless on your dog's paw pads. Desert is beautiful but cacti are sharp, and pulling needles out is no fun.

Remember that you're out there for a good time for you and your dog as well as for some training for both of you. It's okay to stop and enjoy the scenery and let your dog enjoy a stop as well. If your dog voids his bowels, either clean it up in a plastic bag or bury it, depending upon whether you're in a park or suburban setting or out in the boonies.

Plan ahead about water. If there aren't any streams available, you're going to need to carry water bottles for the pooch, too. Dogs catch on pretty quickly to bottle feeding once they realize there's water inside. Resist the temptation to get playful by squirting the water. It could backfire with some dogs, turning into a discipline-breaking game and just waste vital water.

If you've been out long enough to get thirsty, your dog probably is, too. A canine cookie is a fine behavior reward and induces some dogs to take needed drinks they might otherwise neglect in their excitement.

Make sure that dogs are allowed where you're planning to ride. In many places where mountain bikes are welcome, dogs are only allowed on leashes, or only at the trail head.

This brings up whether to run the dogs on a leash or on voice command. Whichever method you use, your dog needs to have been successfully schooled with obedience lessons. Without them, on-leash there will be a lot of frustration as he zigs when you zag, as the leash gets tangled in legs, wheels, etc., or when he surges ahead just as you slow for a technical section. Off-leash, the troubles can be a nightmare, ranging from dog fights to cattle-chasing to hunting-season mishaps.

Dogs that complete off-leash obedience training successfully will most likely train easily to mountain bike running. It depends somewhat upon the strength of the hunting instinct in your breed of dog, but your increased speed and mobility will probably make the dog pay closer attention to heeling. Even among dogs who easily stay with a master, some don't take to following the bike (which is preferable). They like to "race" at your side, especially down every hill. Martha's terrier mix was like that.

> *I taught her to watch out by yelling 'Watch out!' and then running into her with the bike with a controlled hit, more like a bump. A few of those and she jumped at the new command.*—Martha

There's really nothing new about on-leash running. Such roadwork for dogs is an established training and exercise routine with many dog breeders. The benefits to a dog include muscle conditioning (especially for bitches who have recently delivered a litter), ligament tightening, and lessening of hyper-active behavior and stress symptoms.

On-leash

If you decide to ride and run your dog on-leash, there are a few considerations that don't come into play as acutely as when off-leash. Pacing is critical. Never allow a race to develop, at least for any length of time—the dog gets too excited over the competition and tends to forget commands. Racing also drains the dog's reserves so that you find yourself with a pooped pooch. Training the dog to pace correctly is much like walking heeling in obedience class. Forging is corrected by sudden stops or the "watch out" command.

Yuri has a Norwegian Elkhound, who is great on endurance, but who begins with enthusiasm and is too easily overexcited. He also tends to forget about pacing if he hasn't been run regularly and so needs to be retaught pacing frequently.

> *Using the computer on my bike, it's easy to find the pace that my dog is most capable of maintaining and the sort of sprints he can recover from easily. Knowing that and how much exer-*

> *cise Poudre's been getting recently, I know when he may be getting winded or tired and when he's just trying to get me to stop so he can sniff around.*—Yuri

Just as you never want the dog to be out ahead of you, don't run the dog down to where you're dragging him or he's truly lagging out of exhaustion. Such action on-leash constitutes cruelty to animals.

> *I've found medium to wide handlebars give better leash control than narrower models, although narrower bars work well enough with fore/aft handlebar add-ons. For everyday runs, I use a standard, six-foot lead with strong joint construction. I hang the leash loop on the forward pointing add-on, coil it around the left grip, then coil it once or twice around my left hand, with some slack between the hand and the grip-coiled part. This allows me to control the heeling range, grip the handlebar, and work the brake.*—Yuri

Since obedience-trained dogs are trained to heel on the left side, keep the same order when you ride. When approaching people from the other direction, take the left side of the trail well in advance so as to put you and your bike between them and the dog. This isn't always necessary with a well-heeled dog, but it's considerate, especially if there are small children or elderly adults coming the other way. If the trail or path doesn't seem wide enough for this, then just stop and put the dog on a sit-stay until the people pass.

Skijoring (pronounced skee-yor-ing) is a cross-country method of hooking up as many as four dogs on leads attached to a large belt similar to the back-support belts used by weight lifters. The idea is to create a human-canine team whose capabilities complement each other and create a quicker-moving unit.

Mountain bikers interested in adapting this approach, effectively harnessing the dog for added speed or hill-climbing ability, need to use a body harness on the dog rather than a standard collar or obedience training choker. The body harness removes choking pressure on the dog, allowing him to work better and providing lead-centering for dog teams.

Two dogs are not that much more difficult to control than a single dog, assuming strong basic obedience training. Split leads are fairly common dog supplies, and depending on the size of breed, you may not even need a longer lead. But there are some changes from the standard one-dog format.

First, the dogs have to go out front, which means you'll need good voice control and voice projection. This begins to get into dog-sled mushing-type commands for direction, pacing, stopping, and starting.

Secondly, you'll want strong leverage for control of the leash or lead. Here the wider bars come into play. Loop the lead on the right grip and brake or forward projecting bar add-on, then coil it on the left side before it goes out to the dogs.

Running more than one dog multiplies the pacing, watering, and command concerns but opens up an entire world of interspecies communication and teamwork that is uniquely rewarding.

Once you get up to three or four dogs, you can go quite fast on rolling and intermittently steep terrain—you just better be a good rider and relaxed dog handler to do it.

For advice on how to run teams of dogs, much can be learned from dog sledders, who are growing in numbers in the West and Northwest. Many are using mountain bikes for summer conditioning of their dogs, hanging weights off the dogs to mimic snow workloads and keep the situation manageable for the person on the bike.

Body harnesses can be modified to freight harnesses that allow the dogs to perform hauling tasks with the mountain biker. You can even rig up traces.

> *We've hauled driftwood at the beach and logs for firewood, all of us hauling, matching pace. The logging practice came into play one day when a lazy hunter butchered his elk kill on the trail and left its discards, which weighed quite a bit. I bundled the remains in a garbage bag, and we hauled the unsightly mess out of there. A person couldn't have carried it alone.*
>
> —Yuri

Harnesses, leads, and training manuals are available from Rae's Harness Shop, 1524 East Dowling Road, 6, Anchorage, AK 99507.

Mountain bikers have already ridden the entire 1,150 miles of the Iditarod Sled Dog Trail in Alaska. Since skijoring is already well established, who knows where things might lead?

• • Scouts or Louts?

Interacting with Others on the Trail

Mountain bike manners and etiquette are more a matter of common sense and politeness than nitpicking or off-the-wall dos and don'ts. It's the getting-into-the-other-person's-shoes bit, be they a pair of hiking boots, cycling shoes, or deer hooves.

A mountain bike moves fairly silently and can be relatively quick in human terms. That's part of its magic for us. But the same magic can become a potion for disaster if the sudden appearance of mountain bikers panics a horse or stampedes animals, or if riders attempt to pass hikers without any verbal communication.

A bell on your bike, rung when going around corners and approaching people, accompanied by slowing (or stopping and yielding right of way on a narrow trail), a smile, and friendly verbal communication go a long way. And remember that if you've been pedaling hard on the bike, your lungs are working with a lot more force than usual. An attempt at a normal "Hello, nice day isn't it?" may come out sounding loud and aggressive to a pedestrian expecting more subdued vocal projection.

If you come upon a horse, stop while you're still 15 or 20 feet away and coordinate with the rider. Find out how the horse acts around people and cyclists. If possible, learn the horse's name, and talk to it—try to help the animal understand that the strange bike-humanoid thing is actually a person.

Unfortunately, a large number of hikers are just plain prejudiced against mountain bikes, and by extension, the people who ride them. Relentless cordiality and consideration are the only options we have with such people, so regardless of the response, it's always in the interest of mountain biking to break the ice with cheer. Maybe tell them about a special sighting you've just had, be it deer, blooming flowers, or a rewarding view from above the cloud bank higher up on the trail.

Martha has a friend who starts singing as she approaches people. Another starts talking baseball, even to herself when alone.

Mountain bike manners also extend to how you treat other bikers. When you encounter riders going the other way on a hillside shelf-trail, those on the uphill side of the trail should always stop and yield right of way to the outer-edge group. When meeting others in a downhill/uphill situation, climbers have more control, so they should give way to the downhillers, who should slow down.

When you're being overtaken by a quicker rider, hug to the right and let them know you're prepared by saying, "You can go left." If you're the passer, say "track" to let someone know you are there, or "on your left" to tell them you're coming by.

A group ride should be geared to the weakest link, that is, the least experienced or skilled rider. If you organized the ride or are group navigator, it's your responsibility to make sure everyone's up to it. If you invite a friend to another friend's ride, be prepared to stay with that person if he or she can't keep up.

The need for strict discipline regarding litter, shortcuts, and toiletries cannot be overemphasized. People who discard food wrappers while riding don't belong in the sport. Same goes for inner tubes, even in a race. Banana peels do not blend in with many North American biological zones and don't degrade for quite a while. Even something as small as the foil from an inner tube patch can spoil someone's day in the woods. Just pack it all out with you.

Few things are as depressing as coming across garbage in the middle of a mountain bike ride. Worse yet is to be in the midst of some of the too-few acres of unspoilt nature left and come across a Power Bar wrapper that you know a fellow mountain biker left. It's even worse when a discarded inner tube or fender is laying there, too. In some places the combination of food wrappers and inner tubes have been used as exhibits to advocate closing trails to mountain bikers.

If you ride near population centers (resorts or campsites as well as cities) modulate your speed overall to suit the probable number of users on the trail. Sunday afternoons mandate greater caution than weekdays, but don't let the off-peak time of week lull you into a false sense of isolation. A solo hiker may be out there on an off day for the same reasons that you are.

If there's any chance of encountering others unaware of or unprepared for mountain bikes, you can lessen the negative surprise factor by having someone ride ahead as point rider or scout. This is almost mandatory if your gang wants to ride fast. Give the point person plenty of time to warn or advise other users, but not so much time that the other trail users are forced to huddle off-trail for minutes on end waiting for you to come by.

If you come upon wild animals, take immediate calming action. Every wild species has a spook distance, the distance at which human presence begins to worry it. Whether or not an animal overtly displays discomfort or threatening behavior, the considerate thing for humans to do is to withdraw to a greater distance.

Deer usually run first into the brush and stop to look later, but elk often stampede on-trail, looking over their shoulder indecisively. If the lead cow is unsure or not around, an elk who is used to following the leader will panic. Slow down until there's enough distance for the animals to get their senses and get away. Five hundred pounds of crashing elk is not something to mess around with.

Black bears are usually quite people-shy unless startled or surprised in close quarters or unless they have been conditioned to humans by people feeding them. "Park bears" are very unpredictable and should be treated with extreme caution. Sows with young cubs are also more sensitive to human presence. Any bear that begins exhibiting defensive warnings—such as chomping its teeth, standing erect, or lowering its head and bowing its neck—should be given lots of space. Don't move suddenly, but put considerable distance between you and the bear.

Grizzlies and brown bears, a coastal sub-species of the grizzly, are another matter entirely. These animals routinely kill large game for snacking. As one may expect, they are not too impressed by people. If you are riding in grizzly or brown bear territory, be sure to get briefed by local wildlife agency officials on appropriate precautions.

Notes for race promoters

People tend to judge an entire sport by its organized events. It follows then that responsible race promotion can assist mountain bike acceptance and land access—or hurt it. Here are some guidelines for promoting races.

Be legal. Secure the proper permits and don't trespass. This is also relevant for clubs whose traditional training rides have become so well attended and enthusiastic that they should be institutionalized as official events.

Make sure race advertising is responsible. Language that conjures up images of terrain destruction and athletic violence (along with sophomoric macho advertising by the industry) is used by opponents of mountain biking to support their claims that we are crude, rude, street-gang-mentality jocks on wheels out for for a violent speed experience.

Give due notice to the public through channels the noncycling, even nonathletic, populations notice. Stumbling into a race can be a terrifying and dangerous experience for all involved, and noncyclists are more receptive to racing if they simply have the opportunity to plan their use of an area in advance. Who knows? You might even draw spectators to your event.

Use an environmentally responsible course. Many outdoors people quickly notice needless impact from mountain bike racing. Consult local experts and be aware of seasonal conditions.

Don't get totally wrapped up in designing the most awesome mountain bike course in your region. Make sure that the courses are appropriate for each class and category of rider. Ask yourself, "If I'm an expert, sport, or beginner racer, can I ride this at speed? Can I race it?" A course that has every ambulance in the county heading to the hospital, or which causes most of the junior and beginner entrants to drop out, is poorly designed. Reflect on whether your course is likely to give people a positive mountain bike experience for their entry fee or to discourage them from future participation in and enjoyment of the sport.

Mark your course with the standard world mountain bike signage, as follows. Use direction arrows whenever possible. Arrow signs should be at least 30x60 cm, with dark arrows on a white background. Direction arrows or course ribbons should be on the right side at racing eye level (approximately three feet above the ground).

Each intersection should be marked by an arrow 30 meters (35 yards) in advance, another at the intersection, and a third 30 meters later (to confirm the correct direction of travel). A large X can be used to denote "wrong way." Signs with one to three downward pointing arrows should be used to alert racers to course hazards, such as obstacles, changes in surface, water crossings, or other topographic features that increase handling difficulty. These warning signs should also be on the right, at eye level, 30 feet before the hazard, with one arrow for the mildest safety threat and three for the most dangerous.

Take along an instant print camera when installing course markings the day before an event. After installing an arrow or ribbon indicator for a turn, step back in the direction riders will be approaching from and take a photograph. Do this at every turn in the course, and mount the snapshots on a large course map on a billboard near the registration area. This visual preview of turns can do a lot to spare everyone the pain and hassle of lost riders.

Provide adequate marshaling and aid-station staffing. Not only have enough volunteers to manage a safe course, but make sure they are trained to shoulder the responsibilities that arise. The work may

Races for the tiny tikes are a fun finish-line activity for those waiting the return of adult racers and helps build a new generation of mountain bikers.

are great opportunities for us to develop the culture we want our sport to have. Enthusiastic teens will model the behavior they see at races. Though a little humor can do a lot to help make the spectating experience memorable, discourage announcers from celebrating dangerous or reckless racer behavior or encouraging the same with things like the Best Crash Contest, or from using sexist or other vulgar remarks.

Clean and repair the entire course and impacted areas. Sweep the entire course for racer and spectator litter and remove all your markers. Have work crews rake, sweep, and otherwise clean the course and surrounding area as soon as possible after the race.

Build and use community support. Mountain bike events can be good for local business, provide positive activity for youth, and offer a fresh recreational activity for adults. The more community support grows for individual events, the more the sport will be accepted overall.

Provide camping facilities so racers and their friends don't impose on property owners or other users. Provide showers and toilets whether at a campground, hotel, school, or public pool. Get approval for bike storage or maintenance work in hotel rooms and advise attendees of the terms for such activities. Arrange for collective, secure storage if necessary.

In short, be a responsible promoter and the sport—and your race—will benefit.

• • Tender Trails

Riding Techniques for Vulnerable Areas

Truly "Way Rad" riders are dialed-in on skid-free braking, turning cleanly, and climbing with traction. Sure, we've all had our moment of terrified glee as we survived our first outrageous downhill with both tires locked up. But as your skill level increases you'll notice (we hope) that such panic tactics not only destroy the trail, but they're inefficient (slow) and wearing on the rider and equipment.

If you're climbing even a gentle uphill and feel your rear wheel slip (spin a little), you need to correct for the conditions. Use a lower gear, bend over more, and put more weight over the rear wheel, or stop and let a little air out of the rear wheel.

Most riders are responsible, but there have been erosion problems on heavily used single tracks. One rider goes too fast and cuts a corner wide. Someone else follows his line. Horses follow it, too. Soon your nice single track is five feet wide, eroding on one side, and not only ugly but no longer much fun to ride.

Winter riding demands especially responsible and sensitive trail use. Wet trails take a lot more than tricky handling techniques. They should be examined for saturation, stability, and drainage. A trail that's been mucked from edge to edge with gullies of prints and tracks just shouldn't be ridden until drier weather. Riding back to the spot with a hard rake, grooming the wet patch, and ribboning it with trail-marking tape will help ensure the trail will be there come summer.

Dry desert areas are especially fragile. They're slow to grow and slow to mend. Likewise, hillsides composed of saturated, unstable soils will only suffer grotesque erosion and plant-base degradation if scored by footprints or tires.

Those trails already exhibiting erosion scars from irresponsible recreationalists are candidates for rehab work-parties. This is particularly true of waterbars (construction to control runoff) and steps, where impatient recreationalists skirt existing paths, accelerating an erosion problem right where some volunteer or tax-funded (our money) employee has already devoted back-aching labor on our behalf. We've all seen too much damage from both vibram lugs and knobby tires at such places. Contact your local parks and recreation department, outdoor shops, or clubs to find out what can be done to fix various damaged conditions. Consider a work-party part of your upper-body conditioning program.

But taking care of the trails you ride on is best done before accidental damage occurs. As much fun as we have at a trail-repair work-party, it doesn't come close to a great group ride. This means that appropriate-use zoning is important to every mountain biker's riding style.

Appropriate-use zoning means learning to look at terrain and social conditions and adjust your riding style accordingly. For example, find deserted downhill routes on which to get the adrenalin out, and practice high-skill techniques at slow speeds on ground and near vegetation that won't be critically damaged from your trials and errors.

Taking into account grade, traction, and an easy-to-hard technical rating, every route can be put in one of four appropriate-use zones in terms of biological sensitivity and/or social cautions:

C — *Cautious.* Highly sensitive desert areas and alpine tundra are examples. These are to mountain bikers (and other outdoor recreationalists) what school zones should be to automobile drivers. Speeds should be very slow and travel lines kept absolutely on the pre-existing paths.

W — *Within your range of total competence.* These are routes whose sight lines aren't that great, whose topsoil is too thin to handle high-traction demands, or whose geography is too dangerous for testing new skills. Don't try to ride any more quickly or more technically than you could in your sleep.

H — *Hammering allowed.* These are mostly an improvement of sight lines from W, but increased hardness and durability to the trail surface make riding to the furthest extent of your technical capabilities okay. But don't try things you haven't mastered yet.

E — *Experiment or expanding-your-skills territory.* If you're going to get better, you need to push things occasionally. It follows that you might not be in total control or in control of what your bike is doing to the soil while working on skill improvement. Logging roads through clearcuts are prime spots for this work, as are the clearcuts themselves, but so are urban wastelands—abandoned remnants of railroad yards, nontoxic landfills, and huge vacant lots belonging to public agencies.

Appropriate-use zoning would be even more useful if it were part of a uniform trail rating and signage standard.

A uniform signage system

As mountain biking becomes an international sport there is a growing need for a uniform signage language at trail heads, along trails, and on maps. The existence of dozens of different regional trail rating standards means that vacationing mountain bikers still need verbal explanations when attempting to pick routes to ride. Even within regions, the publication of competing idiosyncratic ride guides is generating confusion locally.

From notes taken over the past four years on existing systems, on suggestions made at conferences and at hearings for land management plans, and on rides with land managers, we have evolved a uniform standard we would like to help get adopted by sharing here.

The hope is that implementing a thorough uniform rating language in print and on trail signage will encourage riders to adjust their riding style appropriately to each trail. The system would avoid political complications by being neutral toward the variety of riding styles and premises for riding, be it hammerhead climbing, mountain bike stalking, trials-in riding, or downhill rim bakes.

What is this uniform standard? First off, the appropriate-use zoning codes mentioned above are placed inside ***technical skill*** rating symbols similar to those used to rate ski runs.

Circle—minimal or beginner technical demands
Hexagon—slightly demanding or intermediate handling skills required
Square—advanced, very demanding skill levels required
Diamond—expert trials-in capabilities required

Athletic ability and technical handling prowess are two separate areas, so an overall athletic conditioning or physical fitness rating can be separately indicated with a numerical superscript to the upper right of the ideogram, chemistry chart style. The numercial scale would go from one to five, with five being the high end.

1—simple; manageable for sedentary types on freak outings
2—moderate demand; "decently fit" folks should do okay
3—demanding; requires robust conditioning
4—difficult; studly physiques and a game attitude essential
5—extreme if not Olympian physical abilities and a very healthy sense of humor required

Terrain specifics and hazards on a particular trail can be signified below the principal ideogram in a line of boxes using the International Control Description Symbols for orienteering. There are about 100 symbols, covering directions (north, at the top of, between), geographical features (gully, cliff, pond), man-made features (fence, salt lick, open land), and trail conditions (sandy, marshy).

Club cartographers have also suggested that color can be used to identify the technical difficulty of trails. The following color scheme is proposed:

blue—minimal or beginner technical skills required
green—intermediate skills needed
yellow—advanced riding skills essential
red—expert handling ability necessary

As long as we are discussing club cartography, it also helps if particularly short steep sections of trail are identified on route maps. If your map doesn't have contours, these can be identified by placing two to six chevron wedges on the route line with the point of the chevrons pointing uphill. Two is less severe, and six chevrons is the steepest inclination on the gradient.

With this concise incorporation of symbols, letters, and four colors, a very detailed description of a mountain bike route is quickly communicated, whether at a trailhead, in a ride guide, or on a map. Existing rating systems in different regions may each have various excellent qualities, but the above system has these advantages:

- It communicates the athletic ability recommended to be able to complete the route with what may be called a positive recreational experience.
- It separately indicates the technical proficiency requirements of the route.
- It evaluates the length of sight lines, trail bed quality, and the probablility of social interaction with other trail users, and relates the relevant speeds that should be maintained.
- It is simple enough to lend itself easily to the various architecture standards of different land management agencies' signage, cartography and publication standards, not to mention conversation.
- It allows for identification of route-specific hazards.

The need for uniform trail head signage and a common rating language that incorporates social and environmental concerns as well as athletic requirements grows with every mountain bike sold. The only arguments that have been heard against adopting a uniform rating system involve parochial politics, which certainly pale in light of the need for riders and other trail users to know what to expect on any trail they embark on. And by using such zoning standards, trail degradation can be reduced and user conflicts avoided while still providing outlets for gonzoid urges.

• • What about Wilderness?

Respecting and Preserving Land Use

What it comes down to is this: either we are part of a tradition that thinks it's okay to rape and pillage for self-gratification, or we belong to the body of people who live with respect for the health and well-being of other living things.

If there's anything biological science has brought to our attention over the past 150 years, it's that we humans are just part of a much larger society, or, if you're more comfortable putting it the other way around, other species are legitimate members of our society. Either way, it means that the health and civil protection we recognize as the fundamental inheritance of all men, women, and children also holds true for all other species, amended only by the extent to which our species needs to feed from other living things for its own survival. The development and mass implementation of minimal impact technology that respects this standard of interspecies relations is arguably the challenge of our era.

Mountain bikes are one of the best embodiments of such technology, providing a sound and ethical method for engaging the world. They bring the benefits of a technological culture to outback transportation, with minimal environmental impact and great efficiency (comparable to getting 1,500 miles per gallon of gasoline). Bikes extend the range of outdoor enthusiasts who couldn't walk to places they can reach on a bicycle. And mountain biking campers can have an intimate encounter with nature similar to that of backpacking without the steady jingle of gear next to their ears or the strain on their backs.

So it's ironic that such low-impact devices are banned from parks and reserves (sometimes with political aid from allegedly committed hardcore environmental parties) while the same areas suffer massive injury from the effects of thousands of automobiles (often operated by members of those same organizations).

If we were to compare the impact of motor vehicles and bicycles on wildlife scientifically and honestly, our guess is that it would be apparent that the sensible course would be to combine restrictions on individual motor vehicle access with the development of on-site bicycle and pedestrian access fed by rail transportation. But given our society's bonding of individual libidos to the accelerator pedals of its automobiles and the consequent political probabilities, prospects for the other species on the planet don't seem too great.

There is a glimmer of hope with the advent of legally designated Wilderness Areas. These are the final parcels of North America where the true "real world" still exists much as it did for thousands of years before the industrial onslaught of the past two centuries.

While 90% of Wilderness Areas are validly zoned and should be reserved for nonassisted means of transportation (which also means no horses), not all legally designated Wilderness Areas are truly wilderness. In some there are roadbeds, railway grades, even buildings.

Environmental groups have sometimes chosen to have these areas designated as wilderness because less-extreme legal measures of protection and stewardship were politically unattainable. Unfortunately, that path of action often excludes mountain bikers from areas they might legitimately consider prime riding terrain.

Nonetheless, mountain bikers should support such sincere stewardship-minded people in their efforts to maintain wilderness designation without any potential exploitable loopholes. Sound management of these pieces of our planetary heritage demands strict enforcement both for its own sake and for the precedent it establishes. Let's hope that we can work with these same parties in the future to institute more appropriate and proactive zonings where relevant with less universally restrictive or regressive designations.

Land access politics

The issues and alliances in the national wilderness zoning debate are fairly straightforward, and it's usually pretty easy to identify who is on which side and for what reason. Multiple-use land management, however, is determined by a multitude of user groups, governmental agencies, business interests, and ideological affiliates. The organization that has the interests of mountain bikers at heart in the land-access debate is the International Mountain Biking Association (IMBA).

Almost exclusively rider/member financed, IMBA is an umbrella organization that acts as an information clearing house, conducts rider-education programs, organizes bike patrols and trail-maintenance programs, and represents the mountain bike community in public hearings.

The threats to mountain bike access are many. Some land managers would rather simply deny access than take on the bother of more management work. Traditional users want to protect the tiny niche they've worked so hard to get influence over. Environmental political groups have their own agenda and use the rhetoric of the wilderness debate to limit multi-use recreational zones. In such an administrative free-fire zone, IMBA's efforts have been the most consistent, credible, and forthright on behalf of mountain bikers.

IMBA has been joined in these efforts by the League of American Wheelmen (LAW), whose lobbying and advocacy activity on behalf of cyclists stretches back to the Good Road programs of a hundred years ago. IMBA and LAW hope to improve the lot of mountain bikers by combining the former's expertise with the latter's national network of volunteer activists and lobbyists to effect better representation of mountain bike concerns by coordinating advocacy.

IMBA makes available at cost whatever materials it thinks will help individual and club members. These include University of California studies on reducing safety and user conflicts, Parks and Recreation methods for formulating land-use plans, and the Keptner/Trego Analysis of trail users in a study conducted for the Los Padres National Forest. IMBA also publishes a newsletter, *Land Access Alert*, distributed monthly, and provides concise, informative one-page handouts on such topics as the IMBA Rules of the Trail, ethical race promotion, and organizing a local club.

Unfortunately, although the landscape of public recreation is replete with examples illustrating that in our society recreational sports sustain and thrive only when they contribute to the management of the resources they use, activity by the mountain bike industry rarely goes beyond lip service. So the onus is on local clubs and individuals to keep trail access viable.

Where the call has not been heeded, trails have closed. What has worked is this:

Get involved as early as possible. Get a group together to further mountain bike interests and establish regular meeting times and places. Develop a consensus on appropriate places to ride in your area. Develop rider education and technical-skills training programs to increase public awareness and environmental protection. Get bike dealers to distribute the IMBA Rules of the Trail as well as information on your club's programs.

Provide volunteer trail labor. Nothing works to establish a reputation for caring about the environment like doing grunt work on trails. Offer your club's services to the appropriate land manager or coordinate your efforts with existing outdoors and environmental clubs.

Join a trails advisory group. Identify the decision-makers in land access. Communicate your concerns to them and other user-group leaders about maintaining clean, quiet backcountry access.

> *Attending planning commission meetings is not exactly a lively recreational evening activity, but it takes only slightly more energy that watching television so it fits in well as rest time in the training program, and it reaps great rewards for months and years.*—Yuri

Take agency managers, planners, and other user group representatives on rides and volunteer to accompany them in their activities. Most trail user groups are of the same conservationist-recreationalist persuasion as we are, although the mode of travel varies. Getting in the others' shoes does a lot to break down prejudices and misunderstandings.

Adopt a park as a long-term project for your club or business. By adopting a specific park and having a long-term presence, you make a continued favorable impression for mountain biking and you get to see tangible results for your efforts.

> *I helped lay out trails on Vail Mountain and Beaver Creek Mountain. Now it's really rewarding to ride up there and see the project fulfilled and working. I also help the U.S. Forest Service build and maintain trails in the valley by joining in on work parties to correct or prevent erosion damage.*—Michael

Individual IMBA membership is $15. Clubs can become affiliated with IMBA by sending $75. If your club and members want to join but are starved for cash, get 15 members to donate $5 each for the dues. IMBA then sends 10 or 15 copies of their newsletter to your club.

The address for IMBA is the International Mountain Biking Association, P.O. Box 2007, Saratoga, CA 95080–2007. The address for LAW is the League of American Wheelmen, Suite 209, 6707 Whitestone Road, Baltimore, MD 21207.

If closure looms

If an imminent trail-closure crisis strikes, here's what IMBA recommends.

- Find out where and when public hearings will be. Develop a plan for opposing the closure and work on it.
- Establish criteria for management decisions.
- If public safety is the problem, advocate barricades and safety patrols.
- If user input is wanted, advocate a Keptner/Trego analysis such as the Los Padres National Forest used.
- If the number of affected voters must be pointed out, circulate a petition and start a letter-writing campaign.
- If there's a broad base of trail users, form a coalition with other groups who help in trail maintenance. Volunteer for projects.
- Ask decision-makers if you and others can give oral and written testimony. If necessary, ask for a delay in hearings to gain time to take the actions outlined above.

- Mobilize your group! Hold meetings, attend hearings, provide information to the public and the press.
- Get those who have an economic interest to back you (bike shops, resorts, tourist groups, local businesses, media).
- Show respect and develop a responsible reputation. Learn from the process so that if you don't get what you want the first time, you'll be better prepared in the future.

What history shows us

Sixty years ago outdoorsmen looked around and saw that the things they cherished and that were integral to their recreational activities were at risk. (This was before the success of the New Deal and before anyone would dare suggest that the government fund recreational resource management.) So in the middle of the Great Depression, outdoorsmen, their clubs and organizations, and their respective equipment industries got together, politicked, and passed the Pittman-Robertson Act.

The law established a tax on all hunting and fishing equipment, arms, and munitions, which was used to fund fish and wildlife management and conservation programs. It was the turnaround point for critter and creature survival in America, providing the basis for the multitude of conservation programs and services that have followed, and it continues to be a success today. For example, in the state of Oregon alone, the tax provides $11.8 million per year for wildlife conservation. (The scheme is so successful, that even though the funds collected are legally designated specifically for wildlife conservation, there are politicians and bureaucrats itching to raid that till to pay off mismanaged programs and pork-barrel projects.)

The lesson for mountain bikers is precisely relevant in these days of enormous government deficits and specialized self-interest groups. If we're going to have long-term trail access, there's going to have to be funding for land management, public education, and trail maintenance. Many land management agencies just don't have the money for another major user group. And probably nobody else is going to be excited about paying for our fun.

Besides which, the premise of the self-tax method is fair. We are getting the benefit of the resource, so we should systematically provide for its management. An across-the-store tax on mountain bikes, parts, equipment, and accessories would spread the burden around so that none would feel the pinch, yet those who use the resource the most would pay their appropriate share.

It's worked for fish and wildlife nationally and more recently for off-road motorcyclists in the state of Washington. Maybe we should consider it, too.

• • GLOSSARY

A compendium of terms used in this book, bicycle-related technical terminology, and slang collected from the trail.

aerobic exercise—a level of exercise in which the blood is oxygenated by the increased breathing volume prompted by continuous activity, and which can be continued for an extended period of time without creating an unfulfillable demand for more oxygen.

alignment tolerance—the amount a part of a frameset (frame and fork assembled with headset) may differ in distance from the plane running through the center lines of the seat tube and head tube and still be acceptable as straight—expressed in thousandths of an inch.

anaerobic threshold—the point in physical exertion when lactate levels in the blood rise dramatically in proportion to the workload.

appropriate-use zoning—the rating of off-road routes and trails to indicate the amount of speed and control needed to preserve the terrain in a healthy natural state and to minimize the risk of social conflict with other uses.

athletic rating—a scale estimating the level of physical ability and riding technique needed to manage a route on a mountain bike.

azimuth—a bearing taken relative to magnetic north for purposes of navigation.

bailing out—ejecting from the bike when a spectacular crash is imminent. Also, telephoning for a car ride home.

balanced strength—complementary strength in the entire network of muscles in the body, specifically between active muscles contracting to perform a specific movement and the muscles which stabilize the rest of the body.

bikejoring—the combination of dog mushing and mountain biking in which a dog or team of dogs is harnessed to a mountain biker by a five- to seven-foot lead line.

Blitz—a timed form of chess played with a dual-faced chess clock. Each player has three to five minutes to make all his moves. Good for developing quick thinking and mental stamina.

blowing up—the sudden inability to continue riding at an expected pace. Usually caused by poor pacing (riding too hard early on in a ride), temporary loss of fuel from poor diet management during a ride or the half-day before a ride, and/or dehydration. Sometimes confused with bonking.

bonking—completely running out of fuel, or glycogen, for exercise.

bottomed out—being in your lowest gear, and usually wanting a still lower one.

Braille biking—mountain biking after sunset without lights or with minimally functional lighting equipment due to weak batteries.

bullet-proofing—the outfitting of wheels with maximum protection against punctures, tears, and other flats, irrespective of weight considerations. Commonly Kevlar tires, antipuncture tire liners, and heavy inner tubes.

butted tubing—tubing that has been constructed so that its walls are thick at the ends and thinner in the middle of its length to optimize strength and lightness.

cadence—the rate of rotations of the crank arms and pedals, expressed in revolutions per minute (rpms).

Capacity Heart Range (CHR)—the range of heart rate sustainable for 10- to 40-minute moderately hard efforts, found by factoring resting heart rate.

car wimp—someone who uses an automobile for personal transportation when it only requires a bicycle. Especially a racer who uses his car just to get around when he could do so on a bike.

chainline—the relative angle of the chain between the freewheel cog and chainring; also the relative straightness between the middle chainring and the mid-point of the freewheel cluster (either the middle cog on an odd-count cluster or the space between the middle cogs on an even-count cluster).

chainsuck—when the chain becomes wedged between the chainwheels and the chainstay, stopping forward movement.

chukkar—a period of play in mountain bike polo.

Chryslerizing—equipment that displays one or more of the following faults. It works only with other parts made by the same company. It requires special tools made by the same company. It can't be repaired because parts are universally unavailable, either through lack of distribution, or planned obsolescence cycles that change quicker than popular music. It breaks in common usage but is specifically not covered by the warranty. (Example—mountain bikes marketed specifically as race bikes whose warranties exclude them from coverage once used in competition.)

classic—a race which uses the original mountain bike race format, which combined cross-country, hillclimb, and downhill races in one 30- to 60-mile race course. Such courses were usually either a single loop or ran point-to-point. Less than a handful of the original races from the early 1980s still exist.

cleaning—the successful riding of a section of trail, technical obstacles, or water crossing without putting a foot down, falling, or otherwise stopping.

clear cut—a method of forest harvesting in which all trees within a designated unit are cut. Unit size on public lands in the U.S. range from 2 to 40 acres. Private land clear cuts are often larger, and have been as large as 20 square miles (640 acres = 1 square mile).

clog clearance—the distance between the inner surfaces of the chainstays at the point where the rear tire is widest. A larger measure (more than 65 mm) allows the use of wider tires without getting clogged with mud.

cockpit—the area on a bike between the saddle and the handlebars.

complex carbohydrates—the essential fuel for sustainable mountain biking (or any other athletic activity). Found in fruits, vegetables, and whole grains.

contour map—a topographical map.
cross up—to steer in the opposite direction of a turn while sliding. Also to show up a half-hour or more late on the wrong corner or in the wrong parking lot for a ride.
crotch clearance—air space between one's private parts and the top tube of a bicycle when straddling the bike.
cruisen—a state of euphoria only induced by riding mountain bikes. Often used with the verb to be, as in "Always be cruisen."
dabbing—touching one's foot down when attempting to clean a section, particularly during observed trials.
damping—the rate at which a suspension shock absorber compacts and extends.
death march—a heroically long battle into a headwind on the bike, especially when on the return leg of an already long or vigorous day ride. Also a very steep, protracted hillclimb requiring you to pause numerous times and/or carry your bike.
declination—the difference between true north and magnetic north.
deep reserves—the ability that allows one to repeatedly attack difficult terrain and to recover and continue at race performance pace even after prolonged, continuous, and intense mountain biking.
Desired Heart Rate Formula—the formula for computing the degree of stress at which you want to train, expressed as a percentage of your theoretical maximal heart rate.
dial-in—to get a bicycle or component adjusted to its best operational state and to adjust the mechanics of your riding technique to fully exploit the capabilities of such equipment. Also, to learn the techniques to clean a section or complete a section without fault.
double track—unpaved roadbeds with two parallel motor vehicle wheel tracks.
driving hypotenuse—the distance between the top of the saddle/ center line of the seat tube and the center line of the pedal spindle when the crank arm is perpendicular to and forward of the seat tube. As a measure of leg extension in the power stroke portion of pedaling, an indiviudal's driving hypotenuse should be nearly the same on all his or her bicycles, allowing for differences in shoes, cleats, pedals, and clothing worn on each bike.
eating it—taking a particularly sharp fall, often over the handlebars.

Effective Seat Tube Length—seat tube length that corresponds to the length of your legs for optimal pedaling mechanics. Measured from the center line of the bottom bracket spindle to the center line of the seat tube where it intersects the top tube.

endo—a fall in which the rider is propelled end-over-head over the handlebars. Also known as "taking a header."

Endurance Heart Range (EHR)—the range of heart rate at which you obtain cardiovascular exercise benefit and which you can sustain for long efforts. Found by factoring .75 and .80 into your theoretical maximal heart rate and adding your resting heart rate.

exercise benefit—the positive conditioning effect on the body from the controlled stress of a systematic athletic activity.

flagpole effect—a swaying sensation experienced while in the saddle of bikes with too much exposed seat post and/or seat tube projecting above the juncture of the seat tube and top tube.

front center—the distance from the center of the bottom bracket to the center of the front axle, indicative of cockpit room and fore/aft design balance in a bicycle.

gear count—the number of usable, nonduplicating gears on a bicycle.

gear inch—a single number that expresses the ratio of a particular gearing combination, representing the diameter wheel a 19th-century ordinary bicycle would need in order to cover the same amount of ground with one turn of the pedals.

gear spacing—the amount of change between consecutive gears.

gearing spread—the range of gears available in any drivetrain configuration, from the lowest to the highest ratio.

glass legs—legs whose muscles are totally spent from exertion.

glom—(v) to combine mountain biking with an unrelated or apparently dissimilar activity to form a hybrid activity. Also the ad hoc combination of different vintages, brands, and nationalities of bicycle components in defiance of the recommendations of manufacturers and technical editors, creating a mountain bike that nonetheless works. (n) The resulting bicycle after such parts combination.

gnarly—outdoor activity that's so incredibly demanding it must be fun. Also, the ability to perform such athletic extremism with good humor.

gonzo—non-mountain bikers' term for someone who rides faster or with greater apparent risk than they could imagine themselves doing. Sometimes used negatively to imply irresponsibility. Also used by downhill devotees to describe the riding style of someone, especially another downhill specialist, who rides with great panache.

gram counter or gram cracker—a mountain biker obsessed with component weight to the point of fanaticism.

gravity check—what occurs when a mountain biker falls on his or her face from a dead stop with no apparent cause.

gruppo—traditional term for a component group, from the Italian, referring to the entire collection of drivetrain, brake, and bearing components necessary to make a frameset a working bicycle. Gruppos are manufactured by one company and sold as a uniform package. May or may not include the seat post, pedals, or seat post binder.

gut-bucketing—from jazz, a strong, rhythmical, and vivacious style of riding well into a long ride. Also, specific training regimens for developing such skill.

hammer—riding hard and fast.

hammerhead—a rider preferring to ride hard and fast to the exclusion of all other styles.

happy motoring—pleasantly rewarding, fast riding.

Hike 'n Bike—mountain bike outings in which couples take turns riding and hiking; especially family mountain bike outings in which one parent uses the bike while the other parent hikes with the children on the same trail.

honking—hammering by rising slightly off the saddle with each pedal stroke; also hammering with exceptional ease.

interval ramps—short periodic stretches on a climb which are steeper than the rest of the grade. They often serve to connect contour shelves or benches as a road or trail climbs a ridge.

joust—the initial foray for play on the ball in a chukkar of mountain bike polo.

jungle cross—a route that requires carrying the bike while hacking a trail through the overgrowth.

kneading—in massage, lifting and working the muscles between the thumb and fingers without pinching them.

line—as in "line of travel," the path taken by the bike (and rider), or the best line through a section of trail.

lugged frame—a frame constructed with reinforcement sleeves or fittings at its corners or tubing joints.

Maximum Heart Rate (MHR)—a theoretical maximal attainable heart rate estimated by subtracting your age from 220, or verified by testing in a fitness laboratory.

minute—one 60th of a degree of latitude or longitude.

modulation—the gradient of control in braking.

Mountain Baggers—a registry for mountain bikers who have ridden to the top of mountain peaks on their bikes.

mudsnake—slippery deadfall limbs that lie diagonally across trails.

mulch—to return a bicycle component to its primordial state, as in "I just mulched my derailleur."

observed trials—competitions in which contestants try to ride their bikes through a designated obstacle course without touching a foot, hand, or shoulder to something other than the bike.

opportunistic tightness—a wide selection of nonduplicating gears in a small portion of the gear spread, most commonly sought after by racers who want the most efficient gear ratio for maintaining pedal cadence and power.

orienteering—a competition in which participants race to complete a circuit of target points using only a map and a compass for navigation.

pace—an estimate of average amount of effort, most commonly judged by others by speed, and by oneself through a reading of both speed and subjective feelings of exertion.

pacing—moderating your effort throughout a ride so that you finish it in the amount of time and in the condition you desire, or better.

panniers—packs made specifically for mounting on bikes.

piecemeal compatability—the ability of an individual component to work well with many other components and combinations of components, particularly those of other manufacturers.

pedal leg—a mountain biker's shin or calf that is well decorated with scar tissue from hitting the pedal cage.

point rider—a lone rider or scout sent ahead of a group of riders to inspect terrain and alert other trail users of the group's approach.

point-to-point race—a race course that doesn't loop back on itself and whose start and finish lines are not in close proximity to each other.

preload—the amount to which a suspension system can be set to compensate for rider weight before riding and encountering any bumps or shock forces.

proportional geometry—the slight modification by a manufacturer of frame angles and tube lengths so that all sizes of a model of bike have identical weight distribution, steering, and other performance characteristics.

proportional sizing—the sizing of all parts on a bicycle to lengths relevant to people likely to fit that size of bicycle.

quick release—a mechanical device, usually a lever and cam, that allows the quick tightening or loosening of wheels, seat posts, etc., without the use of hand tools or wing nuts.

Race Performance Range (RPR)—the heartbeat range that reflects the in-season base pace for a racer's training sessions, found by factoring .80 and .85 into theoretical maximum heart rate and adding resting heart rate.

randonneur—a cyclist who completes ultra-endurance cycling challenges within a time control. Also any cyclist interested in particularly long high-performance sojourns.

ratcheting—the pedaling technique of using partial backward strokes to avoid hitting obstacles with the pedals.

reach—the distance between a brake lever and the handlebar grip. Adjustable on quality components.

Rest and Recovery Range (RRR)—the heartbeat range that reflects the minimal exertion level desired for recovery rides after high intensity workouts, found by factoring .60 and .65 into theoretical maximum heart rate and adding resting heart rate.

Resting Heart Rate (RHR)—an individual's heart rate when he or she first awakens, taken before even sitting up in bed.

rig—a high-performance glom of componentry. That is, a mid-range to high-end stock mountain bike that has been customized and accessorized and had nearly all of its original components replaced to the point of becoming a one-of-a-kind vehicle. Regional variants of the term include "Le Rig," "Da Rig," "De Rig," and "De Rig-or."

rise—the height difference between the steerer and handlebar ends of a stem.

saddle height—the distance between the top of the saddle and the center line of the bottom bracket spindle, measured along the center line of the seat post and seat tube.

sand-bagging—occurs when a racer enters a competition in a category much below his skill and expertise level, but for which he is technically registered.

Scott Trials—a race format that combines cross-country trail racing and observed trials competition on a single course in which the trials sections are separated by significant cross-county trail. Named after Alfred Angus Scott, an early British motorcycle manufacturer and inventor who popularized the format that was the predecessor of motocross racing.

screaming legs—over-exercised legs that are beginning to cramp.

shoot an azimuth, or take a bearing—to use a topographic map and compass to plot a line of travel relative to the magnetic North or South Pole.

single track—one- to five-foot-wide trails or paths.

spring rate—a measure of a suspension system's spring stiffness, usually expressed in pounds, describing how much static weight is required to compress the unit one inch.

spud flub—falling over sideways due to the inability to get your feet free from step-in mountain bike pedals.

squirrelly—erratic behavior, usually referring to the line of travel by a cyclist, usually indicating marginal control of the bike for the circumstances.

stiction—short for static friction, the mechanical resistance of two side-by-side units to begin moving independently. In a suspension unit, it is the reluctance of the shock absorber parts to slide and thereby dissipate force.

stylin'—riding with quick, smooth style, as in "stylin' dude."

swarming—the sound effect of many knobby tires riding in a pack on pavement.

Sufficient Cockpit Length—the minimal amount of room needed between a bicycle's saddle and handlebars, measured relative to your upper body and arm lengths.

surface plate—a precision-ground cast-steel or granite plate guaranteed to be flat in that the maximum differences measured along any lines across its surface will be within a stated tolerance. Such plates are used as reference surfaces to check alignment. Grade B tool-room surface plates offer acceptable tolerances for mountain bikes.

targeting—establishing certain rides or races as important times of personal-best performance, and managing participation in other rides or races as training for the important events.

taking soil samples—crashing off the bike, but especially doing an endo, in which you collect pieces of terra firma in your mouth, nostrils, or ears.

talking legs—glass legs that speak to you.

tech weenie—a mountain biker obsessed with having the latest, lightest, most scientifically advanced equipment.

thrashold—the subjective feeling of having come upon a stretch of terrain that demands ultimate athletic exertion and technical prowess for minute amounts of forward progress.

Threshold Heart Range (THR)—the heartbeat range reflecting the exertion level desired while training for the extraordinarily demanding intervals encountered in mountain biking, sustainable for a couple of minutes at 90-rpm cadence. Found by factoring .88 and .92 into theoretical maximum heart rate and adding resting heart rate.

tire patch—the area of actual contact between a tire and the ground at any moment.

toe clips—a metal or plastic fitting that holds the front of your foot to the pedal cage. Use with toe straps (which encircle the middle of the foot and the pedal) to ensure more efficient power transfer from the legs to the drivetrain.

toe-strap buttons—small plastic or metal fittings attached to toe straps so the straps are easier to grip while riding the bike.

topo map—abbreviation of topographical map. A map that illustrates terrain by connecting points at the same elevation with contour lines.

tooth—the ability of a tire to get traction on a surface.

tracking—the ability to ride a specific line. Also following a lead rider's line.

traction—the friction bond between a tire and a riding surface.

travel—in a suspension unit, the distance it will accommodate in axle travel to absorb an impact and dissipate the disruptive force.

unlugged frame—a frame whose tubes are directly joined in the corners without internal or external reinforcement sleeves.

veering—riding in a polo field other than parallel to the sidelines and therefore being excluded from play on the ball

Vinnie Factor—from a humorous text on sport and athletic theory.

The theory is that there are only so many cells in your body to go around and that when you start training and your muscles grow, they have to get cells from somewhere, so they take them from your head. The Vinnie Factor lets you know when you've gone too far. People start yelling "Hey! Yo! Vinnie!" at you, or you no longer remember your roommate's name or the pink flamingos on your lawn.

VO_2 Max—maximal oxygen intake, a measure of your aerobic fitness.

wailing wall—a hillclimb that requires the rider to undergo a profoundly humbling experience.

wankering—to waver from riding to your true abilities, or to ride without gumption, especially while racing.

way-rad—ultimate cool style.

widow-maker—an uphill time trial on a very steep slope.

Wilderness Areas—the legal designation of tracts of land in which protection of the native, nonhuman life from the effects of technological intrusion takes precedence over all other concerns.

wired—securely and serenely assured, confident. Also excited, enthusiastic.

Working Saddle Height—a rule-of-thumb measure for correct distance between the saddle and the crank arms for an individual's leg length. Found by allowing an approximate 10-degree bend in the knee when the foot is at the bottom of the pedal stroke.

zirk fitting—a nipple fitting on a bearing housing that allows the quick-purging of old grease with new grease by use of a grease gun. Non-zirk-fitted bearings require disassembly of the bearing unit for relubrication.

••BIBLIOGRAPHY

BOOKS

The Art of Swedish Massage, Bertil Ravald, 1982, The Bergh Publishing Group.

Athletic Massage, Phaigh and Perry, 1984, Simon and Schuster.

Bicycle Metallurgy for the Cyclist, Douglas Hayduk, 1987, Johnson Publishing Co.

Bicycle Road Racing, Edward Borysewicz, 1985, Vitesse Press.

Bicycling Science, Frank Whitt and David G. Wilson, 1982, MIT Press.

The Complete Weight Training Book, Bill Reynolds, 1976, World Publications.

Cyclo-cross, Simon Burney, 1990, Springfield Books Limited.

Encyclopedia of Modern Bodybuilding, Arnold Schwarzenegger, 1985, Fireside Books.

The Family Fitness Handbook, Glover and Shepherd, 1989, Penguin Books.

Finding Your Way by Land or Sea: Reading Nature's Maps, Harold Gatty, 1983, Stephen Greene Press.

Fit or Fat?, Covert Bailey, 1977, Houghton Mifflin.

The Fit or Fat Target Diet, Covert Bailey, 1984, Houghton Mifflin.

Getting to Yes: Negotiating Agreement without Giving In, 1984, Houghton Mifflin.

Greg LeMond's Complete Book of Bicycling, Greg LeMond and Kent Gordis, 1987, G.P. Putman and Sons.

Health, Fitness Excellence, Robert K. Cooper, Ph.D, 1989, Houghton Mifflin.

How to Stay Alive in the Woods, Bradford Angier, 1962, MacMillan.

Jane Brody's Nutrition Book, Jane Brody, 1981, W.W. Norton.

Ki in Daily Life, Koicgi Tohri, Harper and Row.

Map and Compass Handbook, Randall, Outward Bound Adventure Series.

The Massage Book, George Downing, 1974, Bookworks.

Mental Toughness: Training for Sport, James E. Loehr, 1982, Viking-Penguin.

Mountain Bike! William Healy, 1992, VeloNews Books.

Observed Trials, Bernie Schreiber and Len Weed, 1983, Cleansheet Enterprises.

The Orienteering Book, Steve Andersen, 1980, Anderson World.

Orienteering, The Skills of the Game, Carol McNeill, 1990, The Crowood Press.

The Physiology of Fitness, Sharkley, 1984, Human Kinetics.

Recreational Impacts on Wildlands, USDA, Forest Service, Pacific Northwest Region, R-6-001-1979.

The Recreational Opportunities Spectrum: A Framework for Planning Management and Research, Clark and Stankey, USDA, Forest Service, Pacific Northwest Range and Experiment Station, General technical Report, PNW-98.

Resource Manual for Guidelines for Exercise Testing and Prescription, American College of Sports Medicine, 1988, Lea and Febiger.

Richard's Mountain Bike Book, Charles Kelly and Nick Crane, 1988, Ballantine Books.

Risk! An Exploration into the Lives of Athletes on the Edge, Steve Boga, 1988, North Atlantic Books.

Serious Training for the Serious Athlete, Rob Sleamaker, 1989, Leisure Press.

Skijoring, Carol Kaynor and Mari Hoe-Raitto, 1988, self-published.

Sport Cycling, Michael Shermer, 1985, Contemporary Books.

Stretch and Relax, Maxine Tobias and Mary Stewart, 1985, The Body Press.

Stretching, Bob Anderson, 1980, Shelter Publications.

Surviving the Unexpected Wilderness Emergency, Eugene H. Fear, 1979, Emergency Response Institute.

Training for Sport and Activity, Wilmore and Costill, 1988, Wm. C. Brown.

Training Lead Dogs, Lee Fishback, 1978, Tun-dra, Nunica, MI.

The Woman Cyclist, Elaine Mariolle and Michael Shermer, 1988, Contemporary Books.

PERIODICALS

Bicycle Guide, 711 Boylston St., Boston, MA 02116. A cycling enthusiast's magazine with regular features on mountain biking and equipment.

Bicycling Plus Mountain Biking, 33 E. Minor St., Emmaus, PA 18098. Cycling for the general public with a section in the back about mountain biking.

The Dirt Rag, 5732 Third St., Verona, PA 15147. A bimonthly, exclusively off-road cycling magazine for the Northeast that lets the mud spray where it may.

Outside, 1165 N. Clark St., Chicago, IL 60601. Outdoor recreation and environmental coverage with slant to the hip, yup, and now.

Land Access Alert, International Mountain Bicycling Association, Route 2, Box 303, Bishops, CA 93514. The politics of doing it.

Mountain & City Biking, Box 16149, North Hollywood, CA 91606. The "e-ews!" and "ahhs!" on the latest gear and yummy vacation sites tasted by another gang of L.A. basin riders and an engineer from Bellingham, WA.

Mountain Bike Action, 10600 Sepulveda Blvd., Mission Hills, CA 91345. The shake and bake of way-rad riding practiced with Southern California style.

Muscle and Fitness Magazine, P.O. Box 3739, Escondido, CA 92025-9819. Training and conditioning you're not likely to find in cycling mags.

NORBA News, National Off-Road Bicycle Association, 1750 E. Boulder Ave., Colorado Springs, CO 80909. The official publication of the national race-sanctioning organization.

Running Research News, P.O. Box 27041, Lansing, MI 48909. Training and exercise physiology reports.

Track Technique, 2570 El Camino Real, 606, Mountain View, CA 94040. Exercise physiology.
VeloNews, 1830 N. 55th St., Boulder, CO 80301. America's bicycle racing newspaper.
Women's Sports and Fitness Magazine, 1919 14th St., Boulder, CO 80302. Fitness and recreation for women.

••INDEX

••ABOUT THE AUTHORS

Martha Kennedy is one of America's top women off-road racers, with victories in several major events, including the L.A. 150 in California. She has twice won the 210-mile Iditabike in Alaska and has placed in the top five in the national points series for four consecutive years. Martha lives in Carson City, Nevada.

Michael Kloser has been one of the world's top off-road racers for the past five years. He's a two-time winner of the Iditabike (1988 and 1989) and finished second in the 1989 Grundig World Cup, a season-long series of the world's toughest off-road races. He won a silver medal in the downhill at the 1990 Mountain Bike World Championships. When not competing in Europe, Michael lives with his wife in Vail, Colorado.

Yuri Samer is a longtime off-road rider who makes his living as a freelance cycling journalist and photographer. He's the author of a syndicated cycling equipment column ("Cycle Buys for the Frugal Flyer") and publisher of the *San Francisco Cycling Guide.* His articles and photos have appeared in *Bicycle Guide, VeloNews, Outside, Winning, The New York Times,* and many other publications. Yuri lives in Eugene, Oregon, with his wife Sally and two daughters.